Spirituality *and the* Black Helping Tradition
in Social Work ❋

ELMER P. MARTIN AND JOANNE M. MARTIN

DEDICATION

Dedicated to my grandchildren, Brittnae Nicole Wilson and Kevin Brandon Wilson, and godchildren, Jimi Marchone Lee, Mia Nicole Jackson, Jamin Hill, Elmer Keene, David and Mary Fakunle; Timeka, Terrance Jr., Mykia, and Tamara Sharp; Lance, Chance, and Vance Deleslie.

To Antoine Lewis, a young man whom we have watched grow up in the East Baltimore community, from a young boy to a young man now matriculating to college.

A special thanks to our typist Alice Williams for her diligence and efforts producing this book.

ABOUT THE COVER

On the cover of this book are titles of songs commonly known in the African American community as "Spirituals." During slavery, these songs transmitted messages of encouragement and warning to slaves throughout the South. Our ancestors sang these songs of Zion to keep the faith of a brighter day in a time of darkness. They also knew that the message in these songs would continue to flow from generation to generation.

Today, these songs are still being sung—the tempo may have changed but the message is strong.

Let us never forget...

Spirituality *and the*
Black Helping Tradition
in Social Work

ELMER P. MARTIN AND JOANNE M. MARTIN

NASW PRESS

National Association of Social Workers
Washington, DC

Terry Mizrahi, MSW, PhD, *President*
Elizabeth J. Clark, PhD, ACSW, MPH, *Executive Director*

Cheryl Y. Bradley, *Publisher*
Paula L. Delo, *Executive Editor*
Susan Fisher, *Editor*
January Layman-Wood, *Acquisitions Editor*
Christina Bromley, *Editorial Assistant*
Jodi Bergeman, *Copy Editor*
Sanna J. Thompson, *Researcher*
Susan J. Harris, *Proofreader*
Leonard S. Rosenbaum, *Indexer*

Cover and interior design by Metadog Design Group, Washington, DC

Library of Congress Cataloging-in-Publication Data

Martin, Elmer P.
 Spirituality and the Black helping Tradition in social work /
Elmer P. Martin and Joanne M. Martin.
  p. cm.
Includes bibliographical references and index.
ISBN 978-0-87101-322-4
 1. Social work with African Americans. 2. Social workers—Religious
life—United States. 3. Social service—Religious aspects—Christianity.
4. African American social workers—Religious life. 5. Helping behavior—
Religious aspects—Christianity. 6. African Americans—Religious life.
I. Martin, Joanne Mitchell. II. Title.

HV3181 .M372 2002
361.3'089'96073—dc21

2002021944

CONTENTS

LIST OF FIGURES AND TABLES

DEDICATION
Dr. Elmer Perry Martin, Jr.
1946–2001

Quietly and without fanfare, Dr. Elmer P. Martin, Jr. went about the business of making history. Guided by a determined spirit, a methodical approach, and a powerful vision, he was an advocate for social justice and the imperative of cultural competence. The strong foundations of race pride, commitment to competent practice, and meaningful scholarship were integral to all that he accomplished. The social work profession lost an eminent scholar and dedicated friend on June 14, 2001, when Dr. Martin died in the motherland of his beloved Africa (Egypt).

Dr. Martin earned bachelor's and master's degrees in sociology from Lincoln University (Missouri) and Atlanta University, respectively, and later a doctor of philosophy degree in social welfare from Case Western Reserve University. Throughout his career, Dr. Martin taught at some of America's most prominent colleges and universities including Morehouse College, Case Western Reserve University and, for the last 25 years, Morgan State University.

Providing valuable and critical information essential to understanding family and community, Dr. Martin spent his life teaching, writing, and speaking about the history of African American people and the essential role that history plays in the way that African Americans have lived their lives. He and his wife, Dr. Joanne M. Martin, have published four books, the seminal work, *The Black Extended Family* (1978), *The Helping Tradition in the Black Family and Community* (1985), *Social Work and the Black Experience* (1995), and this posthumous publication, *Spirituality and the Black Helping Tradition in Social Work*.

Dr. Martin's legacy also includes the Great Blacks in Wax Museum, Inc., in Baltimore. Another forum for teaching and honoring history, the museum enhances the visitors' senses of group consciousness and self-efficacy. A multifocused community beacon, the Great Blacks in Wax Museum, Inc., teaches, educates, empowers, and feeds the spirit and the soul. It also provides employment opportunities for young men and women who might otherwise have no knowledge or image of Dr. Ronald McNair, the astronaut who died on the *Challenger* space shuttle, or Dr. W. E. B. Du Bois, a pioneer sociologist, who like Dr. Martin taught about the "souls of Black folks" as critical to understanding the African American experience and its impact on America.

Dr. Elmer Martin's life epitomized what he called "the Black helping tradition"—a largely independent struggle of African Americans to collectively promote survival and advancement. His writings generously provided the science of this tradition to social workers. The museum supplements and supports his scholarship by offering visual, intellectual, and emotional stimulation to the throngs of people who make the North Avenue location their choice for school field trips, homecomings, and reunions. The "race men" and "race women" whose images appear throughout the museum speak of a proud tradition; a life of struggle, joy, and celebration all built on a foundation of mutual aid and support, a fitting parallel to Dr. Martin's life's work.

We will miss Dr. Elmer Martin, who moved through life with a calm, unassuming, but clear focus that was left in his stead legacies and monuments. Our professional ancestors are proud of his contributions, which should ultimately enhance the quality of service that our contemporary colleagues deliver.

Iris Carlton-LaNey

CHAPTER ONE
Introduction

The major purpose of this work is to show how early Black caregivers and pioneering social workers used spirituality in their work with Black people, in their struggle to achieve racial justice and gender equality, and in their efforts to create a truly democratic society. This study primarily takes a historical perspective to demonstrate that earlier generations of Black lay and professional helpers used spirituality as the basis for distinguishing Black people from their oppressors; for critiquing society; for affirming dignity, integrity, and self worth; for promoting interracial cooperation and cultural diversity; and for achieving Black sanity, communal solidarity, and social support. The chief focus of this study is on the implications of spirituality in the Black helping tradition for social workers in the 21st century. The key question is: What is the extent to which spirituality can serve these functions for social work practitioners today?

In the Black helping tradition, spirituality is defined as the sense of the sacred and divine. Spirituality gave Black people the strength to go on when there were threats to their very existence, self-worth, and dignity when oppressive forces were seeking to strip them of their humanity, hope when there seemed to be none, a way when there was no way, and even joy when confronted by nothing but a daily rhythm of hardship, frustration, and pain. In the face of the most demoralizing circumstances, spirituality gave Black people both courage and encouragement, and even in the midst of suffering and death, it gave them a will to live and the determination to make life worth living. Historically, Black spirituality was expressed in countless ways, such as through singing, dancing, moaning, mourning, affirming, worshipping, contemplating, reflecting, shouting, praying, preaching, and testifying. However, most importantly, it was expressed in the way people lived their lives and in the reverence and respect they had for life. Black people historically spoke of spirituality in terms of "lifting the spirit"; of finding that divine spark that would motivate them "to keep on keeping on"; of being "in the spirit"; of living their lives the way they believed God intended human beings to live; and of "feeling the spirit" so deep in their souls that it often made them want to shout. Whatever terms Black people used to captivate the essence of their sense of the sacred, spirituality was their incentive to decency, to respecting life, to treating people properly, and to carrying on their rich Black tradition of helping.

In the urban Black community where we do cultural and social work, demonstrations of black atomization, alienation, and divisiveness are commonplace. A group of Black people attending a funeral are robbed by street denizens. Black preachers have iron bars on the doors and windows of their churches. Elderly people are in constant fear for their safety. Young people find myriad ways to brutalize and disrespect one another. School teachers are often afraid of the children they teach, and mothers are often afraid of their own children. While numerous positive forces also operate in this community, many elders believe that the community has lost something that is vital to the sanity and wholeness of its people. They remember the days when funerals, churches, preachers, old folks, children, babies, teachers, and mothers were sacred. They recall a time when it was considered a divine act to hold these sacred people, spaces, and places in reverence and respect. They believe that something more than social welfare programs calling for Black adjustment to the status quo and more than brick and mortar and money are needed to revitalize and develop impoverished Black communities. They mourn the loss of a time when a strong sense of the holy, sacred, and divine was deep within the souls and social heritage of Black people.

Canda (1997) was correct in his assessment that "during the period of slavery, people of African descent mobilized mutual support and liberation systems inspired by traditional African spirituality and Christian principles under extremely adverse conditions" (p. 300). He was also correct in stating that, "Unfortunately, there is little published information about the impact of these various developments on the formation of professional social work" (p. 300). This work seeks to bridge this knowledge gap. It takes up the concerns of Black elders and explores Black spirituality as a neglected topic in the social work profession.

In our previous work on the Black helping tradition (J. M. Martin & Martin, 1985), we spoke of Black spirituality largely in terms of "religious consciousness." We emphasized that religious consciousness, along with racial consciousness and fictive kinship, were key components to passing the Black helping tradition from one generation to the next. We indicated that enslaved Africans in America believed that religious consciousness was the key to their survival and their endurance. We wrote:

> The worship of God ... gave them a sense of personal significance and worth in a world in which they were defined not as human beings but as property. The belief that God recognized them as equals to [W]hites, that God recognized each of them personally as one of his children, and more important, that God was on their side served as powerful medicine over sick souls and frustrated hopes. (J. M. Martin & Martin 1985, p. 28)

This religious consciousness continued among free Black people during slavery as they built churches to serve as a spiritual refuge. The previous work ended with a discussion of the decline of religious consciousness among Black people. It suggested that although countless generations of Black people believed they had come this far by faith, even the Black church was having problems stemming from the decline of religious consciousness in modern urban Black life.

This new study gives a fuller, more in-depth account of religious consciousness. This work shows that practically all of the early caregivers, from the native healers in traditional Africa to the "race men" and "race women" of the 19th century operated largely from a spiritual frame of reference. It even shows that before social work moved in a purely secularistic, naturalistic, and empirical direction, pioneering Black social workers at the turn of the 20th century had no problem professing their own spirituality, identifying the spirituality of their clients, and working spiritual paradigms into the intervention process. Early Black caregivers and pioneering Black social workers knew that spirituality was so dominant in the lives of Black people that they could not treat it lightly or shrug off this most crucial aspect of Black life as unimportant and insignificant. Moreover, they knew that to keep from becoming alienated from their people, they had to treat spirituality as a serious, normal, acceptable, healthy, and wholesome part of the Black caregiving experience.

Early Black caregivers and pioneering Black social workers were acutely aware that Black people were essentially a spiritual people who defined their reality and structured their lives largely in spiritual terms. They knew that many traditional Africans and enslaved Africans in America saw the spiritual world as the ultimate reality and everything not related to it as an illusion.

Also, they knew that Black people often did not make any clear distinction between religiosity and spirituality. Both spirituality and religiosity in the minds of Black people were concerned with matters of the sacred, eternal, and divine; both dealt with issues of justice and injustice, good and evil, suffering and redemption, death and eternal life, and right and wrong human conduct; and both involved a relationship between a fragile, vulnerable people and an invisible, omnipotent higher power. If Black people made any distinction between religiosity and spirituality, they often associated religion with a religious institution or denomination (such as the Black church) and associated spirituality with one's personal and communal ties to an invisible supernatural realm (whether one belonged to a religious institution or not). In the Black helping tradition, spirituality tends to supersede religiosity. Spirituality is viewed in terms of deep concern for and commitment to the collective well-being; religiosity, at its best, is seen as a manifestation of a spirituality based on human compassion and caring.

This study shows that, historically, religious consciousness by itself did not necessarily lead to enhanced caregiving in the Black family and community. It shows that because many enslaved Africans swallowed wholesale or in part the racist religious mythology and imagery of their slave master, their ability to mourn the plight of Black people and to feel their people were worthy and deserving of the maximum level of care was severely hampered. These enslaved Africans had to break the religious grip that the slave master's propaganda had on their minds and develop a counter spiritual and racial consciousness that would affirm their self-worth and status as human beings. Moreover, many Black people saw their religious conversion primarily in terms of personal salvation, not social salvation. Hence, their religious quest was a private, personal quest that often led less to the higher development of caregiving impulses than to a feeling of self-righteousness, individualism, and moral superiority over Black "unsaved sinners." In the Black helping tradition, a strong sense of caring, communalism, and mutuality went hand-in-hand, reinforcing one another with spirituality as the central, integrating component. This explains why pioneering Black social workers often felt that even the Black church should come under a higher form of Black spirituality that concerned itself with the daily social problems confronting Black people today.

Operating out of this religious and spiritual worldview where distinctions between what is sacred and what is profane were blurred, early Black caregivers had no problem incorporating prayers, Bible readings, sacred songs, tributes to the ancestors, spirit possessions, and even attendance at sacred ceremonies and religious services as part of the remedy to the problems facing their clients. They felt that the spiritual support Black people gave to one another in their mourning work was often the difference between uplift and degradation, sanity and insanity, survival and death. If spirituality in the intervention process did not move political and economic mountains for their clients, early Black caregivers and professional helpers generally felt confident that it would at least quell anxieties and fears, relieve stress, and maybe even instill hope so that their clients could face another day.

So deeply embedded was the spiritual worldview in the psyche of Black people that few pioneering Black helping professionals at the beginning of the 20th century professed a belief in the superiority of the scientific, secularistic worldview over the sacred worldview, neither in terms of explaining, understanding, and predicting nor in terms of controlling and changing social phenomena. Later, of course, this was to change as Black social workers, following the lead of Freudian and other secularistic thinking in professional social work, came to profess a strong belief in the scientific method and even came to see spirituality as an illusion, a narcotic, and a psychic disturbance.

In earlier periods of Black history, a helping, caring person committed to the uplift and well-being of Black people was generally considered to be a spiritual person. In its intimate connection to Black caregiving, spirituality in the Black helping tradition

- promoted a sense of community and social support
- enhanced communal and racial self-development
- established social myths to counter racist mythomania
- laid the foundation for creating a Black strength perspective
- helped Black people to develop the ability to mourn
- served as a major source of inspiration and hope.

Above all else, spirituality in the Black helping tradition was geared toward the promotion of community through Black communal solidarity and social support. Black spirituality sought to integrate the broken, isolated, alienated, atomized, and disconnected strands of Black humanity with the group. It was oriented toward harmonizing human relations, linking

Black people to social support networks, promoting racial cooperation, and bringing those Black people who were seen as social deviants and outcasts back into a Black caring community.

The Black helping tradition also believed that spiritual self-development was a necessary component for developing the caring personality. In fact, caring itself was seen as a spiritual act. A selfish, antisocial, hostile, greedy, socially aggressive, and antagonistic person was considered to be spiritually alienated, if not spiritually dead. Such a person was viewed as a threat to group survival and solidarity and a disturber of cosmic harmony. During the enslavement of African people, the spiritual self also provided the foundation for developing the racial self. No question more profoundly touched the depth of what it means to be Black in a White-dominated society than the question of the Black people's relation to God, nature, and the universe. The question of their relation to the divine was the central question around which other life-and-death questions evolved. What is the meaning of Black suffering? What is the nature of evil? Is God really just? Is God on the side of the oppressed? Is there a better life beyond the present hell some Black people are experiencing? Can Black life be made livable and meaningful under a daily system of relentless oppression?

In the Black helping tradition, a person was considered healthy and whole if the communal self and the racial self revolved around a strong spiritual core. As Figure 1 shows, the racial and the communal selves informed by a central spiritual self were seen as the major components for forming the caregiving personality.

The Caregiving Personality
Figure 1: The Racial Self and the Communal Self
Revolving around the Spiritual Self

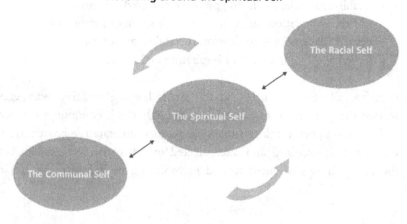

The caregiving personality in the Black helping tradition, then, is a spiritualized, socialized, and racialized personality seeking psychic stability and wholeness and promoting a sense of "we-ness" among the people. Spirituality, racial identity and worth, and communal action go together as the pillars of the Black helping tradition. The spiritual attached Black people to their place and role in the world and determined the extent to which they felt a sense of commitment to the well-being and uplift of Black people.

In our effort to highlight the Black helping tradition, in this book we make considerable use of Black autobiographies, with particular focus on the life stories of early Black caregivers and pioneering Black social workers. What we have found is that the "self" in Black autobiographies is a social, communal, largely prosocial self operating in a specific historical context. As C. L. Martin (1993) stated:

> The self of African-American autobiography is no mere 'lonely sojourner' on the road to life, no isolate with private career, but a soldier in a long, historic march toward Canaan ... a member of an oppressed social group, with ties and responsibilities to the other members. ... The self belongs to the people, and the people find voice in the self. (p. 18)

For example, in her studies of slave narratives, Starling (1981) stated that the narrators "were not telling of themselves alone" but of how their personal destinies were intertwined with the destinies of other slaves (p. 305).

By focusing on African American autobiographies, we seek to avoid presenting a helping experience based on historical abstractions. We seek to capture the essence of Black spirituality in the Black helping tradition by focusing on real, flesh-and-blood people operating in real historical situations. We seek an in-depth exploration of how spirituality works its way through the lives of Black individuals and transforms them from victims and dependents to agents and doers fashioning a better world for themselves and their people. By using autobiographical and biographical material we not only show the individual career as a microcosm of wider communal and caregiving commitments, but we also rescue from relative obscurity the biographies of some early Black caregivers and social workers who have made outstanding contributions to the Black helping tradition and to the social work profession.

A very important function of spirituality in the Black helping tradition was to create social myths to counter racist propaganda. In contemporary society, the word "myth" is generally synonymous with lies, half-truths, and distortions. However, we use it in respect to its older usage, as an expression of eternal truth through tales rich with metaphor and symbolism. In traditional Africa, people relied heavily on a collection of myths dealing with history, cosmology, supernatural beings, totems, animals, ancestors, and heroes to express eternal truths and to highlight sacred tradition. Although African myths are usually "phantasmagoric tales of gods and demons, exaggerated humans, improbable animals, impossible places, and unbelievable series of serendipitous events" (Ford, 1999), they served to inform and shape the worldview of African people, gave sanction to their customs and beliefs, and helped them to establish moral order and authority. Myths were used to impart proverbs, stories, metaphors, examples, and teachings, which served to promote group cohesiveness and ancestral connectedness and to give African people a unique sense of their identity and place in the world. Enslaved Africans and oppressed but free Black people in North America also felt a need to develop social myths that were powerful enough to combat the all-powerful racist mythomania deeming Black people inferior. They felt the need to free their spirit—their souls—from the baggage of egotism, cultural amnesia, and internalized racist propaganda. By drawing from stories from the Holy Bible, and from their own pantheon of historical heroes, folktales, and legends, Black people were able to create their own body of social myths that allowed them to view service to a higher power and helping others as actualizing and transcending values. By creating their own social myths, based on their spiritual strivings and beliefs, they were able to lay claim to their own larger-than-life historical and mythical heroes. These people were also able to develop the idea that they were not only part of a vast, divine force that was bigger than their troubles in this world but also a firm belief that no human power, no matter how ruthless and cunning, could deprive them of the dignity, integrity, and self-worth they received from the divine.

By creating positive social myths to counter racist mythomania, early Black caregivers also developed a strength perspective. Their spirituality allowed them to believe that Black people had special gifts and talents that were given to them by God and their ancestors, not by their oppressors. They believed that if Black people cultivated their God-given and ancestral genius, they would shape the destiny of Black people and make a major contribution to the world. Black caregivers strongly believed that one of their most important roles was to help Black people realize and cultivate their God-given gifts and become more fully and wholly African people.

Black elders today believe that, in essence, Black people should mourn the loss of their sense of the sacred. They should mourn the loss of their African homeland, African gods, and the millions of ancestors who died in the middle passage (the Maafa). They should mourn the thousands of Black people who fill the modern-day slave ships called prisons and the daily, senseless deaths of Black young people on the pavement of big-city streets. They should mourn the loss of their spiritual life, which keeps them centered and connected and which provides them with a rich, creative process of collective empathy, therapy, and social support. Many Black elders today believe that as Black people lose their sense of the sacred, they lose their ability to mourn. They lose hope. They lose the fire in their souls, and they need Black leaders who lift their spirits. These elders sense a time when the chief role of Black caregivers from the traditional African leaders to the early pioneering Black social workers was to instill hope and inspire Black people to more liberating visions of themselves and their possibilities. The renowned African novelist, Armah (1978), believed that inspiration was the major source of power to traditional African healers:

> We healers do not fear power. We avoid power deliberately, as long as that power is manipulative power. There is a kind of power we would all embrace and help create. It is the same power we use in our work: the power of inspiration. The power that respects the spirit in every being, in every thing, and lets every being be true to the spirit within. Healers should embrace that kind of power. (p. 309)

Inspiration was important to Black ministers, the chief helping professionals in early African American history. It was the primary tool of their work. Early Black social workers also believed that inspiration was crucial in circumventing the rise of alienation, defeatism, bitterness, and despair among Black people. To what extent have Black social workers today lost the power of inspiration for more manipulative methods of intervention?

As we explore spirituality in the Black helping tradition from a historical perspective, we are acutely aware that although spirituality in the past was the driving force behind Black caregiving, social work gradually shook off the remnants of its spiritual and religious roots to become fundamentally a secularistic profession, operating almost solely from a naturalistic perspective. We are well aware that currently there is a schism between Black spirituality and social work similar to the conflict Mendes (1982) recognized earlier between Black religion and psychotherapy. Mendes held that psychotherapy had come to explain physical and social phenomena in the empirical world solely in terms of natural causation and remedies and to view "humanity, not God or some other supraempirical reality" as "the center of life" (p. 206). Black people, of course, operated from a religious and spiritual perspective that saw "God-determination, rather than self-determination" as "the highest value" (p. 206).

Social work also abandoned the God-determination helping paradigm for a more secularistic approach. This way of viewing reality gained momentum among Black social workers during the Great Depression years of the 1930s. By the end of World War II, Black social workers had practically given up any reference to spiritual needs as an area of consideration for social work practice. Black social workers followed other social workers in the psychodynamic direction and began to view social problems not in terms of religious and spiritual values but in terms of value-neutrality, objectivity, and empirical observation. Black people also began to behave as if the secular techniques of social work were universally applicable to all people, regardless of color, culture, or historical circumstance.

The 1990s saw a resurgence of spirituality in social work, sparked in part by the growing interest people tend to have in religious matters and apocalyptic thinking on the eve of a new millennium. Smith (1997) stated that the relatively recent interest in spirituality is due in part to so many people of all races feeling that they are spiritually uprooted refugees with few attachments to community and little emotional support from deeply held religious beliefs (p. 39).

Because spiritual "rootlessness" is part of a deeper malaise operating in mainstream American culture, spirituality is destined to become an integral part of the social work curriculum. The key question of this study is: To what extent are social workers today equipped to revive spirituality in the Black helping tradition and to use spirituality as a vital instrument for strengthening and empowering Black individuals, families, and communities?

As we pursue the historical significance and contemporary relevance of spirituality in the Black helping tradition, the key concepts of this book are defined as follows:

- *The Black helping tradition* is defined as the largely independent struggle of Black people to collectively promote their survival and advancement from one generation to the next.
- Black spirituality is the sense of the sacred and divine that inspires, motivates, and uplifts Black people and endows them with dignity, self-worth, meaning, purpose, and hope as they seek to transcend and transform soul-destroying, life-threatening systems.
- Black religiosity is a manifestation of Black spirituality that is often viewed in terms of organized religion and denominational ties. In the Black experience, the lines between religiosity and spirituality are often blurred. Spirituality in the Black helping tradition supersedes and overarches religiosity.
- The caregiving personality comprises the spiritual, racial, and communal selves as components of the total caregiving or helping self.
- "Race work" was an effort by 19th-century Black people to advance the survival, liberation, and well-being of Black people. It was Black people's form of social work in the 19th century.

With these concepts as the chief organizing principles of the book, the chapters are organized as follows:

- Chapter 1 provides an introduction.
- Chapter 2 examines the role of spirituality in traditional African helping practices by following a case example.
- Chapter 3 discusses how conjurers and slave preachers used religion and spirituality on the slave plantation to give enslaved Africans a feeling of some control over their lives and to inspire them to seek freedom.
- Chapter 4 explores spirituality among enslaved Africans in America and the torturous process of freeing themselves from the slaveholder's religious mythomania, propaganda, and imagery and developing a sense of racial self-worth conducive to serving their own communal interest as a people.
- Chapter 5 analyzes race work and spirituality among 19th-century freed Black people during and after slavery.

- Chapter 6 discusses the attempt of early Black scholars such as
W. E. B. Du Bois and Alexander Crummell to shape race work into
a sophisticated, systematic social philosophy to serve as a strength
perspective to bridge race work to the new profession of social work
and to guide the advancement and liberation cause.
- Chapter 7 draws from the biographies of four Black pioneering male
social workers—Reverdy C. Ransom, R. R. Wright, Jr., Edmund Haynes,
and Monroe N. Work—to explore how they used the race work spiritual
paradigm in their social work practice with Black people.
- Chapter 8 discusses the leadership role of four pioneering Black female
social workers—S. Willie Layten, Eva Bowles, Mamie De Mena, and
Thyra Edwards—in their attempts to form fictive kinship (communal) ties
with Black women in a quest for gender empowerment and community.
- Chapter 9 evaluates the limitations and strengths of mainstream social
work in dealing with issues of Black spirituality, and provides a framework
for incorporating Black spirituality into contemporary social work practice.
- Chapter 10 reviews the efforts of the American-centered and the
Black experience-based social work paradigms to revive spirituality in the
Black helping tradition. The chapter also shows how these paradigms use
spirituality in the intervention process on the micro, mezzo, and macro levels.

Overall, spirituality in the Black helping tradition might appear in some
sense to be a relic of the past with little usefulness in a rapidly changing secular, postmodern age of information. However, there are already numerous
empirical studies (Hill, 1997; Jagers & Mock, 1993; Mattis, 1997; Potts, 1991)
suggesting that religious or spiritual orientation may be crucial to the
prevention of antisocial behavior and other negative life outcomes of Black
people, particularly young Black people. To untold numbers of Black
people over the generations, spirituality in the Black helping tradition has
been a powerful tool for survival, sanity, group solidarity, and liberation.
Historically, Black people believed that spirituality and caring were the twin
pillars of racial and communal consciousness. The new century affords yet
another opportunity for Black people to get back in tune with the sacred
heritage that they believed for hundreds of years represented the best
within themselves.

CHAPTER TWO

Spirituality and the Traditional African Helper

T raditional African helping professionals, such as diviners, herbalists, healers, medicine specialists, priests, prophets, rainmakers, wise elders, and even sorcerers, had no difficulty bringing spirituality into the helping process. No problem they faced, whether physical or emotional, private or social, was outside the spiritual domain. Even "accidents" were generally assessed by them in terms of supernatural causation and rectification, underscoring that the traditional African spiritual approach was a holistic approach. Traditional African helpers believed that even small, routine problems could have universal significance, that any human suffering could be a sign that evil was winning over cosmic good in the battle to regulate human affairs.

Traditional African caregivers had to have a greater understanding of the African spiritual worldview than the laypersons they were called upon to serve. They had to have thorough knowledge of the spiritual forces that operated to do harm or good and mastery over the techniques that put good spiritual forces on the side of their clients. For example, a case cited by Ogbonnaya (1994) of a sick man who came to an Igbo diviner illustrates the importance of spirituality in traditional African helping practices. (A diviner in traditional Africa was a helping professional whose primary concern was diagnosing the spiritual cause of affliction and prescribing a remedy designed to restore psychic balance and physical and emotional health.) People came to diviners seeking help for numerous persistent and unexplained afflictions: illness, barrenness, haunting dreams, poor crops, suspicion of being hexed, sudden death of loved ones, and so on. The traditional African diviner is the forerunner of the modern psychotherapist and the clinical social worker. In this case, the sick man came seeking a cure for his unexplained ailment after Western doctors failed to assess what was wrong with him.

Ogbonnaya (1994) said that the diviner first started his case by having members of the sick man's family peer into a calabash filled with water and tell what they had seen. He then asked the sick man to do the same. The sick man said that he had seen nothing in the calabash and the diviner told him that that was his problem, an inability to see. The diviner then proceeded to engage the sick man in a lengthy interview, asking the sick man about his dreams, his relationship to his ancestors, his parents, his family, his children, and his totem. (A totem is a symbolic representation in nature of one's soul. It could be an animal, a plant, the moon, the sun, or any other natural object considered to be related symbolically, metaphorically, or spiritually to an individual, family, or clan.) After the diviner had exhausted the process of inquiry, he discovered that the sick man had not paid proper attention to his dead grandfather, who represented the sick man's reincarnated self. The sick man knew where his grandfather was buried, yet he had never paid a visit to the grave site of this most important ancestor. He had never paid proper respect or homage. The diviner also discovered that the sick man was having problems with his father and that one of the sick's own sons was angry with him. Furthermore, he discovered that the sick man had killed an animal that represented his totem and had sold the carcass. Finding that the sick man was not in spiritual harmony with a significant ancestor, his father, his son, and his totem, the diviner said to the sick man, "You have been scattered all over the place" (Ogbonnaya, 1994, p. 85). After manipulating sacred objects of his trade, he began to prescribe a remedy.

First, the sick man was to make peace with his reincarnated self. The diviner prescribed that the sick man go to his grandfather's grave and spend three nights there performing several appeasement rituals (outlined in detail by the diviner) to placate the wrath of the sick man's grandfather. The sick man could never expect to get well physically or emotionally until he corrected this spiritual imbalance with his reincarnated self.

Second, the diviner indicated that the bad soul of the sick man's father was operating against him. The sick man must get his father to withdraw his bad soul and replace it with his good soul. This would bring the sick man back into harmony with his parental self. Traditional Africans believed that each child inherited a part of the soul of his or her parents. For example, among the Akan people of Ghana, the "Mogya" is the mother's spirit that is part of the child's blood, and the "Sunsum" is the father's spirit transmitted via his semen to his offspring. Traditional Africans believed that when the parents were out of harmony with themselves or with each other, this situation could seriously affect their children's emotional, mental, and physical health. In fact, diviners generally looked first at the situation of the parents whenever a child was having any type of problem requiring ritualized assistance. In this case, the diviner prescribed that the sick man must buy a goat and give it to his parents to appease the bad parental self of his father.

Next, the sick man was to withdraw his own bad parental soul from his son to ease his son's anger toward him. The sick man realized that he should make sure that he and his wife were in harmony with each other because their parental souls could adversely affect their children. The sick man was told that he must have a feast for his family and make special overtures toward his angry son.

Finally, the diviner told the sick man that he had to make peace with nature. By destroying an animal that symbolically represented his own character and personality, he had damaged that part of his soul that dwells in nature. In other words, he had committed a sacred taboo. The sick man was instructed to go to the spot where he had killed the animal and build an altar to the animal that represented his totem. It was only then that he would restore a harmonious relationship with nature.

After holding the sick man responsible for carrying out the special rituals and tasks designed to bring him back into harmony and balance with his ancestors, his extended family, his immediate family, and nature, the diviner was certain that the client's sickness would leave him and he would regain his health. It was clear to the diviner that the man's sickness was not a physical ailment, but an ailment of the spirit. The diviner told the sick man to "call back your souls from where they have gone. Be at peace with the world. Be at peace with yourself" (Ogbonnaya, 1994, p. 85).

Although this case of the sick man was fairly recent, it was handled by the diviner in much the same way that it would have been dealt with thousands of years ago. Traditional African helping professionals have so meticulously and resolutely carried on their tradition that their helping professions are the longest surviving caregiving professions in the world. The religious and spiritual worldviews that are the driving force behind the African helping tradition are thousands of years older than Judaism, Islam, and Christianity—the world's three major religions. Although we speak of traditional African spirituality and helping tradition in the past tense, the sick man's case indicates that we could very well be describing helping practices that are still in full force on the African continent today.

THE AFRICAN SPIRITUAL UNIVERSE

Traditional African helping professionals operated in a spiritual universe in which there was no clear distinction between the sacred and profane. Whether traditional African people were pastoralists or cultivators, raiders or nomads, whether they belonged to fishing societies or trading societies, or were governed democratically by family or clan elders in simple villages or by autocratic kings and queens in complex nation–states, they operated largely from a spiritual outlook. In the world of traditional African people, the family and community were sacred. The children, the elders, the ancestors, nature, and the gods were sacred, and the chief role of helping practitioners was to help African people maintain a sacred covenant with these divine entities. Traditional African helpers were guided by the belief that all human life was animated by a vital spiritual life force. To diviners and other helpers among the Yoruba people of Nigeria, for example, this spiritual dynamism was known (as it still is today) as "Ase," meaning the power of transformation or the power to make things happen. Traditional African people among the Ashanti people of Ghana called this spiritual essence "Okra," meaning the eternal breath of life. Traditional African helpers also believed that this spiritual force was so vast that it dwelled in nature. Many of the African gods and spirits had refused to dwell in something as puny and limited as human beings and chose instead to reside in nature where they could have dominion over the forest, the sky, the weather, the sea, and so forth. Traditional African helpers not only had to tap into this spiritual force to ensure that their clients were in harmonious relationship with themselves, their families, and communities but also harmonious with the natural environment around them. Traditional African helpers were also well aware that the spiritual force that gave vitality, energy, and life could also find a place in inanimate objects such as stones or wood. African people were known for their wood carvings of masks and figurines and other objects that held the spirits of their gods and ancestors. For example, the Golden Stool of the Ashanti people was viewed as the dwelling place of the soul of the Ashanti nation. Even today it is considered to be so sacred that it is never to touch the ground and even the Ashanti King is forbidden to sit upon it.

THE HIGH GOD

Traditional African helpers operated in a spiritual universe that was hierarchical. At the top of the hierarchy was a high God—the creator, ruler, and ultimate life force of the universe. This high God was viewed in some societies as a male and in some as a female. In many African societies, it was viewed as having both male and female qualities. Whatever way the high God was viewed anthropomorphically, this ultimate life source of the universe was generally considered to be so remote and distant from human affairs that it was largely unapproachable. Although they generally built shrines to the high God, many groups believed that the high God should be approached only in times of special need. Some groups feared any contact with the high God. They believed that the high God's power was too awesome, that any closeness could result in serious illness or some natural calamity such as a hurricane or drought. Some groups, such as the Gikuyu people of Kenya, were extremely cautious of approaching their high God, Ngai, their creator and giver of all things. Kenyatta (1965) stated that although Ngai had a temporary earthly home on mountains (his chief residence was in the sky), Ngai was not primarily concerned with the well-being of individuals. Therefore, individuals had to be extremely cautious in approaching and disturbing Ngai with their petitions and prayers lest they incur his wrath. Ngai was somewhat concerned with the well-being of the community on the whole. However, even then traditional African helpers were to "turn to God and offer sacrifice only in serious matters such as drought or outbreak of an epidemic, and great distress, as with serious illness" (Kenyatta, 1965, p. 230). Helpers among Gikuyu people could also approach Ngai during "the four main crises" of life—birth, initiation, marriage, and death.

AFRICAN DEITIES

Below the high God on the African spiritual hierarchy were the lesser gods and deities; they were generally who traditional Africans turned to for problem solving and to serve as intermediaries between humans and the high God. Kenyatta (1965) wrote:

> There are occasions in each man's life, apart from the four crises, when he requires spiritual assistance. He may have broken a taboo; he may attribute some ill luck to such an infraction. This is reckoned as an individual matter, and Ngai is not approached. The man's purification or absolution is achieved by means of the medicine man, who will work by establishing contact with such of the ancestral spirits as may be thought involved. (p. 226)

Traditional African helpers were not lacking in gods to call on to help them solve their problems. Some African religions had only a few deities in their pantheon, but others had more gods than the people could sustain. For example, although Yoruba folklore focused attention around several major gods (such as Ogun, Shango, Yemoja, Obatala, Elegba, and Oshun), the Yorubas in actuality had hundreds of deities covering practically every aspect of nature, human relationships, and the universe. Most traditional Africans had their own personal gods or spiritual guardians, their family gods, and the major gods of their clan to serve and to turn to for help. Also, in traditional Africa, there were numerous nature gods, such as gods of mountains, forests, rivers, streams, trees, and hills. While the nature gods were seldom worshipped and often could not expect a temple, shrine, or altar to be built in their honor, few Africans dared to ignore them altogether. If, for example, Africans were to enter a forest or travel on a particular river, they at least had to pay proper respect to, and even get permission from, the gods who ruled those two natural domains. With so many spiritual entities in their world, traditional Africans often created an extensive body of social myths pertaining to major deities. These social myths guided ethical and moral choices and informed human conduct.

ANCESTORS

Below the numerous lesser gods on the African spiritual hierarchy were the ancestors. In the family, ancestors were the deceased family elders who were the most important members of the African extended family. In the community, the ancestors were mythical and historical heroes, heroines, and founders who were revered by community members and often treated as if they were gods. Just as traditional Africans were not lacking for gods, they definitely were not lacking for ancestors. As the Senegalese poet, Birago Diop (1975) suggested in his famous poem, "Spirits," the ancestors were ubiquitous. The poem reads in part:

Those who are dead are not ever gone
They are in the darkness that grows lighter
And in the darkness that grows darker.
The dead are not down in the earth;
They are in the trembling of the trees
In the groaning of the woods,

In the water that sleeps
They are in the hut, they are in the crowd:
The dead are not dead.

The ancestors were still considered to be among them, although not in the flesh. B. Diop (1975) wrote:

Each day they renew ancient bonds
Ancient bonds that hold fast
Binding our lot to their law,
to the will of the spirits stronger than we
to the spell of our dead who are not really dead,
Whose covenant binds us to life
Whose authority binds to their will ....

Ancestors were powerful because they intersected the profane and the sacred world. They were the chief intermediaries and intercessors that could be called on to carry the petitions, prayers, pleas, supplications, and sacrifices of their living descendants to the gods and to act as cosmic spokespersons on their behalf. For these cosmic favors, the ancestors demanded that their relatives show them the proper deference and respect. Above all else, ancestors demanded that their living descendants remember them. In this respect, Mbiti (1970) stated that ancestors are best understood in terms of two traditional African concepts of time, a "Sasa period" that is the period of the here and now and of the immediate future, and a "Zamani period" that is the period of a prehistory, remote past, or mythical time (pp. 28–29). Mbiti (1970) stated that as long as deceased family members are remembered by their relatives and friends who have survived them, as long as they recall their names and remember their personality, character, words, incidents, and deeds, the departed are not really dead. They are among what Mbiti calls "the living dead" (p. 32). The living dead, according to Mbiti, are physically dead but alive in the spirit world and in the memories of those who know them. The longer the living dead are recognized by name, the longer they remain in the "now-moment" period of Sasa. However, after their names and deeds are no longer recalled or recognized among the living, they are in effect completely dead as far as family ties are concerned. They pass beyond the horizon of the Sasa period and enter into the time zone of

Zamani, where they become unknown spirits merged with other spirits whose names are no longer uttered and whose deeds are no longer recorded or recalled in the present time.

Through remembrance, the ancestors achieve a kind of personal and collective immortality. As long as relatives do not let them slip out of the Sasa period, they can call on their ancestors to intercede in the spirit world on their behalf. Therefore, in traditional Africa, it was in the interest of the living to always invoke the names of their ancestors at birth and naming ceremonies, weddings, funerals, and all significant family and community events. It was in their interest to pour libation to them, build altars and shrines in their honor, make animal sacrifices on their behalf, feed them ritual meals, conduct community feasts and festivals in their honor, show obeisance, and dramatize their exploits in stories, dances, and songs. If their departed loved ones died in a strange land, it was also in their interest to carry their bodies or their bones back to the land of their birth. This also would ensure that their sacred ties, binding them mystically and spiritually to the sacred world, would continue. Traditional African helpers were often called on to help living descendants regain communion with their ancestors. This was not done just out of fear of the wrath the ancestors could mete out or because the ancestors were the connecting link to the spiritual universe and to the cosmic good but also because the living descendants were the issue and heir of the uncounted multitudes of ancestors. Pride in one's ancestry was considered in and of itself a reason to honor and remember them.

MYTHICAL HEROES AND HEROINES

Traditional African communities often had a host of heroes and heroines in which to take pride. Deceased community founders, noble warriors, wise rulers, and other heroic clan members were honored on the community level with the same fervor that family ancestors were honored on the family level. In many instances, these community heroes and heroines were put on the same level in the spiritual hierarchy as the gods. Their lives and exploits took on mythical proportion as they were extolled in stories, poetry, music, and dance, and through dramatic rituals and reenactments. In many instances, it was difficult to tell whether the African heroes and heroines actually walked the face of the earth as real, flesh-and-blood people or if they were just archetypal figures created out of a rich, fascinating African imagination. It was often difficult to tell because traditional African griots (storytellers) often had these heroes and heroines wrestling with mythical beasts, descending into the depths of the underworld, conversing with animals, or forming sexual liaisons and marriages with the gods.

Ford (1999) stated that African social myths represented the values and norms of the ancestors and that these myths came in numerous forms. There were myths about death and resurrection, sacred warriors, sacred animals, the African goddess, demons, the beginning and end of creation, and so forth. Whatever form social myths took, they were an intimate part of the traditional African spiritual worldview and were considered to be key to group cohesiveness and continuity.

African social myths were not only designed to answer timeless questions of humanity and to convey eternal truths of the universe but also to convey to the African people the customs, beliefs, practices, and outlooks their ancestors wanted them to adhere to for the continuation of the group. By using the timeless messages of the ancestors to inform and guide the present generation, myths included riddles, symbols, and metaphors. For example, Ford (1999) stated that a social myth that was prevalent among traditional African people was about the savior-warrior hero that descended into the belly of some ogre or monster and freed his or her people from being totally annihilated or devoured. For example, griots in early Benin told lively tales of how the founder of the Dahomean Kingdom came to his people out of the belly of a leopard through the threshold of death to freedom and prosperity. Such social myths are rich in metaphor pertaining to the African American experience. They convey images of Black people in the dungeons of the slave forts, in the hold of slave ships, and in the grips of the monstrous slave plantation. During the civil rights era, such a metaphor conjured up images of Black Americans trying to liberate themselves from the evil monster of segregation and third-class citizenship. Such myths also address the needs of African Americans as individuals and as a group to look within themselves to find the courage and the strength to face and free themselves from their own internal demons.

Traditional African helpers had to immerse themselves in their people's culture, history, cosmology, and mythology. They had to have greater knowledge than laypersons about their people's songs, prayers, fables, rituals, folklore, and values. In some cases, traditional Africans were trained in secret societies, where they underwent special rites of passage and were given all the esoteric knowledge pertaining to their people's life, history, mythology, and culture. For example, it takes African trainees seeking to become Yoruba Ifa diviners between 10 and 20 years to master and memorize word for word the monumental literary corpus of Ifa, which is divided into 256 distinct volumes and subdivided into numerous chapters. Their memories are stretched to an almost limitless extent for the retention of knowledge about Ifa divination myths that are needed to master the traditional art of healing.

Because traditional African helpers were specialists in their people's history, culture, and mythology, it was their chief duty to ensure that much of what they knew was passed on to African families. Unlike literate cultures, such as that of the Yorubas, most traditional African cultures had no written traditions. Wisdom had to be passed from generation to generation by storytelling, songs, celebrations, and initiation rituals from birth to death. Through hours of listening to elders and other helping professionals discuss practically every aspect of life both past and present, African people could become well-versed in their people's history and culture and in the major life issues of the day. Much of what African helpers had to teach was directed to the children and their parents. Both were often willing to sit for hours at the feet of these helpers listening, talking, and discussing all aspects of their people's experience. Parents, particularly, had a responsibility to immerse their children in their culture and history. Kenyatta (1965) told how Gikuyu women used songs to immerse their children in their history:

> The education of very small children is entirely in the hands of the mother and nurse. It is carried on through the medium of lullabies. In these the whole history and tradition of the family and clan are embodied and, by hearing these lullabies daily, it is easy for the children to assimilate this early teaching without any strain. This is one of the methods by which the history of the people is passed on from generation to generation. (p. 100)

When children are older, Kenyatta (1965) stated, they are given "memory training" (p. 100). Similar to most traditional African peoples, the Gikuyu people relied heavily on the oral tradition to transmit their culture and history. This required processing huge amounts of information about one's cultural heritage through memory. Memories of the group's history, values, and culture were reinforced through initiation rites for girls and boys of various ages. In "rites of passage," young people were not only steeped in their history and culture, but special care was also devoted to physical development, health and hygiene, the use of different medicines, sex education, and issues regarded by the Gikuyu as taboo. Parents were held accountable as the chief judges of how well their children had absorbed the lessons taught by their elders. Very strong criticism was directed at the parents whose children did not behave according to the approved tribal law of conduct. Such parents were considered to have neglected the important task of preparing their children to become worthy members of the community (Kenyatta, p. 101).

MANAGING EVIL

The lowest entities on the traditional African spiritual hierarchy were evil spirits. Overall, spiritual power was seen as basically good, but evil was recognized as a stark reality in the world. Traditional Africans believed that in some cases supernatural power could be used maliciously by both spiritual and human agents to wreak havoc on human life. Some African spirits were angry, hostile, and evil by nature. Some generally good spiritual forces, which wanted nothing more than happiness, peace, and contentment, could become angry and express their outrage by exacting misery on human life. For example, the ancestors generally worked on the side of their living descendants. However, they could be very stubborn and act with stiff judgment, iron will, and brutal wrath when they believed they were neglected or disobeyed. The harsh wrath of the family and clan gods often came in the form of epidemics, locusts, poverty, and other major calamities. Traditional African helpers were frequently called on to help their people neutralize the forces of evil. Many traditional African helpers had to undergo years of specialized training in learning the ways of evil in order to have a wide range of flexible options to combat it. They often had to master special rituals outlining the use of potent medicines and the techniques for calling on the power of the ancestors and the gods to help them in their battle to ward off evil.

Witchcraft was one of the chief evils traditional African helpers were called on to put in check. Nothing instilled a greater sense of terror and dread in traditional Africans than this evil. Witchcraft was seen as a malevolent supernatural force that depended on human agents to bring it into the world. Through magic and other forms of spiritual manipulation, evil human agents could harness power from the underworld. Witchcraft was seen as having no other purpose than to work against whatever aims good individuals and groups were trying to achieve. Witchcraft sought to create disharmony when there was harmony, divisiveness when there was unity, and social antagonism when there were peaceful relations. It was dreaded because it was not easily controllable by divination, sacrifice, magic, or medicine after it was unleashed on the world. Many traditional Africans felt some reassurance that witchcraft, hopefully before it did too much damage, could eventually be overcome by the infinitely superior forces of cosmic good. Others did not feel safe until every person thought to be a witch was hunted down, tortured, and brutally and ritually murdered. Even today one reads from time to time about the beheading or burning of witches in some place on the African continent.

Many traditional African helpers believed that the only assurance that evil would not win over the forces of good was for the community to practice moral, ethical, and altruistic behavior as the highest good. They were taught throughout their lives that the ancestors and the gods were pleased with moral, prosocial, principled acts that promoted community. They were taught that nothing angered these good cosmic forces more than divisive, antisocial, selfish acts that brought disharmony to the communal bond. Traditional Africans believed that when a person was out of harmony with his spiritual–communal intrapsychic selves, he or she was out of harmony with the community. Mental, moral, and spiritual imbalances and disharmony in social relations opened the gates from which all kinds of evil flowed. Traditional Africans believed that witchcraft thrived on disharmony and that greed, selfishness, and violence could cause cosmic disturbances in the form of drought, an outbreak of plague, and other natural disasters.

Many traditional African groups guarded against any antisocial act that showed even a hint of upsetting the fragile threads of a harmonious communal life. For example, the Taita people of Kenya believed that any expression of anger not only disturbed the ancestors and gods and disrupted communal harmony, but also had the potential to destroy human life (Harris, 1978). Even a child's anger toward his or her parents was viewed as having the potential of bringing about the parents' death. Therefore, everybody was divined for anger. The Taita people believed that anger had to be detected before it manifested itself in sorcery and witchcraft. To the Taita people, casting out anger was a central theme of their cultural and spiritual lives. Hidden anger, believed to be the most dangerous and insidious kind, was particularly to be pinpointed and removed through an anger removal process the Taita people called "Kitasa." Kitasa was designed to assure the community that "cool heads" and "good hearts" would prevail. Only "cool

Spirituality and the Black Helping Tradition in Social Work

heads" and "good hearts" could be victorious over sorcery and witchcraft, assure the blessings of the ancestors and the gods, restore intrapsychic balance, and maintain the communal bond.

AFRICAN ROYALTY AND THE TRADITIONAL HELPER

African kings, queens, princesses, princes, and other royalty often conceived of themselves as being in power because of divine decree. Therefore, they also took their places on the African spiritual hierarchy, believing that they were not only endowed by God with material superiority but also with spiritual superiority. Believing that they were closer to the ancestors and the gods than their subjects and that their own power and authority emanated from the spiritual world, they believed they were in a better position to tap into spiritual sources to advance their own needs and the needs of the people. Traditional African religions gave sanction to the power and authority of African royalty.

In traditional, pre-colonial Africa, African monarchies and empires were present everywhere on the African continent, covering vast territory and ruling over a vast number of people. Even some of the smaller clans and villages living in remote areas often came under the authority of African monarchy. African people became accustomed to looking at the royal family, the king in particular, as the divine authority on earth working for balance and harmony between the sacred and the profane worlds. Diop (1987) wrote:

> Within the framework of this universal harmony, in which each being has his place, the king has a precise function, a definite role: he must be the one with the greatest vital force in the whole kingdom. Only in this way can he serve as mediator - he being sacrosanct with the superior universe, without creating any break, any catastrophic upheaval within the ontological forces. If he is not a legitimate king, fulfilling those exact conditions of established filiation, and appointed according to the rites of tradition, all of nature will be sterile, drought will overtake the fields, women will no longer bear children, epidemics will strike the people. (p. 61)

Because the kings were viewed as the sacrosanct mediator between the people and the god, their duties and obligations were strict. They, above everybody else, were expected to follow the traditions of the ancestors and the examples of the founders. They, above everybody else, were to display the strength, courage, and character of mythical African heroes and pay tribute to the ancestors and gods. In some cases, in traditional Africa, when a king showed a sign of bad health, loss of strength, weakening of the mind, or even a physical deformity, he was put to death actually or symbolically; in either case, he was dethroned and a stronger person with an enhanced level of spiritual energy and vital force succeeded him.

To maintain his power, the king and other members of the royal family had no choice but to work closely with traditional African helpers. They had to turn to priests, medicine men, herbalists, diviners, and so forth to help them manipulate forces in the spiritual world. For example, even before a king waged a war on another king, the war first took place on a spiritual plane long before the physical battles took place. Priests and others familiar with the ways of nature, the gods, and the ancestors would have to be consulted, and the vital forces of the universe had to be marshalled in the king's favor. Only then could the king be assured of victory. Also, kings needed traditional helpers to ensure that the gods and the ancestors were appeased. An angry god could cause a drought or famine that could result in the people losing confidence in their king and the king losing his throne.

Some traditional African helpers were vital parts of the king's court. This could prove to be a prosperous position as long as things went well. However, after things became out of balance and the king was no longer at ease, the traditional African helpers generally were the first scapegoats and the first to be persecuted. For example, Armah (1978) depicts in his novel, *The Healers*, scenes where an African king ordered healers who were not under his control to be executed. Although this is a fictional account, it shows that real traditional African healers were in a very vulnerable position. They could be accused of sorcery and witchcraft, mixing poisons from secret formulas to poison the royal family, or placing a hex or curse on them.

Traditional African helpers who were not under the influence of African royalty often found themselves in an oppositional position. Steeped as they were in the people's history, culture, customs, and values, they could see more clearly than the average citizens when the king and other members of the royal family were acting contrary to the sacred ways of the ancestors and violating sacred decrees. They were in a better position than most members of society to see the corruption and evilness of African royalty. African royalty already wielded tremendous power. They would expropriate land, enlist soldiers, mobilize labor, collect taxes, appoint administrators, mete out punishment, wage war, and repress any forces that presented a threat to their power and authority. Ideologically, traditional African helpers who were part of the royal court operated from an ideology that was antithetical to African royalty. Many traditional African helpers lived in villages where communalistic, egalitarian, democratic, and proletarian clan ties were radically opposed to aristocratic, monarchic tendencies on moral, traditional, and spiritual grounds. For example, under a system of communalism, African people (by virtue of being family and community members) were assured of sufficient land to meet their needs. African royalty had a tendency to appropriate the best land for themselves and to turn the people into tenants from whom they exacted rent and taxes and a portion of the agricultural products the people produced. Also in communalistic tribal societies, every individual had an obligation to promote the welfare of the group, and every individual could expect and even demand that the group also obligate itself to his or her well-being. Under African monarchy, royal families were primarily concerned with luxurious living, extending their empires, and enhancing their own power and status even if it meant exploiting and abusing the people.

Traditional African helpers could tolerate royal families who showed concern for the well-being of the people. However, when kings and the royal court used their power to make human sacrifices to appease the gods, when they held Black people hostage for ransom, and when they sold their own people into slavery, traditional African helpers generally were at war with African royalty. In turn, royalty was very suspicious of them, not because they were strong economically, militarily, or politically but because they were strong spiritually. It was the spirituality of the people in general that African royalty feared most. This explains why a King of Dahomey who sold his people into slavery had them walk several times around what was called "the tree of forgetfulness" before they passed through the gate of no return and boarded the slave ships. The hope was that if they forgot their ancestors and their gods and, most significantly, if they forgot what their king had done to them, they would not place a curse on the king and his family.

MULTIPLE SELVES AND SPIRITUAL SELF-DEVELOPMENT
Traditional African helpers not only had to take into consideration gods, ancestors, evil spirits, mythical heroes, and African royalty in the outside environment, but they were also concerned with the inner spiritual

self-development of the African individual. Traditional African helpers sought to develop a personality that corresponded to the spiritual universe. Not only did traditional African helpers believe that Africans had a biological connection to ancestors and a spiritual connection to the gods, but they also believed in a psychological connection to both. They believed that the African personality consisted of multiple selves that reflected an intrapsychic link to the spiritual world and to the communal bond (the family, the clan, and the community). Centuries before the esteemed psychologist William James (1890) theorized that a person is made up of several selves (an empirical or material self, a social self, a spiritual self, and a pure ego self), traditional Africans had conceived of the person as a composite of multiple selves. As the case illustrated earlier showed, the sick man had to come to grips with his fragmented selves that determined the nature of his spiritual and human relationships. The prominent social psychologist, George Herbert Mead (1934) discovered that, "We divide ourselves up in all sorts of different selves in reference to our acquaintances" (p. 142). The acquaintances of the multiple African selves just happen to include ancestors, gods, and other forces in the spiritual world. The gods and the ancestors were said to have found a place in an invisible, supernatural realm and in the head of each African person. To speak of an ancestral self was to imply that people had a kind of spiritual antenna within their own psyche that put them in touch with reincarnated ancestors and guardian spirits. When they were not in harmony with these supernatural entities, the gods and the ancestors would surely be disturbed and the people would surely suffer the consequences, physically, morally, and psychologically.

The number of spiritual selves recognized by traditional African helpers depended on the ethnic group. However, Kamalu (1998) stated that the selves that recurred most frequently in traditional African societies were "the destiny self" [often referred to as "the spiritual double"], "the transcendent self" [often seen as the soul, breath, or life force], "the thinking or feeling self," "the ancestral/reincarnated self" [often seen as the ancestral guardian], and "the dream self" [often referred to as "the shadow"] (p. 52). Ogbonnaya (1994) identified "the ancestral self," "the destinal self," "the parental self," "the totemic self," "the emergent self," and even "the mischievous self" (pp. 81–82). Whatever specific selves particular African groups recognized, spiritual self-development was a major goal of the traditional African helping legacy. Self-development worked hand-in-hand with the effort of traditional African helpers to promote community. The intrapsychic multiple selves reflected the person's relationship to the family, the ancestors, the natural environment, and the gods. Ogbonnaya (1994) wrote: "If the person is a community of selves, an image of the greater community, then ... not only is the person participating as a whole being in the community of beings, but the person is a community of selves in interplay" (p. 82). Each self incorporated in the psyche of the individual had to be in harmony with other selves for the individual to be in harmony with the community.

Overall, then, as intimated by the case of the sick man that was illustrated earlier, a chief role of the traditional African helping professional was to help the individual get in tune with his or her higher, most significant, and enduring self. Armah (1978) wrote:

> Yes, we have more than one self. The difficulty is to know which self to make the permanent one, and which we should leave ephemeral. You set one of the passing selves above your permanent self: that's doing violence to yourself. Things will go wrong then, and you'll never know why as long as you remain in the same situation and don't move out of it. (p. 82)

False selves grew out of the demands and expectations of other people who did not have their best interest at heart. Traditional African healers believed that when people embraced false selves they were not only in danger of having these false selves dominate and do great violence to their real selves, but they were also vulnerable to having their real or true selves killed. After their spirit was broken, stifled, or killed, they were susceptible to all kinds of afflictions of the mind, body, and soul. One way of helping people rediscover their true selves was to put them in touch with their spiritual destiny.

THE DESTINAL SELF AND COMMUNITY

When James (1890) discussed the multiple selves of the personality, he explained that the spiritual self is the central, integrating, "most enduring and intimate part of the self" and can be considered "the self of all other selves." (pp. 296–297). James wrote that when the spiritual self is weakened, the individual's ability to argue and discriminate, his moral sensibility, and his conscience and will also are weakened, and the person becomes alienated from the self (p. 296). If any self in traditional Africa was said to be the central, integrating, most enduring self of all other selves, it was the destinal self. The destinal self was extremely important to traditional Africans because it oriented the other selves around the fulfillment of a person's life mission. Kamalu (1998) wrote:

> The orientation of all the … selves in us is provided by the self known as destiny. Obviously these selves merge into one another and cannot always be distinguished from one another easily, but the destiny or double self has the special function of not only directing the whole person towards his purpose in life—it also … is the part of ourselves associated with an unrealized future and the unfolding of a 'higher' or 'better' self.… However we come about this destiny, it is a life-changing discovery. (p. 78)

Because of the significance of the destinal self, all traditional African societies had a name for it. In ancient Egypt, it was called "Ka"; among the Asante people of Ghana, the destinal self was called "Kra," and among the Akan people of Ghana, the concept "Okra" was used. Kuba people of Zaire called the destinal self "Ido"; the Fon people of Nigeria called it "Se"; the Bini people of Nigeria called it "Ehi"; the Igbos of Nigeria called it "Chi"; and the Yorubas of Nigeria called it "Ori." Abimbola (1997) wrote that, "The Yoruba regard Ori as … the greatest god of all. Every man's Ori is regarded as his personal god who is expected to be more interested in his personal affairs than the other gods who are regarded as belonging to everybody" (p. 114). Whatever the destinal self was called in traditional African societies, it was seen as the essence of God in human beings and all living things, as the divine substance that endows individuals with intelligence, energy, drive, and willpower as they move toward the fulfillment of their destiny. Traditional Africans believed that people acquired their destinal selves in the spiritual world even before they were born. Once in the world, the destinal self was significant throughout a person's life cycle. Therefore, from birth until death, a person was to take every opportunity to pay special tribute to the destinal self. Somé (1998) said that the Dagara people of Burkina Fasa paid particular attention to the destinal self, which they called "Siura." He explained:

> Your Siura is behind you, trying to work with you as closely as possible to keep you on the path of your purpose, speaking to you through your inspiration, your dreams, and your instincts. An offering to your Siura

now and then at an ancestor altar or any altar is appropriate, a token of appreciation for the diligence and leadership they have shown toward your purpose. (p. 34)

When one was out of harmony with the destinal self, the other selves were in danger of becoming disjointed and fragmented; without this intrapsychic antenna linking him or her to a nurturing spiritual world and a life's mission, one's personality was in danger of disintegrating. Without the destiny, traditional Africans believed, there was a danger of the volatile cluster of forces (which make up the person) falling out of balance and into anarchy, causing the individual to lose sight of his or her higher purpose and suffering inner instability and threats to his or her health and well-being (Kamalu, 1998, pp. 73–74). The destinal self was to guide other spiritual selves in achieving harmony with one another, with the family, with the community, and with the natural environment.

The role of the destinal self was to orient the other selves around a person's life mission for the purpose of creating community. This means that the destinal self was not an individualistic self pursuing the individual's interest above the community's interest, but a communal self that sought to make the individual's interest and the community's interest one. Traditional African helpers believed that people were born with a spiritual mission or purpose. Even if they were uncertain about what their life's mission was, they knew that it had something to do with group survival, group identity, group solidarity, harmonious social relationships, mutuality, and reciprocity, because these were all values that the ancestors and the gods had extolled and that all Africans must have embedded in their personality if they were to be sane, happy, healthy, and whole.

PRACTICAL CONCERNS

Although traditional African helpers sought to create a socialized, spiritualized, and communal self, their religious and spiritual beliefs were highly pragmatic and practical. Traditional African helpers were less concerned about getting them to live righteously so they could reap the rewards in an afterlife than they were in getting them to live morally so they could solve problems of human existence in the here and how. Traditional African gods and ancestors were not called upon to free people from eternal sin and damnation. When they were called on to intervene on a person's behalf, it was not only to restore balance to their souls but also to provide practical things they needed in their daily lives such as food, water, shelter, good marriages, wise leaders, cures for their ailments, children, and protection from their enemies. Often, traditional African helpers would bring people together as a community to pray and petition for good crops; protection against famine, drought, floods, and other natural calamities; and safe, dry places during the rainy season. However, even the most mundane, seemingly insignificant problems of day-to-day living were not outside the scope of spirituality in the African helping tradition. As we indicated earlier, in traditional Africa there was hardly such a thing as an "accident." If a person fell or broke a toe, such an incident could be attributed to any number of failures on the part of the individual to perform routine spiritual tasks or, as the case of the sick man showed, to fulfill routine spiritual obligations. An ancestor might be angry with the person because of a failure to pay proper homage and respect. A person might be out of harmony with his or her own spiritual and destinal self. As the case of the sick man illustrates, even physical illness was likely to be assessed in spiritual terms and likely to require spiritual intervention.

In traditional African religiosity and spirituality, the general belief was that much of what happens to a person, whether good or bad, was the result of his or her own doings. Traditional Africans believed that a person's immoral, selfish, avaricious actions could bring down evil not only upon his or her head but also upon the heads of all of his or her acquaintances. Therefore, traditional African helpers seldom called on a cosmic savior or messiah to resurrect sinful people and to restore a sick, fallen, decadent world. They held individuals and the community, both the living and the dead, responsible and accountable for their actions. They forbade their clients to wait until they stood before a final authority beyond the grave for judgment, atonement, or justice. They wanted their clients to confront their own actions and behaviors while they walked the earth, to make amends for their own immoral, unethical, and evil deeds before they received the brutal chastisement of the ancestors and the gods. Individuals and groups were expected to pay careful attention to any of their actions. Even the smallest person or public imbalance could disturb the sacred order and bring calamities and misfortunes on individuals, families, and communities.

Traditional African helpers saw themselves as partners with their clients in helping to solve daily problems and to keep alienation, divisiveness, and social chaos from subverting community. Working as partners with their clients, traditional African helpers emphasized engaging the client in the intervention process. The sick man's case presented earlier demonstrates that traditional African helpers were highly task-oriented. They sought to transform their clients into "doers," who would seek problem resolution through their own action and activity. They sought to engage their clients in the process of fashioning their own destiny and realigning them with their higher communal-spiritual selves. By engaging their clients in the intervention process, they sought to strengthen their clients' confidence in themselves, to boost their morale, and to strengthen their self-discipline.

AFRICAN SPIRITUAL SURVIVALISM

African people wanted to be close to their ancestors and gods. They wanted to feel their presence in their homes and in every aspect of their daily lives. They wanted to feed them and to build altars and shrines to them. They wanted to feel them through singing, praying, chanting, and dancing. They wanted their gods to possess them to put them in an altered state of consciousness so they could sing and dance with them and receive their sacred messages and advice. African people were not interested in making their religions universal. Therefore, there were few African evangelists or missionaries that would attempt to convert people to their traditional African spiritual worldview. Traditional African religion typically was the sole province of particular persons belonging to a particular group in a particular, sacred place. For the most part, it was not tied to a building, an organizational structure, denominational connections, or a holy book. However, the African idea of a sacred world and sacral cosmology was as basic, natural, and self-evident to traditional African helpers as breathing, eating, or seeing through their own eyes.

For thousands of years, traditional Africans have used their own spiritual traditions to tackle the cosmic problems that confront their daily lives. For thousands of years, their spiritual beliefs and practices have sustained them through wars, famine, plagues, slavery, colonial exploitation, and death. They have withstood holy jihads; being called "pagans," savages, and devil worshippers; and being forced at the point of a gun, a bayonet, and a sword to renounce and repudiate all signs, symbols, thought-forms, and rituals of their own religious worldview. They have seen objects and symbols related to their religious practices publicly burned or displayed out of context in museums. They have emerged from the belly of cultural myopia, religious deluge, and hardness of heart to pass their spiritual and religious worldview down to the generations through two centuries of religious persecution and repression. Today, their spiritual worldview has leaped across the African continent to be embraced by thousands of people in South and North America and the Caribbean. Even as they have sought to make peace with the world's major universal religions, they cling tenaciously to their own. Even when they are converted to Islam and Christianity, they very seldom give up their old religious and spiritual beliefs which connect them to a people and a place and link them to their own inner selves, to the essence of their being, and to an infinitely profound spiritual universe.

On United States slave plantations, Black caregivers used spirituality in the helping process. A host of conjurers, slave doctors, fortune tellers, preachers, elders, and freedom fighters sought to marshal the resources of higher powers to relieve Black misery and suffering. Like their counterparts in Africa, enslaved helping practitioners were guided by a complex, sacred cosmology that was more real and enduring to them than the objective conditions of the physical or material world. Slaves typically lived in a world of spirits, charms, magic, sacred medicines, ghosts, and all manners of evil forces seeking to dominate human life. Even though several generations removed from their place of origin—decentered, so to speak—African influences continued to be evident everywhere in the enslaved African's style of worship, spiritual perceptions, music, dance, folklore, mastery of the oral tradition, reliance on spiritually potent magic and medicine, and the tradition of calling on forces from the spiritual depth to solve the practical, personal, and communal problems of daily life.

This chapter focuses on the most prominent caregivers on the slave plantation, namely the conjurer and the slave preacher. It seeks to shed light on the efforts of these Black helpers to harness the forces of nature, the energy of spirits, the authority of the dead, and the power of God to help their troubled people confront the harsh realities of plantation life. However, before we bring these two important enslaved African caregivers on center stage, it is necessary to establish the social context in which they sought to use spirituality in their therapeutic, relief, and emancipative work.

From the outset, we can say that the helping tradition among Black people in slavery was profoundly impacted by three major spiritual influences:

1. African spiritual survivalism
2. the slaves' adoption of Christianity
3. the racist religious propaganda and mythmaking designed to keep Black people content with their servile status.

AFRICAN SURVIVALISM IN THE "NEW WORLD"

Enslaved African helpers throughout the diaspora were heirs to the African spiritual worldview that crossed the Atlantic Ocean on slave ships. Although this African sense of the sacred did not arrive in the "New World" unadulterated and complete, even in its fragmented form it became a dominant motivating influence in the lives of enslaved African people. Key pieces of the puzzle were missing and key actors necessary to give African spirituality its full strength and potency were absent; nevertheless, enslaved Africans maintained a sense of the sacred in their memory, firmly rooted in their personalities and deeply embedded in their consciousness.

African spiritual survivalism did not take solid roots in the United States as it did in Cuba, Jamaica, Haiti, Trinidad, Brazil, and other slave countries. With the exception of the "voodoo" gods called "loas," which were brought from Haiti to New Orleans, West African deities such as the orishas of the Yoruba, the voduns of the Fon, and the abosems of the Ashanti hardly touched North American soil. Even in fragmented form, African spirituality proved to be amazingly resilient, flexible, and adaptable because an unbroken chain of African spiritual survivalism continues today. African gods are being served right this very moment in the Candomblé in Brazil, Santeria in Cuba, Vaudou in Haiti, and the Shango cults in Trinidad, appealing not only to African people but to thousands of Latin American people as well.

Unlike the situation in Catholic slave countries including Brazil, Jamaica, Trinidad, and Haiti, enslaved Africans in North America during the 16th and 17th centuries found themselves a minority among a growing White Protestant majority that was intent on destroying all but the most harmless features of African spirituality and religiosity. In South America and the Caribbean, the huge size of the African population alone, not to mention the steady influx of even more slaves being brought from Africa, made it difficult for the minority White Catholic population to suppress African spirituality. Therefore, in South and Central America and Caribbean countries, Africans were not only able to build religious organizations around an African priesthood and around their own national identities but were also able to ingeniously fortify their religious worldview with Catholicism.

North America did not have a steady influx of slaves coming from Africa. North American enslavers ensured a steady supply of slave laborers by using their own plantations along with special farms as breeding stations. Thus, with each passing generation of these homegrown slaves, the memory of the

African spiritual heritage grew more dim, and it was not long before enslaved Africans in North America lost memory of their African gods and gradually grew closer to the God of Christianity (Raboteau, 1978, p. 92). Enslaved Africans did not immediately adopt or receive instructions in Christianity when they first arrived in America during the 16th century. For more than a century and a half, enslaved Africans in America primarily adopted the spiritual worldview of their traditional African ancestors. Their world was one where the supernatural intersected their earthly existence and often impinged on their daily lives in both good and evil ways, making vague and indistinct any dichotomy of the sacred and the profane.

White enslavers were a major reason that enslaved Africans did not immediately turn to Christianity. White enslavers feared instructing their slaves in Christianity principles because of their general belief that such instructions would make enslaved Africans stubborn, insubordinate, and recalcitrant. This belief was generally accepted by early American slaveholders as an indisputable truth. Enslavers believed that Christian teachings would instill in their slaves dangerous notions of freedom and of being the equal of White people in the eyes of God. American enslavers also strongly believed that Black people were inherently savage, innately barbaric, and stupid and that it would be a waste of time to try to convert them to something so refined, dignified, and civilized as Christianity. Enslaved Africans were considered to be chattel property, no higher than an ox or a plow as an instrument of utility at the disposal of their masters. Early colonies went so far as to avoid the baptism of people of African descent out of the belief that Black people were a subhuman species who did not have souls.

While White enslavers were extremely reluctant to impart Christian teachings to their slaves, they simultaneously waged a vicious campaign to eradicate the most conspicuous and threatening expressions of the slaves' own African religious beliefs and practices. For instance, they forbade their slaves from using drums, which were the key musical instrument in traditional African religious ceremonies and rituals. They knew that African people were skilled at using drums to beat out secret messages that White people could not understand. They forbade their slaves from making animal sacrifices to the gods. They forbade enslaved Africans from forming secret societies and making blood oaths. Such bonds among slaves held threats of insurrection. They forbade slaves from building altars and shrines to African gods. This kind of communal memory could fuel a collective nostalgia that could interfere with work. They forbade slaves from sculpting wooden figurines that represented the ancestors. The enslavers saw this as "fetish worship." Also, as Herkovits (1941) pointed out, "slaves were brought to be worked, and the leisure essential to the production of plastic art form was entirely denied them" (p. 138). American enslavers forbade slaves to engage in rites of passage that were so prominent in Africa. White people in colonial America had no interest in advancing socialization rites that would make African people more fully and consciously African and more concerned about their own group survival than the economic interest of White people. Their interest was in creating a species that was neither fully human nor fully animal, and neither wholly African nor wholly White, but a different kind of species altogether—obedient, docile slaves whose only purposes in life were to work and obey.

Early American enslavers believed that African spirituality at its best was crude, barbaric, childlike, and even comical at times. At its worst, they believed it was an insidious form of Satanism and devil worship. Whatever the case may be, they believed it prudent and wise to keep vigilance on Black people and their ignorant "superstitions." Only the less harmful manifestation of Black religiosity and spirituality was to be accepted, or tolerated. For example, White enslavers generally believed they could be lenient toward Black people in their singing, dancing, foot-stomping, and hand-clapping, etc. that were significant expressions of their religious worship. These "joyful noises" were not seen by White enslavers as serious and sacred encounters with a spiritual universe. They were viewed as a form of entertainment that served White people as much as it served Black people. Such entertainment, they believed, helped to lighten the workload of the slaves in the fields and helped to keep them happy and content in the slave quarters. A content slave was an obedient slave. White people themselves were often amused and entertained by these allegedly playful and childlike outbursts.

White enslavers also showed a degree of tolerance for enslaved Africans' usage of sacred magic and medicine in their confrontation with the spirit world. Although they believed it was their duty to put down any effort on the part of enslaved Africans to create poisons and other instruments of evil, White people themselves were no strangers to "hexes," "lucky numbers," "fixes," omens, signs, guardian spirits, and love potions. Being prominent features of their own folk beliefs and practices, efforts to manipulate the forces of nature were not outside White people's own cultural purview.

Furthermore, White slave masters learned that they could exploit Black "superstitions" and effectively use them as instruments of social control. For example, White people became quite adept in creating a huge body of ghostlore designed to take advantage of Black beliefs in evil spirits. Most White ghost stories were designed to get Black people to believe that ghosts (often called "night doctors") were fond of lurking around wooded areas, cemeteries, swamps, caves, and rivers, waiting to pounce on Black people and inflict harm and destruction. It was no accident that the ghosts in these tales happened to have a deep affinity for those places where enslaved Africans were likely to go in an attempt to escape. White "night riders" often dressed in white hoods and pretended to be ghosts themselves. These "ghosts" sought to bring to reality the ghosts White people created in the minds of Black people (Fry, 1991). These human ghosts beat, terrorized, and killed Black people caught outside the designated zone, reinforcing in the minds of incredulous Black people that the ghosts that the slavemasters so often talked about really existed. White slaveholders also saw Black medicinal practices as being in their own interest. They could be spared the huge expenses of bringing in outside White physicians if they had Black "doctors" attending to the health needs of their slaves. White people generally welcomed any medicine that was an improvement over their own, whether it came from the Native American medicine man or from the Black American "root doctor." It must be remembered that this was during a time when medical ineptitude ruled the day in White America, a time when leading White medical experts saw bloodletting as the most effective method of curing most illnesses and diseases. White people did not pretend racial superiority regarding medical advances that were superior to their own medical practices. After all, they were in the position to take credit for any medicines they borrowed from their slaves and claim them as their own.

Overall, White people's preoccupation with their own "superstitions" and their own health concerns allowed enslaved helping specialists to use magic and medicine in ways that would have been quite familiar to their African ancestors.

THE ADOPTION OF CHRISTIANITY
Christianity was born on African soil long before the mass enslavement of African people by Europeans. In its infancy years, it found refuge in Carthage, Egypt, Nubia, and Ethiopia as it fled the dangers of extinction

because of the systematic persecution of early Christians in Greece and Rome. Although Christianity established solid roots in North Africa, the enslaved Africans brought to America came primarily from West Africa and had little exposure to it. For nearly a century and a half, enslaved Africans on North American soil had fashioned their beliefs and practices out of their own African spiritual worldview. Enslaved Africans did not come to Christianity in large droves until they were swept up into the Christian revivalist tide known in American history as "The Great Awakening."

The Great Awakening began approximately in 1734 as an evangelical revivalist movement that sought to accelerate the pace of religious conversion among people in the North American colonies. Not long after it began, it swept through the colonies like wildfire, causing flocks of White people to experience conversion with a fervor that was unprecedented. The leader of the awakening revivals was George Whitefield, who led a group of other itinerant evangelist preachers, including a few Black ones, across the country to preach a simple, inspiring, democratic Christian message that had tremendous appeal to the lowly, the downtrodden, and the illiterate, which included the slaves. The message of Whitefield and the other "awakeners" sought to put the brotherhood back in American Christianity that the slaveholders had so insidiously removed. Whitefield and other awakeners voiced strong condemnation of slaveholders for their cruelty to slaves and for their neglect of slaves' spiritual needs. While their message fell short of calling for the downfall of the institution of slavery altogether (particularly because a few of these evangelists themselves owned slaves), it did cause some awakened slaveholders to free their slaves or to undertake the task of providing them with religious instruction.

Whether their masters were awakened or not, hundreds of enslaved Africans and free people of color attended these revivals and experienced conversion with or without the permission or approval of the White enslavers. Now several generations removed from Africa and with African gods almost totally erased from their collective memory, Black people at this juncture in history stood ready to fully accept their new God known by the name of Jesus Christ. West (1982) wrote:

The existential appeal of Christianity to Black people was the stress of Protestant evangelicalism on individual experience, and especially the conversion experience. The 'holy dance' of Protestant evangelical conversion experiences closely resembled the 'ring shout' of West African Novitiate rites: both are religious forms of ecstatic bodily behavior in which everyday time is infused with meaning and value through unrestrained rejoicing .... The conversion experience initiated a profoundly personal relationship with God, which gave slaves a special self-identity and self-esteem in stark contrast with the roles imposed upon them by American society. (pp. 35–36)

Raboteau (1978) held that "The Great Awakening represented 'the dawning of the new day' in the history of the conversion of slaves to Christianity" (p. 128). Campbell (1998) maintained that "aftershocks of the Awakening continued to rumble through the last half of the 18th century, propelling ever more African Americans into the burgeoning evangelical churches" (p. 5) and prompting Black people to establish independent Black churches under the leadership of Black evangelical preachers.

Overall, the spiritual and cosmological worldview that enslaved West Africans brought with them showed remarkable receptivity to Christianity, making it easy for them to embrace this new faith as their own and interpret it within the context of their own traditional practices and beliefs. West Africans in the so-called New World were particularly receptive to the Christian concept of God. In West Africa, God was often placed on such a high transcendental plane that He/She was remote from daily human affairs and largely unapproachable. Deren (1953) wrote that "when Christianity taught that such a primal figure was concerned with human affairs, and was to be personally and intimately addressed, this was accepted as a welcome modification of the African tradition" (p. 55). She said that "the Christian deity who was subject to persuasion by prayer, and who might interfere as a supernatural force—was much easier and more comfortable than the usual High God of Africa, whose absolute objectivity placed him beyond the pale of human reference" (p. 55). Drake (1970) wrote that "the concept of the West African 'high god' who did not interfere in human affairs was replaced by that of a God 'who's got the whole world in his hands' and who at the end of time, will judge all men" (p. 22).

It was extremely significant to enslaved Africans that they had found in Christianity a God that they could reach personally through prayer, particularly because their enslavers strictly forbade them to call for the intervention of the ancestors and the gods. It was also important to enslaved

Africans that they could praise this Christian God without having to perform any specialized rituals, particularly because they were punished severely on the slave plantation for any attempt to commune with their gods. Because West Africans already had a rich tradition of praising their own historical, religious, and mythological heroes, heroines, ancestors, and gods in song and epic drama, it was easy for them to praise the Christian God in song and rich, dramatic displays of emotionalism. Just as they had looked to the ancestors as exemplary figures to be emulated, they could, through their new hybrid Christian faith, identify with biblical heroes and heroines who themselves were struggling against oppressive forces.

Moreover, enslaved Africans were starkly aware that under the oppressive yoke of slavery they were constantly needing God's care. Therefore, like their traditional African counterparts, they needed to feel a personal and intimate relationship with their God. Traditional Africans were able to experience this immediate closeness with the divine through rites of spirit possession. After a person was possessed and had his or her character, personality, and behavior taken completely over by a god, everyone involved in this communal exercise could not only touch their god and see their god in action, in the flesh, but join with the god in singing the god's favorite songs, dancing the god's favorite dance, eating the god's favorite foods, and otherwise experiencing the joy of the god's divine presence.

Spirit possession ceremonies in traditional Africa were intensely emotional and physically draining sacred events. The drumming, dancing, singing, and shouting would often reach feverish heights as the devotees and priests sought to match with their own human bodies the incredible feats, frenzied activity, and convulsive energy of the gods. Enslaved Africans experienced being possessed by the spirit in their quests to "feel the spirit," in their desire to create a sacred space, a spiritually charged atmosphere, where they could engage in unrestrained rejoicing until they felt the immediate presence of "the holy ghost" deep down in their souls. Enslaved Africans also sought to reach the ecstatic state that spirit possessions often brought to traditional Africans. "Feeling the spirit" helped them to experience a profound joy in a hostile, joyless world. It helped them to grow closer not only to their God but to one another in this profound Black communal exchange. Most significantly, it confirmed in their hearts that the slave master might have control over the bodies of Black people, but he did not have control over their souls.

While the rhythms of drums, so important in traditional African spirit possession were forbidden to the slaves, their singing, dancing, fainting, hand-clapping, foot-tapping, rhythmic preaching, and call-and-response communication as they felt the holy ghost were no different from those associated with spirit possession in Africa. Raboteau (1978) wrote that "while the North American slaves danced under the impulse of the Spirit of a 'new' God, they danced in ways their fathers in Africa would have recognized" (p. 65).

It is important to note that even as the enslaved African helpers sought to dynamically transform the religious beliefs of Christianity into a functional caregiving faith to console them in their world of sorrow, they were confronted with their enslavers' brand of Christianity, which propounded notions of absolute Black inferiority and permanent Black servitude. In the next chapter, we show how difficult it was for some of Black history's leading enslaved caregivers and freedom fighters to free themselves from their masters' spiritual and religious grips.

CONJURERS

The Black caregivers who were the most liberated from the spiritual shackles of the slaveholders were the conjurers. W. E. B. Du Bois (1903) concluded that despite the devastating impact slavery had on African survival in America,

> Some traces were retained of the former group life, and the chief remaining institution was the priest or medicine man. He early appeared on the plantation and found his function as the healer of the sick, the interpreter of the unknown, the comforter of the sorrowing, the supernatural avenger of wrong and the one who rudely, but picturesquely, expressed the longing, disappointment and resentment of a stolen and oppressed people. (p. 144)

When Du Bois talked about the priest or medicine man as "the chief remaining institution" (as in, the primary carryover) from Africa, he was speaking for the most part of that slave caregiver known as "the conjurer."

The conjurer was a throwback to both the traditional African diviner and the medicine man or herbalist. Similar to the traditional African diviner, the conjurer had the knowledge and skills to tap into, manipulate, and use for either good or evil purposes the forces, powers, and energies permeating the entire universe. Both the conjurer and the diviner had the ability to link the living to the living dead (the ancestors) and to the spirits. Like the traditional African medicine man or herbalist, the conjurer often had extensive knowledge of the medicinal value and spiritual potency of different herbs, leaves, juices, minerals, plants, dust, roots, fruits, barks, grasses, bones, feathers, seeds, powders, insects, shells, eggs, and even animal excreta. Their extensive knowledge of the natural environment earned conjurers the title of "root doctor." The conjurer was also referred to as the "voodoo" or "hoodoo" man because of his historical connections to the system of magical practices associated with the legendary voodoo priestess, Marie Laveau, and her followers in New Orleans. New Orleans was the capitol of the religious cult known as voodoo that was brought during the late 18th century by Haitian Black people fleeing Toussaint Louverture's slave revolt. The system of voodoo magical practices enjoyed wider influence among slaves in the colonies than the religious system of voodoo itself. Voodoo men and voodoo women became known for their ability to put a "fix" (curse or spell) on people or to take a "fix" off of them. The conjurer enjoyed a great reputation for being able to take strands of hair, nail clippings, or a personal item such as a shirt or a button and use these personal items to cause people severe mental or physical distress or even death as they fell totally under the spell of the conjurer.

Enslaved Africans generally were in awe of the conjurer's reputation for fixing and attributed all kinds of supernatural abilities to the conjurer. As one ex-slave reported: "I saw a root doctor cut out of a man's leg a lizard and a grasshopper, and then he got well. Some conjur ain't to kill, but to make a person sick or make him have pain" (Steiner, 1990, p. 379).

Whether the conjurer was called the "root doctor" or the voodoo man, most slaves, even those who deeply feared him, often found their way to the conjurer to get him to harness the powers of the universe on their behalf. Slaves appealed to the conjurer to use his magical and medicinal powers to solve numerous problems. They came for charms to bolster courage; roots to prevent floggings; powders to enhance sexual potency; graveyard dust to remove hexes and spells; love potions to attract desired love objects; good luck charms to protect them from evil spirits; voodoo bags to prevent being separated from their loved ones; teas to cure a host of illnesses; and poisons to exact final solutions. Many enslaved Africans sought out the conjurer to have him prepare small bags of roots, graveyard dust (called "gooper" dust), herbs, and so forth that they would wear around their necks or have somewhere on their bodies to ward off all kinds of evil spirits and to attract good ones. These bags were called various names such as "hand," "toby," "ju-ju," "greegree bags," and "voodoo bags." It was not unusual to find practically every slave, young and old, on a given plantation wearing a "hand" or some other type of charm prepared for them by the conjurer. For example, on one slave plantation it was the custom for the infants to wear "moles' feet and pearl buttons around their necks to insure teething" and to have "their legs bathed in a concoction of wasp nest and vinegar if they were slow about learning to walk" (Webber, 1978, p. 120). The older slaves on this plantation "wore voodoo bags ... handed down from generation to generation ... to keep witches away" (Webber, 1978, p. 120).

Basically, the conjurer was the most important caregiver on the slave plantation primarily because he made oppressed people believe that they were not totally at the mercy of the natural environment and not totally subjected to the oppressive whims of the slave master. Through the work of the conjurer, diseases could be cured, evil could be warded off, good luck could come their way, and slave masters could be made kinder and even removed. The conjurer conveyed to enslaved African people the message that regardless of how downtrodden and oppressed they were, they had some control over a vicious, precarious, and capricious existence. They gave enslaved Africans some measure of predictability over a chaotic existence and over the future courses their lives would take. Following in the footsteps of traditional African helpers, who used divination, water gazing, and the reading of animal intestines to fortell the future, conjurers also were expected to bring the future of their clients into the present. Through reading signs, interpreting dreams, watching the stars, paying careful attention to the weather and changes within their own bodies, and listening to the messages conveyed by the wind, the clouds, and the trees, the conjurer functioned to simplify a complex world, to make it intelligible and manageable. The conjurer was expected to be a prophet, visionary, and fortune teller all rolled into one.

Conjurers were often thought to be the only Black person on the plantation considered to have more power than the slave master. Blassingame (1972) held that the conjurer was "often the most powerful and significant individual on the plantation" (p. 109). It is emphasized that the conjurer was not the most powerful Black person on the plantation but the most powerful individual whether Black or White. Many enslaved Africans firmly believed that the slave master's earthly power over them was puny in comparison to the powers the conjurer had at his command. Even the slave master, most slaves believed, had to walk lightly around the conjurer less he incur the conjurer's wrath and become a helpless slave himself to the conjurer's will. When a conjurer actually demonstrated power over the slave master, he was practically worshipped by other slaves as a god. For example, Blassingame (1972) cites a case of a conjurer named William Webb who used his power to make a cruel master kind to his slaves (p. 110). He said that Webb had grown tired of seeing his people groaning under the cruel infliction of the slave master. Therefore, he secretly visited the slave quarters, prayed with the slaves, and then began to collect various roots. After his potions were mixed and bagged up, Webb marched around the slave cabins several times and then pointed several bags of roots in the direction of the master's house. Slaves soon noticed that the master started treating them with a kindness that overwhelmed them. After that, Blassingame (1972) wrote: "The slaves were completely in Webb's power: They regaled him with sumptuous meals nightly, and the women were especially attentive" (p. 110). Webber (1978) cited a case of a conjurer called "old gran' pap," who took matters into his own hands against an overseer who was deeply dreaded by the entire slave community (pp. 119-120). Old gran' pap too grew tired of watching his people suffer at the hands of the overseer and decided to do something about it. Old gran' pap chanted incantations against the overseer night after night and it was not long after old gran' pap had told the people that their problem would soon be solved. Then the overseer fell off of his horse and died. Old gran' pap became an instant hero, and every slave on the plantation was thoroughly convinced of the power of old gran' pap's conjure (Webber, 1978, p. 120).

Some conjurers, knowing that their masters were just as afraid of them and their powers as the slaves were, decided to live a carefree existence and do whatever they pleased in utter contempt of their masters' authority. For example, Blassingame (1972) reported that a conjurer named Dinkie "never worked, never received a flogging, and was never stopped by the patrollers" (p. 113). Everyone in the neighborhood, Black and White, was terrified of Dinkie's conjuring powers and more than happy to stay out of Dinkie's way.

Most conjurers did not have to chastise their masters, kill overseers, or terrify White people, however, to demonstrate their powers. Enslaved Africans could see with their own eyes that White people too often came to the conjurer for advice, love potions, good luck charms, and even "hands" to ward off evil spirits. Slaves could also see that the conjurer was practically the only Black person on the plantation who was considered to have greater ability and intelligence than White people. This was particularly the case regarding medicine, because Black "doctors" (typically conjurers in their role as "root doctors") often administered to White families as well as to slaves. Slaves dreaded White medicine and White doctors and were elated when they found Black doctors in charge of their care. Owens (1976) wrote:

When masters were unable to effect a cure by their own methods they might send for a Black "doctor," maybe a conjurer skilled in folk medicine. This was necessary because some sick slaves often showed a complete lack of confidence in a master's or White physician's ability to cure them, while they might place themselves willingly in the care of another slave. Many of these Black "doctors" displayed great confidence in their ability to cure the sick. (p. 34)

Owens (1976) went on to say that the medical abilities of slave doctors "bothered those [W]hite practitioners who found their skills on the short end of comparison" (p. 34). He said that a few White doctors "adopted some of the slave methods, and others followed" (pp. 34-35). Owens (1976) maintained that when enslaved Africans saw the White people placing their very lives in the hands of the slave doctor their egos were "inflated with pride" and they could imagine seeing one of their own children one day "rising to a similar rank" (p. 35).

While the dependence of the White people on the conjurer put the conjurer in great standing with Black people, nothing ruined the reputation of a conjurer quicker and more lastingly than slaves seeing him getting whipped, worked, and treated by the slave master as if he were just as powerless and helpless as any other slave. They reasoned that if he could not protect himself with his alleged conjuring powers, then he probably was a fake or was pretending to be a genuine heir to the healing powers of Africa.

THE SLAVE PREACHER

As we stated earlier, many slaveholders experienced conversion during The Great Awakening and began to allow their slaves to receive religious instructions. The standard practice was to have their slaves accompany them and their families to White churches. Although enslaved Africans attended church with their slave masters and their families, this was far from being an integrated atmosphere because the lines of division were clearly drawn right there in the house of God. Wilmore (1998) said that enslaved Africans attending White churches were promptly seated "in the 'African Corner,' in seats marked 'B. M.' (Black Members), or in the increasingly crowded galleries" (p. 116).

With enslaved Africans present in churches, White ministers were prompted to take extra precautions in what they preached and how they interpreted biblical passages. White slaveholders might have undergone a religious awakening compelling them to give their slaves religious instruction, but they wanted to be certain that they were in full control of the type of instructions their slaves received. In fact, the chief reason for bringing their slaves to churches with them in the first place was to ensure that the Christianity they received would advance the interest of slavery.

White preachers, who had long reconciled their brand of Christianity with slavery, became skilled in finding messages to direct to the slaves. All the messages, teachings, and biblical interpretations that came from the White preacher's lips were geared toward instilling in enslaved Africans the need to obey and love their masters. The most important biblical teaching of the slaveholding brand of Christianity came from Ephesians 6:5-9 which read:

> Servants, be obedient to them that are your masters according to the flesh, with fear and trembling, in singleness of your heart, as unto Christ; not with eye-service, as men-pleasers; but as servants of Christ doing the will of God from the heart; with good will doing service as to the Lord, and not to men; knowing that whatsoever good thing any man doeth, the same shall he receive of the Lord whether he be bond or free. (*The Holy Bible: Contemporary English Version*, p. 1728)

White ministers found myriad ways to present this message to their enslaved African members. At the same time, they avoided such biblical passages as that which came from Leviticus 25:10 calling for the year of jubilee in which "Ye shall hallow the fiftieth year, and proclaim liberty throughout all the land unto all the inhabitants thereof; it shall be a jubilee unto you; and ye shall return every man unto his possession, and ye shall return every man unto his family" (*The Holy Bible: Contemporary English Version*, p. 211).

Despite being inundated by these teachings, enslaved Africans often worshipped with a fervor that proved to be quite unsettling to White worshippers. Many White churchgoers were disturbed by the slaves' unrestrained display of religious emotionalism. While White people in the evangelical Baptist and Methodist churches and camp meetings could also be highly emotional, they could very seldom match the emotional intensity of the slaves. Even when their masters struggled to constrain the slaves' torrent of religious ecstasy, slaves often sang songs with such enthusiasm that their voices completely drowned out the voices of their fellow White Christians. Also, because of their cultural heritage, slaves had a tendency to add their own words to standard hymns. They would generally change the words of a song at the very moment the song was being sung. Blassingame (1972) said that "Even when slaves did model their songs on those of [W]hites, they changed them radically" (p. 137). White people who were accustomed to following the lines of a song word-for-word as they were written in hymnals were often totally taken aback by this audacious and licentious display of Black improvisation. White ministers sometimes also became unsettled as they found their White congregation getting drawn into the religious vortex of enslaved Africans. The singing and clapping and shouting of the enslaved African congregants was sometimes so intoxicating that White people themselves could not help but respond by swaying their own bodies and shouting "amens" and "hallelujahs" unto the Lord with all the emotional fervor they could muster. For example, one White church member reported that after witnessing the "shouts, and groans, terrific shrieks, and indescribable expressions of ecstasy, of pleasure or agony, and even stomping, jumping, and clapping of hands" of the enslaved African worshippers, "I was once surprised to find my own muscles all stretched, as if ready for a struggle, my flace glowing, and my feet stomping, having been infected unconsciously" (quoted in Raboteau, 1978, p. 62). White ministers wanted their White church members to follow the preacher's lead in religious worship, not the undignified exhibitions of the slaves.

White slaveholders who had grown tired of chastising their slaves for their emotional outbursts in churches and camp meetings began to explore other alternatives to providing religious instructions to their slaves. Many allowed itinerant White preachers to come before their slaves in what was called "plantation missions," but they had to keep great surveillance over these ministers from the outside because some were not committed to preaching the standard sermons and those who were, generally preached with little enthusiasm. They seemingly wanted to hurry and tell the slaves what the master wanted them to hear, get paid, and get on the road before sundown.

As one ex-slave explained "the preacher came and ... he'd just say, 'Serve your masters. Don't steal your master's turkey. Don't steal your master's chickens. Don't steal your master's hawgs. Don't steal your master's meat. Do whatsoever your master tells you to do.' Same old thing all the time" (Fisk University Social Science Institute, 1945, p. 134).

Many masters were so disgusted with the slaves' lack of response to the White itinerant preachers that they decided that they themselves would instill their own brand of Christian principles in their slaves. In this regard, slave masters not only were creative in presenting the obey-your-master sermon in practically every conceivable way, but they also created their own catechisms to instruct the slaves:

Question:	Who gave you a master?
Answer:	God gave him to me.
Question:	Who says you must obey him?
Answer:	God says that I must.
Question:	What did God make you for?
Answer:	To make crops.

There was absolutely no way for the slaves to "feel the holy ghost" when their masters instructed them in such a dry, pedantic manner. It was no great consolation whatsoever for the slaves to constantly hear from their master-turned-preacher that they would go to heaven just like White people if they were good and if they obeyed. It did not warm their souls when their slave masters preached that although there would be a wall between them and White people in heaven, that there would be holes in the walls permitting them to look out and see their master and mistress when they passed by (Raboteau, 1978, p. 213). The last people enslaved

Africans wanted to see in heaven were the master and the mistress. It definitely did not inspire religious fervor when their master told them that they would occupy the "kitchen" in heaven and would continue to be blessed in serving him and his family there just as they were blessed to serve them on earth (Raboteau, 1978, p. 360). In short, enslaved Africans grew weary of constantly hearing about how they shalt not lie, they shalt not steal, they shalt not disobey the master, they shalt not kill the master, nor his family, nor his ox, nor his manservants, nor his maidservants. They wanted to hear about Jesus and not from an oppressor who could be telling them about the mercy and love of God one minute and be flogging them senseless the next.

Enslaved Africans generally found any excuse not to attend the plantation worship with their master or some other White man as preacher. A chief concern of slave masters was how to keep their slaves from stealing away at night and engaging in what they called "hush harbor" worship. The secret meetings held in the woods, gullies, swamps, and other hiding places allowed enslaved Africans to worship God without constraints to their desire to gain unmitigated personal closeness to the divine. However, to slave masters these "hush-hush" meetings severely disrupted work activity, were clearly in defiance of the master's authority, and were too ripe with potential for insurrection to be ignored. Slave preachers were generally the products of a deeply felt need on the part of slave masters to put the masses of slaves in check and to stop flagrant acts of insubordination.

Generally, slave preachers lived and worked on the plantation along with other slaves before they were handpicked by their masters to perform a service on their masters' behalf. Called upon to serve as a buffer between their masters and their fellow slaves, slave preachers had to have somewhat of a reputation for being spiritual men who had the respect of other slaves. At the same time they had to have a solid history of demonstrated loyalty to their masters. Besides being persons whom other slaves admired and having an unblemished record as "good niggers," another chief criteria for being selected to preach was very significant. Slave masters wanted slave preachers who were illiterate. They could be eloquent, passionate, and even charismatic, but they must not be able to read and gain their own understanding of the Holy Bible. They had to be open to being spoon-fed by their masters the bits and pieces of the holy book their masters wanted them to digest and to regurgitate.

After respected, loyal, good-natured, and illiterate slave preachers were selected, their chief duty was to preach the typical sermons except they were expected to do it with a flair, with a style that would move the masses to the intense emotional highs they were accustomed to in their religious worship. As long as slave preachers never mentioned the word "freedom," never dwelled upon the Hebrew people coming out of bondage in Egypt, and never gave slaves even the slightest impression that they were the equals of White people in the eyes of God, they would be amply rewarded. They could expect for their loyalty a drastic reduction in their workload, better clothes than the average slave; better living quarters; and greater freedom of mobility. If they proved to be able to excite the slaves right there on the plantation and make them feel that running away at night to their "invisible churches" was unnecessary, a select few of them might be fortunate enough to be hired out to preach to slaves on other plantations, and even given a small portion of the proceeds.

For these rewards, many slave preachers were so content with the status of being in a position of authority that they did their masters' bidding without any deviation from their assigned roles. Blassingame (1972) stated: "Sometimes obsequious to a fault, a few Black preachers, so valued the rewards and the marks of respect they received from [W]hites they occasionally voluntarily advised the slaves to be content with their lot in life" (p. 132). History amply shows that slave preachers were men, for the most part, with a double consciousness. They were men who wore the mask.

As caregivers assigned by their masters to address the spiritual needs of the slaves, slave preachers were men walking a tightrope. Many of them became masters of the art of deception, of "puttin' on ole massa." When the masters were present, few could match the enthusiasm of slave preachers in exhorting the slaves to be obedient to their masters. However, when the master was not around, and the slaves could fully worship God in their own way, unrestrained by their master's interference, Thurman (1975) held that those same slave preachers told the slaves "you are not slaves, you are not niggers, you are God's children" (p. 17).

Slave preachers also were very deceptive in terms of their knowledge of the Holy Bible. Most of them were indeed illiterate and those who were not, pretended that they were. They knew that a literate slave was considered to be a dangerous slave who had to be kept under strict surveillance whether he was a holy man or not. Raboteau (1978) stated that "illiteracy proved less of an obstacle to knowledge of the [B]ible than might be thought, for biblical stories became part of the oral tradition of the slaves" (p. 241). Slave preachers often had keen native wit and insight. They were usually adept in committing to memory every part of sermons, prayers, and talks they had heard concerning the Holy Bible. Many were capable of committing to memory entire chapters of the Bible and passages of scripture that they had heard from oral instructions in Sunday school, camp meetings, and even secretly listening to their masters read from the holy book. As one missionary to the slaves stated: "To those who are ignorant of letters, their memory is their book" (quoted in Raboteau, 1978, p. 241). The chief means of remembering Bible stories was to repeat them time and time again in songs called the spirituals. Slaves said that their sacred songs were called spirituals because the spirit of the Lord revealed these songs to them. Spirituals were born in the slaves' most profound moment of religious excitement and ecstasy. As one slave said:

Us ole heads use ter make 'em on de spurn of de moment, after we wressle wid de Spirit and come thoo. But the tunes was bring from Africa by our grandaddies. Dey was tis 'miliar song ... dey calls 'em spirituals, case de Holy Spirit done revealed 'em to 'em. Some say thoss Jesus taught 'em, and I's seed 'em start in meetin.' We'd all be at the prayer house de Lord's Day, and de white preacher he'd splain de word and read what Ezekiel done say. Dry bones qwine ter lib again. And honey, de Lord would come a-shing thoo dem pages and revive dis old nigger's heart, and I'd jump up dar and den and holler and shout and sing and pat, and dey would all catch de words ... And dey's all take it up and keep at it, and keep a-addin to it an den it would be a spiritual. (quoted in Raboteau, pp. 244-245)

Slave preachers generally had an entire repertoire of biblical knowledge drawn from the spirituals. Their sermons were often little more than spirituals delivered in the poetic and dramatic style, rich with vivid imagery, highlighting the parallels between the Hebrew people of the Old Testament and the African people in the fiery furnace of American slavery. One 19th-century author, A. M. French, attested to the ability of the slave preachers to preach from the Holy Bible. French (1862) wrote:

The real spiritual benefit of these poor colored people, instrumentally, seems to have been mostly derived from a sort of local preachers, colored, and mostly slaves, but of deep spiritual experience, sound sense, and capacity to state scripture facts, narratives, and doctrines, far better than most, who feed upon commentaries. True, the most of them could not read, still, some of them line hymns from memory with great accuracy, and fervor, and repeat scripture most appropriately, and correctly. Their teaching shows clearly that it is God in the soul, that makes the religious teacher. One is amazed at their correctness and power. They say: "God tell me 'you go teach the people what I tell you; I shall prosper you; I teach you in de heart.'" (p. 131)

Although the chief role of slave preachers was to keep their people in check, most slave preachers were too close to their people to be an instrument of their oppression. As the traditional Black call-and-response preaching style suggests, slave preachers and their Black congregations were generally one in spirit, with one responding to and feeding off the religious fervor of the other in a quest to feel the spirit. Slaves generally knew that slave preachers had to wear the mask when they were around their masters and they expected to hear the slave-obey-your-master sermons. However, in their own spiritual space, they knew that their relationship with slave preachers was one of spiritual support and communal exchange. Slave preachers in turn could not help but realize that their own greatest source of spiritual energy, support, and reinforcement was their people. They knew that they could continue to be one with the people so long as they were genuine and sincere. Anyone starting a song in the highly spiritually charged atmosphere of the slaves could soon have all slaves joining in, singing and shouting, relieving pent-up frustration and rage, and ready to face the trials and tribulations of another day. Just the singing of a spiritual created instant, spontaneous community among the slaves. With the slaves, a sacred space could be anywhere: in the fields, on the broken wooden stairs of a slave cabin, in the kitchen of the big house, or down by the riverside. Despite the master's agenda, many slave preachers were clear that their chief roles were to bring their people closer to God; keep them from giving up and going insane; guide them through life crises such as births, baptisms, weddings, and funerals; and give them a sense of the sacred. The slave preacher was well aware that there were many slaves who were not religious. There were some who had come to believe that a just God could not possibly exist, dare not exist while Black people suffered slavery. It was the role of slave preachers to bring these Black people back into the fold by inspiring them to higher conceptions of themselves and their possibilities and raising them to a spiritual plane higher than their alienation, bitterness, defeatism, and despair. The slave preachers had the awesome responsibility of keeping hope alive in the slaves in an extreme situation where it seemed that hope was only a possibility in imagination while suffering, misery, and despair ruled the day. Raboteau (1978) said that slave preachers "kept hope alive by incorporating as part of their mythic past the Old Testament exodus of Israel out of bondage" (p. 311). By turning enslaved Africans backwards toward the mythical sojourns of the Hebrew people and turning them forward toward Jesus and the coming kingdom, the new Jerusalem on earth, slave preachers sought to impart the message of hope, that things are not fixed in the universe forever, that life is worth living, and that a change is going to come.

While the most important duty of slave preachers was to inspire hope, their most profound function as slave caregivers was to help give the slaves a feeling of spiritual advantage. If the masters were superior in wealth, wrath, and weapons, slave preachers made slaves understand that they had the moral and spiritual advantage. Slave preachers more than anybody on the plantation were able to point out the religious hypocrisy of the slaveholders, the contradiction between their professed beliefs in Christianity, and their stealing of human beings from their homeland and holding them in bondage. Raboteau (1978) held that "as early as 1774 American slaves were declaring publicly and politically that they thought Christianity and slavery were incompatible" (p. 290). By giving the slaves a point of reference where they could make judgments on the world, the slave preachers had much to do with enslaved people developing this worldview. In fact, few slaves thought it was possible for any slave master or mistress to get into heaven as long as they continued to subject Black people to hell on earth (Raboteau, 1978, pp. 291-292). While the slave master brought slave preachers on the plantation to reinforce their masters' own brand of Christian teachings, the slave preachers were generally the very ones who were leading the charge to help slaves distinguish the hypocritical religion of their masters from true Christianity, to reject the master's moral precepts, and to adopt the revolutionary idea under slavocracy that White people were no better than Black people in the eyes of God.

THE CONJURER AND THE SLAVE PREACHER:
A BRIEF COMPARISON

While conjurers and slave preachers were often rivals competing for the minds of their fellow slaves, they typically coexisted peacefully. Conjuring stemmed from the voodoo religious cult out of New Orleans that embraced Catholicism. Therefore, conjurers were not hostile toward Christianity. The more obsequious slave preachers, of course, had to view conjurers in much the same way their masters did—as practitioners of idolatry, fetish worship, and Satanism. However, for the most part, slave preachers coexisted well with the conjurer. In many cases, slave preachers played a dual role as a conjurer and vice versa. For example, Levine (1977) held that the authority of Uncle Aaron, a Virginia slave, "was enhanced by the slaves' belief that in addition to being a Christian preacher he was a conjurer who could 'raise the spirits'" (p. 58). The results were often cataclysmic when the slave preacher and conjurer came together. This was powerfully demonstrated in the preacher-conjurer collaboration in the Gabrial Prosser, the Denmark Vesay, and the Nat Turner slave revolts. For the most part, however, neither conjurers nor slave preachers were insurrectionists. They were slave caregivers trying to help slaves make life livable under an extreme situation.

Overall, when one compares the slave preacher with the conjurer, one can say that the slave preacher was a spiritual artist while the conjurer was a spiritual technician. In his role, the conjurer was able to give the slaves some feeling of control over an oppressive and chaotic environment. The conjurer helped to reconnect Black people to the world of their ancestors, who believed that the universe was governed by spiritual laws, making the cosmos predictable, explainable, and controllable. The right spiritual technicians with the right knowledge and skills could manipulate the power and energy of the spirit world and use it for evil or for good. The conjurer maintained the traditional African heritage of being a spiritual technician. The slave preachers, on the other hand, had to master the art of inspiration, the art of eloquence, and the art of delivering the word of God in order to give their oppressed people hope and a spiritual advantage. Both the conjurer and the slave preacher felt it was important to link Black people to a mythical past—the conjurer to the African ancestors and spirits and the preacher to the Hebrew people of the Old Testament—so they could continuously draw strength from the spiritual energy and life forces of those who came before them. Both also sought to instill in Black people that their status in the world is not fixed forever, that evil forces can be controlled or removed, and that good can prevail. Stated another way, both sought to bring the enslaved African people back into the flow of human history by linking them to a past they could turn to for nourishment time and time again and by focusing their eyes on a future where soon they would be done with the troubles of the world.

CHAPTER FOUR

Religious Mythomania and the Fight for Freedom

The great majority of the slave preachers and conjurers were not seeking to overthrow slavocracy or to plot insurrection. Their chief role was to help enslaved Africans maintain their humanity and integrity against oppressive forces seeking to demoralize and dehumanize them. However, there were caregivers on the slave plantation who wanted nothing less than the total freedom of Black people. These were the freedom fighters who devoted their lives not only to putting an end to their people's suffering but also to economically bankrupting the slavery system by taking away Black laborers, its most vital product. Some of these freedom fighters would participate in the Underground Railroad, assisting runaway slaves to freedom. Others emerged as great antislavery spokespersons, seeking to strip slavery of its ideological, intellectual, and moral underpinnings.

This chapter examines the lives of four Black freedom fighters who rose from slavery to become legendary caregivers in the Black experience: Josiah Henson, Sojourner Truth, Frederick Douglass, and Harriet Tubman. With the exception of the lesser known Henson, the others (Truth, Douglass, and Tubman) are archetypal ancestors widely revered in Black history. This chapter makes the case that even before these great Black freedom fighters could liberate themselves, let alone help to emancipate others, they had to overcome the power their slaveholders' religious mythomania had over their minds. By "religious mythomania" we mean the lies, distortions, and exaggerations slaveholders used to give religious justification to slavery. As Cox (1948) held: "It was during the days of slavery that the most insistent attempts were made to develop a religious rationale for [W]hite, ruling class policy" (p. 436). This chapter shows how effective White racist religious mythomania was in controlling the minds and actions of enslaved Africans. It shows that even before the most celebrated Black freedom fighters could fully discover their true promise, potential, and destiny as caregivers, they had to break the stranglehold of White religious propaganda that deemed them cursed, damned, unworthy, and inferior. They had to counter White racist religious mythmaking with an independent spiritual worldview conducive to the development of a race-conscious, communal-oriented, caregiving self.

WHITE RACIST RELIGIOUS MYTHOMANIA

While religious mythomania was more than the typical servant-obey-your-master propaganda that was pounded daily into the heads of enslaved Africans, it involved the total racialization of Christianity. Before the late 15th century and the advent of the slave trade, Europeans seldom stigmatized the entire Black race as morally, mentally, and spiritually inferior. They showed little antipathy or disdain toward Black skin color, and they had not yet institutionalized racism in their social structures. Moreover, slavery had not become synonymous with Black people. Before the European slave trade devastated Africa, practically every race on the planet had experienced slavery in one form or another. In fact, the word *slave* itself was derived from the widespread servitude of Slavic-speaking people of Europe (such as the Russians, Ukrainians, Serbs, Croats, Czechs, Poles, and Slovaks) during the Middle Ages. Black people, during that time, had not become associated with slavery. In fact, religiously in Europe, from approximately the 10th to the 15th century, thousands of Europeans looked upon Black patron saints, Black Madonnas, Black magi, and other Black Christian icons as their spiritual heroes, heroines, and saviors. Statues, paintings, and other artistic images of Black religious figures were standard features of European churches and cathedrals. With the rise of the European slave trade, however, these images of Black religious icons rapidly disappeared and Black people were transformed from being children of God to being children of the Prince of Darkness.

Baltazar (1973) explained that the essence of White racist religious mythomania lay in Europeans taking the color symbolism in the Holy Bible that was previously applied to the condition of the soul and applying it to Black skin (p. 25). The biblical idea of the soul coming out of the darkness of ignorance, depravity, and sin into the divine light of purity, truth, and redemption was twisted to associate Black skin color with ignorance, depravity, sin, defilement, and death and to associate White skin with innocence, beauty, truth, chastity, and all that is pure, sweet, sacred, and divine. With this skin color symbolism, Baltazar (1973) believed, there was a "progressive Aryanization of Christ" and all those associated with him

(p. 32). The Christ that was once thought to be dark skinned with dark hair and big dark eyes underwent a "bleaching process" in which his hair and beard became blond, his eyes became blue, and his garments became white (Baltazar, p. 32).

The whitening of biblical figures went hand-in-hand with the propagation of the Hamitic myth. According to this myth gleaned from bits and pieces of nonbiblical Jewish and Islamic folklore, Ham, Noah's son, had looked upon his father's nakedness, and he and his descendants were cursed with a Black skin color that was shameful and grotesque. They were doomed not only to be slaves forever but also to roam throughout human history as an apelike, thick-lipped, kinky-haired, savage nation of thieves, fornicators, and liars (Drake, 1990, p. 22).

In America, the Puritan-Calvinistic-Protestant Christian denominations, and, to some extent, even the more liberal-minded Quakers, incorporated the racist mythomania into their religious doctrines and practices. Puritans, with their great fear of carnality, believed that any sexual contact with Black people was contact with the sin, stain, and pollution of Satan in the flesh himself. White Calvinists, viewing the economically successful and powerful as the elect of God, transferred skin color symbolism from theology to economics. With their spiritual-economic worldview, White American Christian slaveholders advanced the notion that the prosperous and the powerful were the paragons of hard work, thriftiness, sobriety, ambition, sexual morality, and other virtues alleged to be held in the highest esteem by God. They viewed Black people as lazy, wasteful, slothful, immoral, and promiscuous. In other words, they viewed Black people as a people who were clearly the complete negation of God-inspired virtues.

Freedom to many of the liberal White humanitarians meant not bringing Black people out of the house of bondage but leading them back into the house of God. As for the slaveholders, slavery was a holy crusade. Years later, when they were to defend it with all the martial forces they could muster, they would do so with the fervor and fanaticism of a holy war.

While White people were fashioning a religion that made them feel comfortable enslaving darker people, all the forces of White racist religious propaganda were marshaled and backed by law and brute force to instill in Black people that they were immoral, stupid, and ugly and that Blackness represented a super savage body cursed by God to toil, to sweat, and to serve. So brutal, deliberate, systematic, and persistent was the notion that God

Almighty Himself made Black people to serve White people forever that a great number of enslaved Africans had become thoroughly convinced that White people were indeed the elect of God. Many had come to believe that their White masters were gods themselves. The servant-obey-your-master religion that was pounded daily into the heads of enslaved Africans was designed to create Black people not in the image of God but in the image of the "Black Sambo" in White people's imaginations.

In traditional Africa, Black people had incorporated in their psyche their ancestors and their gods, and it was those spiritual entities that directed them toward the fulfillment of their destiny and the development of community. In slavery, a White man, not Black ancestors and not Black gods, was deeply ingrained in the heads of Black people, deeply entrenched in their souls, the essence of their being. This White man in their heads was telling them that they were slaves, that they would be slaves forever, that their children and their children's children would be slaves, and that they might as well become content with their lot in life.

In traditional Africa before the coming of Europeans as enslavers and colonizers, African people developed a concept of multiple selves to correspond to their social environment and spiritual world. However, one self that they did not have to cultivate or develop was the racial self. Certainly, they had their own ethnic differences and their "tribal" warfares, but whatever contempt they had for African people who were not like them was not based on notions of inferiority and superiority because of skin color. They had not categorized groups into a rigorous dichotomy of Black and White races. However, after Europeans introduced the concept of race, it became brutally real in its consequences. Whether the Africans were enslaved or free, race became the dominant, most overwhelming, and most enduring reality of their lives. It meant that spiritually and religiously, Black freedom fighters during slavery had to completely destroy the White man in their heads before they could discover a positive, authentic concept of racial self that would allow them to develop the maximum level of compassion and care.

As the case of Josiah Henson and other great Black caregivers will show, the extent to which enslaved Africans incorporated this belief as fact or truth in their own personalities was the extent to which they would participate not in helping their people break their chains, but the extent to which they would participate willingly or unwillingly in holding them back.

THE NARRATIVE OF JOSIAH HENSON

Josiah Henson, born a slave in Maryland in 1789, gained international fame as the prototype for Harriet Beecher Stowe's fictional character "Uncle Tom." Henson had risen from slavery to become one of the leading Black caregivers of the 19th century. After gaining freedom in Canada, Henson established the Dawn Institute and Settlement, which gave hundreds of fugitive slaves a fresh start in life. The formerly enslaved Africans of the Dawn Settlement built homes, schools, churches, lumber mills, and other enterprises, and harvested crops on farmland that they themselves owned, becoming an economically self-sufficient, all-Black Canadian community. Henson became a leading antislavery advocate, traveling to Europe where he met with the Queen of England as he pleaded the cause of Black people still in captivity. Henson also became an active participant in the Underground Railroad, risking his own life and freedom by going back into slavery time and time again. As a result of his efforts, he rescued more than 800 enslaved Africans, 500 more than famed Underground Railroad conductor Harriet Tubman. Henson (1849/1962) said, "I was perfectly satisfied in being permitted to be the instrument of freeing such a number of my fellow creatures" (p. 149).

Spiritually, Henson was a deeply religious man who had become a Methodist minister. His chief message to oppressed Black people was that God was a deliverer and a liberator and that they must become active partners with God to forge the path to their own freedom. Henson (1849/1962) said that every time he took a band of escaped slaves safely to freedom, he took the time to impress upon them that they had two obligations: "first, to God, for their deliverance; and then, secondly, to their fellow men, to do all that was in their power to bring others out of bondage" (p. 145). Henson saw God's presence everywhere in human history and everywhere in the daily lives of Black people. He attributed to God every good thing that happened to him or his people. Once, when he and a group of Kentucky runaways found themselves on the banks of a flooded Ohio River, Henson and his group searched for hours trying to find a low tide that would allow them to wade in the water. After they saw a cow walk straight across the river without swimming, Henson (1849/1962) told the group that God had sent the cow to show His troubled children the way (p. 155). Henson dedicated his life to being an instrument of God to show his people the way.

If one read about the latter part of Henson's life, they would have been astonished to learn that before he became a settlement founder, an abolitionist, an underground railroad conductor, and a minister of God, he was an enslaved African who was so indoctrinated that he believed his master was God. Henson's earliest recollection of his childhood in slavery was one of trauma. He had become a witness to White men flogging his father, cutting his father's ears off, and selling his father to the dreaded "Deep South." Henson also remembered that his mother was a very religious woman, a "woman of piety," who instilled in him and his brothers and sisters a sense of religion (Henson, 1849/1962, p. 10). While Henson's mother wanted religion to serve as a source of solace to her children in slavery, she also had to instill in them the slave master's brand of religion, which demanded obedience to the slave master as if it were obedience to God. It was for the sake of their children's survival that Black slave mothers felt compelled to teach their children this compromising kind of religion. Henson himself as a young boy had incorporated these kinds of religious teachings into his soul. Although his mother was a devout, praying woman, all six of her children were taken from her and sold. Only Josiah was returned to her because he had become so physically ill that the buyer returned him as damaged goods. Neither Henson nor his mother would see their loved ones again. While Henson adored his mother, it was Isaac Riley, their master, whom he had come to view as a father figure to whom all praises were due.

Henson (1849/1962) said that to ingratiate himself to Isaac Riley, his master, he sought "to out-hoe, out-reap, out-husk, out-dance, out-everything every competitor .... One word of commendation from the petty despot who ruled over us would set me up for a month" (p. 19). Henson became such a loyal, hardworking, obedient slave that Isaac Riley made him an overseer. Henson said: "I was promoted to be superintendent of the farm work, and managed to raise more than double the crops, with more cheerful and willing labor, than was ever seen on the estate before" (p. 23). Henson looked for every opportunity to prove his loyalty to Riley. Once when his master was in one of his frequent drunken brawls, Henson was so badly beaten while trying to rescue him that it took Henson several months to recover from his injuries. He was not killed but he was left permanently maimed in his shoulders. Henson said he was willing to give his life for his master.

Henson's loyalty to his master did not keep him from gaining the love and esteem of his fellow slaves because Henson also felt compelled to relieve their burden as much as it was in his power to do so. He said, "I early learned to employ my spirit of adventure for the benefit of my fellow sufferers"

(Henson, 1849/1962, p. 21). He explained that it was not unusual for him to run down one of his master's chickens or drive a mile or two into the woods and clandestinely slaughter a pig or sheep "for the good of those whom Riley was starving" (pp. 21–22). This "divinity of a sympathetic heart," he said, made him feel "good, moral, heroic" (p. 22). He said it was "the luxury of doing good" that he esteemed "among the best of my deeds" (p. 22). Even though he worked the slaves harder than the former White overseer, his good work among them earned him their trust and respect.

When Henson was 18 years old, he experienced a religious conversion that awakened him to a new life, heightened his "consciousness of power and destiny" and made him feel he could "bear all things" (Henson, 1849/1962, p. 30). Henson had become deeply affected when he heard a White minister utter the words "That he, by the grace of God, should taste of death for every man." These words "for every man," he said, made him realize that God's love was for everybody. This included the rich as well as the poor, his master Riley and himself, "a poor, despised, abused, creature deemed fit for nothing but unrequited toil" (p. 28). Henson wrote that after his religious conversion he became interested in all things religious and began to preach among his fellow enslaved companions. The kind of message Henson preached was clear. He wanted them to love the master as much as he himself loved him. He wanted them to love their master as much as they loved God. While Henson's conversion brought more peace within himself, it did nothing to alter his relationship with Riley. In fact, it made him love and worship his master even more. Henson said: "I loved my enemies and prayed for them that did spitefully use and entreat me" (p. 29). He wrote of his master:

> I had no reason to think highly of his moral character; but it was my duty to be faithful to him in the position in which he placed me; and I can boldly declare before God and man, that I was so. I forgave him the causeless blows and injuries he had inflicted on me in childhood and youth, and was proud of the favor he now showed me, and of the character and reputation I had earned by strenuous and persevering efforts. (p. 41)

For years, Henson's loyalty to his master never wavered despite how cruel Riley was to Henson and to the other slaves. When Henson was 36 years old, he experienced the greatest of his loyalty to his slave master. By this time, Isaac Riley was in financial trouble. Creditors were threatening to take everything he owned and a drunken, desperate Isaac Riley was having difficulty managing his affairs. Riley believed that the only way to keep his most valuable assets, his slaves, was to ship them down to Kentucky to Amos Riley, his brother. Thus, out of sheer desperation, Isaac Riley did something that was virtually unheard of in the world of human bondage. He entrusted another slave to leave the plantation without being under the authority of a White man, and to take other slaves with him. Of course, his most loyal, trustworthy, and obedient slave was none other than Josiah Henson. To interest Henson in taking this journey, Riley told Henson that the move was the only way he could guarantee that the slaves on his plantation would remain together as intact families. Isaac Riley ensured Henson that sending his slaves down to Kentucky was purely out of his desire to keep them from being sold separately to the dreaded Deep South. Henson (1849/1962) wrote:

> Solicited in this way, with urgency and tears, by the man whom I had so zealously served for over thirty years, and now seemed absolutely dependent upon his slave, impelled, too, by the fear which he skillfully awakened, that the sheriff would seize everyone who belonged to him, and that all would be separated, or perhaps sold to go to Georgia or Louisiana, an object of perpetual dread to the slave of the more Northern States, I consented, and promised faithfully to do all I could to save him from the fate impending over him. (pp. 46–47)

Thus, armed with his master's pass authorizing him to take slaves through several states, Henson took off with 18 comrades plus his own family (his wife and two children) on a nearly 1,000-mile trek on foot, taking his people from slavery in Maryland to deliver them to slavery in Kentucky. Because of Henson's intelligence and resourcefulness, the trip went without much trouble and Henson's ego received a great boost from the White people who stopped him and his band along the way.

Because of Henson's determination to please his master, everything went smoothly until he and his fellow travelers reached Ohio. Black people there, particularly those in Cincinnati, reminded them they were on free soil and that it would be stupid for them to keep traveling the road to bondage. Henson (1849/1962) said: "They told us we were fools to think of going on and surrendering ourselves up to a new owner; that now we would be our own masters, and put ourselves out of all reach of pursuit" (p. 51). Henson's band began to get restless and showed signs of insubordination, and even Henson began to feel the temptation to take freedom for himself and his family. He wrote:

> Freedom had ever been an object of my ambition, though no other means of obtaining it had occurred to me but purchasing myself. I had never dreamed of running away. I had a sentiment of honor on the subject. The duties of the slave to his master as appointed over him in the Lord, I had ever heard urged by ministers and religious men. It seemed like outright stealing, and now I felt the devil was getting the upper hand of me. (pp. 51–52)

Henson's band was growing excited, but they offered no resistance. They were willing to put their fate in Henson's hands. After all, he had been their companion and leader for years and they were accustomed to obeying his orders. In their ignorance and degradation they had no full comprehension of what freedom really meant. Henson felt burdened by his dilemma, but after giving it more thought, he resolved that Satan was trying to tempt him and that it was his duty to himself and God, not to mention Riley, to do all he could to resist Satan. He said that his notion of right was against taking freedom in Ohio. Henson (1849/1962) wrote:

> I had promised my master to take his property to Kentucky, and deposit it with his brother Amos. Pride, too, came in to confirm me. I had undertaken a great thing; my vanity had been flattered all along the road by hearing myself praised; I thought it would be a feather in my cap to carry it through thoroughly; and had often painted the scene in my imagination of the final surrender of my charge to master Amos, and the immense admiration and respect with which he would regard me. (p. 52)

Black people in Ohio hurled "a shower of curses" on Henson as he led his charges up the gangplank to the steamboat for the final leg of their journey (Henson, 1849/1962, p. 53). Henson did deliver Isaac Riley's property to Kentucky and, just as Henson had imagined, Amos Riley was exhilarated. In fact, he was so pleased that he made Henson an overseer.

Henson was pleased with his life in Kentucky. He was serving his new master just as loyally and faithfully as he had served his old master. He had started to make a few dollars preaching. He added two more children to his family and was planning to settle down in Kentucky for life. His only regret was that Isaac Riley had not yet kept his promise to come to Kentucky to join them.

After three years of contentment on Amos Riley's plantation in Kentucky, something happened that would provoke Henson's consciousness to the core. Isaac Riley had broken his promise not to sell Henson's companions to the Deep South. These were the people Henson himself had escorted to Kentucky thinking his actions were the surest guarantee that the families would stay together. However, Henson was betrayed; all his companions were sold. Only Henson and his family were spared. Isaac Riley needed the money. Henson was stunned. He said it was as if all "the torments of hell" had seized upon him. "This, then, was the reward and end of all faithfulness to my master," he said (1849/1962, p. 60). Henson started feeling intense guilt for not having allowed his fellow companions to take their freedom in Ohio:

Oh! What would I have given to have had the chance offered once more! And now, through me, were they doomed to wear out life miserably in the hot and pestilential climate of the Far South. Death would have been welcome to me in my agony (Henson, 1849/1962, p. 60)

Henson said that with his master's betrayal, his eyes were wide open. "From that hour I saw through, hated, and cursed the whole system of slavery." He also said, "one absorbing purpose occupied my soul—freedom, self-assertion, deliverance" (Henson, 1849/1962, p. 60).

After Henson's companions were sold off, he attempted to gain freedom by the only method he felt was honorable, which was to purchase himself and his family. He got permission to go see Isaac Riley and was surprised to learn that Isaac Riley was agreeable to his plan. Riley wanted $450.00 for Henson and a total of $650.00 for Henson's family. Henson put $350.00 down on himself and was eager to get back to Kentucky so he could earn the rest. After he was back in Kentucky, he began to preach and work with more fervor than ever before.

Henson was even more convinced that he had chosen the right time and the right path to freedom after accompanying Amos Riley's son, Amos, Jr., on a flatboat trip to New Orleans. When they stopped in Vicksburg to sell produce, Henson got permission to visit some of his old companions who were on a plantation nearby. Henson (1849/1962) said: "It was the saddest visit I ever made" (p. 84):

> Four years in an unhealthy climate and under a hard master they had done the ordinary work of twenty. Their cheeks were literally caved in with starvation and disease, and their bodies infested with vermin. No hell could equal the misery they described as their daily portion. Toiling half naked in malarious marshes, under a burning, maddening sun, and poisoned by swarms of mosquitos and black gnats, they looked forward to death as their only deliverance. Their worst fears of being sold down South had been more than realized. I went away sick at heart, and to this day the sight of that wretched group haunts me. (pp. 84–85)

After seeing his companions in such wretched condition, Henson (1849/1962) said: "My faith in God utterly gave way. I could no longer pray or trust. He had abandoned me and cast me off forever. I looked not to him for help. I saw only the foul miasmas, the emaciated frames of my Negro companions; and in them saw the sure, swift, loving intervention of the one unfailing friend of the wretched, death!" (pp. 86–87).

When Henson, Amos, Jr., and the three White men accompanying them reached New Orleans, his faith in God was shattered even more. He discovered that the purpose of the trip was not only to sell a boatload of pigs, cattle, poultry, corn, and whiskey at various stops along the Mississippi River, but also to sell him. "After all I had done for Isaac and Amos Riley. After all the regard they professed for me," Henson (1849/1962, p. 87) cried. He was so outraged that he seriously contemplated killing Amos, Jr., and the other White men while they were on the boat asleep. That night, he had actually got an axe and was about to bring it down on Amos, Jr.'s head when suddenly the thought came to him: "What! Commit murder! And you a Christian?" (p. 90). Henson laid down his axe, thanked God that he had not committed murder, and left his fate in God's hands as he prayed for God's intervention during the interminably long and sleepless night. The next day when he was about to be inspected, auctioned off, and sold, young Amos Riley suddenly took seriously ill. Being among a city of strangers, he called on Henson to nurse him and to take him back to Kentucky, which, of course, Henson was thrilled to do. He believed God had heard his cries for deliverance.

When they returned to Kentucky by steamboat, Amos, Jr. told his family that if it had not been for Henson, he would have died. Henson said that he had received more accolades and commendations from Amos and Isaac Riley than ever before. It seemed as if the Riley family had totally forgotten that they had planned to sell Henson, and thus separate him from his family, just a few days ago. Now they were giving him praises that Henson would have died to have received before. Henson went about his chores seemingly with the same loyalty and enthusiasm he had shown for more than 40 years. Then one night, he, his wife, and their four children took off for Canada.

The life story of Josiah Henson shows that it is not enough to assume that Black religiosity and Black caregiving naturally go hand-in-hand. Henson underwent a life-changing religious conversion and became a slave preacher. Yet he could not come to terms with his own Blackness or overcome White religious judgments.

Sigmund Freud's concept of "disavowal" seems to apply well to Henson. Disavowal is a kind of splitting of the ego where one perceives a reality but simultaneously plays down the psychological significance or impact of it in order to achieve pathological meaning to one's own life. Freud (1893) described it as "blindness of the seeing eye in which one knows and does not know a thing at the same time." Henson knew his people were suffering. He could see it with his own eyes. However, through his own torturous process of accommodating himself to slavery and compromising his integrity, dignity, and manhood, he played down the psychological impact of his people's misery. He could only see his own selfish need to be constantly stroked by the master. He could help his people in ways that made him feel good, moral, and heroic, but he could not fully mourn with them. Henson had to create a fantasy structure of denial and disavowal that kept him from seeing the full reality of slavery. Disavowal kept him always intending to be free but never taking the risk of making actual steps in freedom's direction. For more than 40 years, Henson went through this excruciating process before his consciousness was finally so provoked and outraged that he could no longer disavow the harsh realities of slavery and no longer ignore the full suffering of his people. His ego was no longer split. His spirituality was no longer fragmented. He now knew fully where his loyalties were. Religiously, Henson had to go through a process of worshiping Whiteness, bowing down to Whiteness, and suffering deep spiritual fragmentation before finally relinquishing the White man's conception of God and discovering a God of liberation.

In comparing Henson's life with the lives of Sojourner Truth, Frederick Douglass, and Harriet Tubman, we find that these other great, enslaved caregivers also had to reconcile their religious worldview before they could reach a higher level of spirituality and racial self development, and before they could truly mourn with their people and devote their lives completely to their cause.

SOJOURNER TRUTH

Religiously, racially, and communally, Henson's life reads much the same as the life of the legendary Black matriarch, Sojourner Truth. Truth's mother had also sought to instill in her children the religion of accommodation. She told her children to always obey the master, always work hard to please him, and if he was mean to them just pray to God to make him good. Isabella (her name before she took on the name of Sojourner Truth) had prayed to God to make her first master and mistress good because they had subjected her to constant whippings, grueling labor, and mental torture, but she had to finally admit that "it didn't seem to do no good" (Bernard, 1967, p. 22). When Truth was sold to a kind master, named John J. Dumont, she believed that her prayers had been finally answered and she believed more strongly in her mother's religious teachings than ever before. Fauset (1938) wrote:

> Her mother had taught her well, religiously … Isabella readily accepted the relative positions of master and slave without trying to perceive any injustice in that relationship. With all her intelligence and independence, she nevertheless continued to believe that slavery was right and honorable … Isabella looked down contemptuously upon anyone who decried the injustice of slavery … It was risky to speak against slavery in front of Isabella. She was apt to think that it was her God-given duty to report the matter to the proper authorities … Isabella made little distinction between preachment by the master to the slave, and inconsistent practice by the master of the things he insisted that the slave should scrupulously observe. For, in her mind, God and the institutions of this world were so interrelated as to be practically synonymous. Had not her mother taught her so? (p. 25)

Truth not only swallowed wholesale the notion that the enslavement of African people was ordained by God, but she became even more convinced that her master, Dumont, actually was God. To her, Master Dumont was the "Mighty Being" her mother had told her about (Bernard, 1967, p. 41). After all, did not Dumont "jot down in a great book every action of his slaves, to keep as a record? Did he not order one about, and reward when one was good, or punish when evil arose?" (Fauset, 1938, pp. 25–26). When Truth prayed, she believed she was speaking to Master Dumont.

Believing that Dumont was God, Truth did all she could for him. Like Henson, she lived for her master's praises and tried to outwork all her other enslaved companions. "Sometimes, intoxicated by such praise from her master, Belle would refuse her complaining body its rest, forcing herself to work on through the night. Only when she could work no more, would she lean for a moment to rest against the wall. And often, leaning there, she would fall asleep and never know it until her head hit the floor" (Bernard, 1967, p. 37). Unlike Henson, Truth never gained the respect and admiration of the other slaves. Truth worked so hard to please Dumont that other enslaved Africans dubbed her "the White man's pet" (Bernard, 1967, p. 37). They constantly reminded her that "working hard ain't gonna free any of us, just kill us sooner, that's all" (Bernard, 1967, p. 37).

Truth was not able to free herself from the idea that her master was God until Dumont sold her son Peter. She was outraged because he had promised never to sell any of her children away from her. Truth had been told that there was one thing God never did and that was to lie. For the first time in her life, Truth openly opposed her master. Trembling with fear, she stood firmly in front of him and begged him not to send her son away, but to no avail. She was so disheartened and disillusioned that she ran away from this man she thought was God and became the paid servant of a Quaker couple, the Van Wagenens.

Shortly after her cruel discovery that Dumont was not God but just another cruel slaveholder looking out for his economic interest, Truth experienced a religious conversion. She said that by being born again "I began to feel such a love in my soul as I never felt before—love to all creatures ... Lord, Lord, I can love even the [W]hite folks" (Bernard, 1967, p. 67). Like Henson, even with her conversion, she could not completely rid herself of the idea that Jesus Christ was a White man who would return to earth in the flesh to create his Kingdom. Driven by these beliefs, Truth became attracted to a White religious cult called "the Kingdom" because she was convinced that the cult leader, a White man named Matthias, was the true Jesus Christ. She became so devoted to Matthias that she donated to the Kingdom all the money she had saved as well as several pieces of furniture she had accumulated over the years. She took up permanent residence as the only Black member in the Kingdom's cooperative community. She soon became one of the most devoted followers and defenders of the Kingdom. Fauset (1938) wrote:

> Nothing that he does or says is wrong, even though in the latter phase of the Kingdom she does begin to develop doubts and misgivings. Even her doubting is of the wavering variety, however and naturally so. For her seriously to doubt Matthias was to forfeit everything which she had created in her mind about the divinity of Matthias and of his Kingdom. (p. 95)

After several months in the Kingdom, there were things about Matthais, his followers, and his Kingdom that even she could not totally ignore. It appears that Matthias was openly having an affair with the wife of one of his followers, and the Kingdom itself was being attacked in the media as advocating free love. "Neighbors ... gossiped that Matthias slept with all the women at Zion Hill and saved Black Isabella for Sundays" (Painter, 1996, p. 60). Also, Truth could see that with all the quarrels and infighting among the leaders that the Kingdom was clearly not practicing the love and truth that it preached. Furthermore, as far as cooperating in this so-called cooperative community, nobody seemed to be doing the cleaning, cooking, and laundering but her. Matthias told her that although his body was not there, his spirit was there with her helping her do all the cleaning and other chores. Truth soon discovered that Matthias, who had called time and time again for the abolition of slavery and for racial equality, was beginning to act like a slave master himself. Like a slaveholder, he reserved for himself the right to make all the key decisions affecting the lives of people in his charge. Matthias referred to his followers as his children. Like a slave master, he felt it was his God-given right to inflict corporal punishment on those who violated his commands. Painter (1996) wrote:

> As Robert Matthias he had beaten his wife and children, and as the Prophet Matthias he beat Isabella for the infraction he considered abominable in women: insubordination. On the occasion when she was

not feeling well—already the apparent proof that she was possessed by a "sick devil"—she had intervened when Matthias was punishing one of his young sons. Matthias lashed her with his cowhide whip, shouting "Shall a sick devil undertake to dictate to me?" (p. 54)

Matthias, who claimed his kingdom was egalitarian and opposed to slavery, further reserved a right for himself that slaveholders took for granted: the right to have sex with anyone under his charge. Painter (1996) held that, "there is little doubt that a potent erotic current ran between Isabella and Matthias" (p. 60).

Although Truth could clearly see that all was not as it was supposed to be at the kingdom, she nevertheless continued to believe in Matthias's divinity. Even as the kingdom spiraled downward when Matthias was placed on trial for murder, Truth stood by his side. Matthias had been charged with poisoning one of his followers so he could sleep with the deceased follower's wife. A deeply hurt and humiliated Truth became the star witness testifying on his behalf. She became so close to Matthias that one newspaper reported that she herself had mixed the poison that killed the follower. However, the prosecutor could not prove his case. Matthias was acquitted, and Isabella won a lawsuit for slander and was awarded $125 in damages, which she split with Matthias.

Matthias, with his kingdom in ruins in New York, decided that a change of scenery was in his best interest. He decided to go out West and build a new kingdom in the wilderness. Naturally, Truth wanted to go with him. Thus, she continued to give him every cent she had "even after the commune broke up and it was plain to others that he was a charlatan" (Painter, 1996, p. 55). It was not until he took her money and headed out West without her, his truest believer, that she began to believe that "Matthias was no more Jesus than John Dumont had been God" (Bernard, 1967, p. 103). Painter (1996) held that, "a chasm seems still to separate the strong, canny person who would create the legendary Sojourner Truth from the woman who stayed with a scoundrel who beat her up, suppressed her preaching, took her money, and made her do his housework for nothing, who lay abed with another man's wife and proclaimed that his spirit was helping with the floors and the laundry" (p. 59).

Isabella was 48 years old when she said that God gave her the name "Sojourner Truth." With her new name came a new sense of racial and gender identity and a new sense of spiritual independence and destiny. With her new name establishing her mission in life, Truth was determined to speak her own mind and not let a Dumont or a Matthias speak for her. She was determined that no one would ever again oppress, beat, exploit, and abuse her, that she herself would become God's mouthpiece against oppression, exploitation, mistreatment, and abuse. For more than 30 years, Truth traveled the country speaking the "Truth" about the conditions of enslaved Africans and the plight of women. Although she was illiterate, Truth said: "You know, children, I don't read such small stuff as letters, I read men and nations. I can see through a millstone, though I can't see through a spelling book" (Loewenberg & Bogin, 1976, p. 289). Truth enlisted children to read the Holy Bible to her every chance she got. She said that she could no longer trust adults to read it to her without interpreting it for her as well. Truth was determined "to know the entire Bible by heart exactly as it was written and to interpret it for herself" (Bernard, 1967, p. 128). All of her life, she had conducted her affairs according to the idea that some White man or the other was God. It was not until she was nearly 50 years old that she overcame such an immobilizing and self-defeating notion and developed a newfound spiritual consciousness and racial and gender awareness that would make her, an illiterate enslaved African woman, a legendary figure in world history.

FREDERICK DOUGLASS

Frederick Douglass, a Maryland slave, developed a hatred for slavery early in his life. He grieved over how his grandmother was treated in her advanced age. She had raised her master, her master's father, and her master's children, only to watch her own children being sold like cattle, never to hear from them again. When she became too old to work for her master, he built her a cabin out in the woods and turned this sickly, feeble old woman loose to fend for herself, literally leaving her to die. Frederick Douglass (1881/1963) reported: "My grandmother was all the world to me" (p. 17). Since the day she was separated from Douglass, he hated slavery with a passion.

Douglass's early hatred of slavery kept him from coming under the spell of his slave master's religion. Douglass was influenced at an early age by the preaching of a White Methodist minister who made him feel that in God he had a friend, and Douglass' conversion to Christianity lightened his burden, relieved his heart, and made him love all mankind, even the slaveholders. But, unlike Truth and Henson, F. Douglass (1881/1963) said that with his conversion he abhorred slavery more than ever (p. 82).

Douglass never adopted the idea that God sanctioned something as evil as slavery. He became quite contemptuous of Black people who accepted and taught that idea. F. Douglass (1881/1963) wrote: "I have met many good religious colored people at the South who were under the delusion that God required them to submit to slavery and to wear their chains with meekness and humility. I could entertain no such nonsense as this, and I quite lost my patience when I found a colored man weak enough to believe such stuff" (p. 77). Douglass was well aware of how religion was used to adapt enslaved Africans to their lot in life. He wrote: "To make a contented slave, you must make a thoughtless one. It is necessary to darken his moral and mental vision, and as far as possible, to annihilate his power of reason. He must be able to detect no inconsistencies in slavery; if there be one crevice through which a single drop can fall, it will certainly rust off the slave's chain" (F. Douglass, 1881/1963, p. 187). Douglass felt that his own master was proof that slaveholders were not gods. He said that his master's house was literally a house of prayer and that hymns and prayers were heard all day long (p. 102). However, Douglass discerned that "if religion had any effect at all on him, it made him more cruel and hateful in all his ways" (p. 103). To Douglass, the highest proof slaveholders could give to enslaved Africans that they had truly found God was to free their slaves (F. Douglass, 1881/1963, p. 102).

Douglass had no intentions of becoming a contented slave, one who was convinced that his enslavement was divinely ordained. Unlike Henson and Truth, Douglass was fortunate to have right there on the plantation not one, but two elderly Black men who were happy to serve as spiritual advisors to the young Douglass. One of Douglass's spiritual advisors was a man named Charles Lawson, whom Douglass affectionately called "Uncle Lawson." F. Douglass (1881/1963) wrote:

This man not only prayed three times a day, but he prayed as he walked through the streets, at his work, on his dray—everywhere. His life was a life of prayer, and his words when he spoke to anyone, were about a better world. Uncle Lawson lived near Master High's house, and becoming deeply attached to him, I went often with him to prayer meeting, and spent much of my leisure time with him. (p. 83)

Uncle Lawson became "my chief instructor in religious matters" F. Douglass (1881/1963) said (p. 83). "He was my spiritual father and I loved him intensely, and was at his house every chance I could get" (p. 83). Douglass said that Uncle Lawson instilled in him a deep feeling of self-worth and fanned his already intense love of knowledge into a flame by assuring him that he would be a useful man in the world (p. 84). Lawson assured Douglass that the Lord would make him free because he had a "great work" for Douglass to do. It had been shown to Lawson that God wanted Douglass to preach the Gospel. Douglass said, "This advice and these suggestions were not without their influences on my character and destiny. Thus assured and thus cheered on under the inspiration of hope, I walked and prayed with a light heart, believing that my life was under the guidance of a wisdom higher than my own" (F. Douglass, 1881/1963, p. 84).

Douglass also had as a spiritual advisor an old Black man named Sandy. Douglass said that Sandy was "a man as famous among the slaves of the neighborhood for his good nature as for his good sense" (p. 132). He wrote:

I find Sandy an old advisor. He was not only a religious man, but he professed to believe in a system for which I have no name. He was a genuine African, and had inherited some of the so-called magical powers said to be possessed by the eastern nations (F. Douglass, 1881/1963, pp. 133–134).

Sandy, in other words, was a conjurer. F. Douglass (1881/1963) wrote:

I had a positive aversion to all pretenders to "divination." It was beneath ... my intelligence to countenance such dealings with the devil as this power implied. But with all my learning—it was really precious little—Sandy was more than a match for me ... I saw in Sandy too deep an insight into human nature, with all his superstition, not to have some respect for his advice; and perhaps, too, a slight gleam or shadow of his superstition had fallen on me. (p. 133)

Douglass often turned to Sandy for spiritual advice and for magical potions. On one occasion he turned to Sandy for a root to keep the slave breaker from punishing him. Douglass said that it worked for a while. Douglass also consulted Sandy when he and five other young enslaved Africans planned an escape. Sandy warned against it because he had seen Douglass in a dream in the claws of a huge bird, surrounded by a large number of birds of all colors and sizes pecking at him (F. Douglass, 1881/1963, p. 169). Although Sandy's dream had a powerful effect on Douglass, he and the others went on as planned and had not gotten too far before they were surrounded by a mob of armed White men. The mob commenced to make sport with their captives, picking at and jeering them. Douglass said, "As I looked upon the crowd of vile persons, and saw myself and friends thus assailed and persecuted, I could not help seeing the fulfillment of Sandy's dream" (p. 169).

Uncle Lawson and Sandy were not only the young Douglass's spiritual advisors and mentors, but served also as his father figures. F. Douglass, (1881/1963) wrote, "in my loneliness and destitution I longed for someone to whom I could go, as to a father and protector" (p. 82). In Uncle Lawson and Sandy he found two fathers and two protectors. This was significant because his own father was a White man who had no compunction whatsoever in consigning his own child to slavery.

Douglass was not only fortunate to have Uncle Lawson and Sandy guiding his moral, religious, and spiritual life, but he also found the other slaves on the plantation extremely supportive of him and of one another. In Truth's early years, she never got along with her fellow slaves in general because she was too willing to do her master's bidding. Henson got along well with the slaves on Master Riley's plantation but his love for them was always self-serving, geared just as much toward winning him favors with the master as it was toward developing true friendships based on genuine affection and love. F. Douglass (1881/1963) wrote:

I am indebted to the genial temper and ardent friendship of my brother slaves. They were every one of them manly, generous and brave ... It is seldom the lot of any to have truer and better friends than were the slaves on this farm. It was not uncommon to charge slaves with great treachery toward each other, but I must say I never loved, esteemed, or confided in men more than I did in these. They were as true as steel, and no band of brothers could be more loving. There was no mean advantage taken of each other, no tattling, no giving each other bad names to Mr. Freeland, and no elevating one at the expense of the other. We never undertook anything of any importance which was likely to affect each other, without mutual consultation. We were generally a unit, and moved together. (p. 151)

Douglass said that his greatest obstacle to running away to freedom was the thought of having to leave behind the people whom he loved and who loved him. After consulting with his spiritual advisors, Douglass sought to escape again. This second time he succeeded, as Sandy had predicted. Douglass did go on to become an ordained minister of the African Methodist Episcopal Church, just as Lawson had prophesized, but he did most of his preaching against slavery as the foremost abolitionist lecturer in the country. In fact, he gained international fame for his oratory skills. Douglass used powerful religious imagery, symbolism, and metaphors to express his intense hatred for slavery and his intense love for his people and their freedom. Douglass became particularly adept in pointing out the great contradiction between slavery and White America's most professed beliefs in Christianity and democracy. For example, in his famous 1847 Fourth of July address, he declared emphatically that "slavery is not divine, that God did not establish it" and that "that which is inhuman, cannot be divine" (in Foner and Branham, 1998, p. 257). Douglass asked:

> What, to the American slave, is your Fourth of July? I answer: A day that reveals to him, more than all other days in the year, the gross injustice and cruelty to which he is the constant victim. To him, your celebration is a sham; your boasted liberty an unholy license; your national greatness swelling vanity; your sounds of rejoicing are empty and heartless; your denunciation of tyrants brass-fronted impudence; your shouts of liberty and equality hollow mockery; your prayers and hymns, your sermons and thanksgivings, with all your religious parade and solemnity, are to him mere bombast, fraud, deception, impiety and hypocrisy— a thin veil to cover up crimes which would disgrace a nation of savages (in Foner and Branham, p. 258).

HARRIET TUBMAN

Like Douglass, Harriet Tubman, (who was born Araminta Ross in Maryland) was not convinced that God ordained the enslavement of Black people. It seems that her enslaved parents did not instill in her the typical servant-obey-your-master teachings that many slave parents believed were crucial to their children's survival. Freed of this baggage, Tubman developed a close, personal relationship with God. Her biographer and close friend, Sarah Bradford, wrote:

Brought up by parents possessed of strong faith in God, she had never known the time, I imagine, when she did not trust Him, and cling to Him, with an all-abiding confidence. She seemed to feel the Divine Presence near, and she talked with God 'as a man talketh with his friend.' Hers was not the religion of a morning and evening prayer at stated times, but when she felt a need, she simply told God of it, and trusted Him to set the matter right. (Bradford, 1869/1971, p. 23)

Tubman had become steeped in the folk-thinking and spirituality of Black culture, which called for creative expression, communal support, social mobility, and a liberation ethic. While Tubman was a Christian who underwent a powerful religious conversion in which she "prayed without ceasing" (Bradford, 1869/1971, p. 24), she, like a number of enslaved Africans, blended traditional African religious practices into her beliefs. Therefore, Tubman was just as apt to rely on charms, amulets, signs, numbers, and so forth as she was to rely on prayers. Tubman particularly relied on dreams and visions to gain insights from the spiritual world. When Tubman was a young girl, an overseer hurled a two-pound weight at another slave, but it struck Tubman with a stunning blow on the head. It took months before Tubman recovered and she was scarred for life. After recovering, Tubman would often slumber into a deep trancelike stupor. It was when she was in this lethargic state that she would receive her clearest visions. Although these spells would put her into a deep sleep, Tubman saw them as her most wonderful and glorious entry into a heavenly Jerusalem. Biographer Bradford (1869/1971) wrote:

When these turns of somnolence come upon Harriet, she imagines that her "spirit" leaves her body, and visits other scenes and places, not only in this world, but in the world of spirits. (p. 51)

Not only did Harriet rely on these apocalyptic visions from the spirit world to guide her, she also relied on dreams. She often had horrible dreams of enslavers chasing down terrified Black women and children and selling them deeper into slavery. She had recurring dreams of the infamous Middle Passage. She could vividly see the agony her people suffered on the death ships. These dreams of Black suffering and oppression gave her a powerful sense of ancestral connectedness. They also greatly agitated her and made her want to take action on behalf of her people.

Tubman had always been what slaveholders called a "stubborn slave." Unlike many enslaved Africans who had made their peace with slavery, Tubman always questioned why things were the way they were and whether there would be deliverance for her people.

While Tubman intensely felt the weight of her people's suffering, past and present, she was especially motivated as a caregiver out of her concerns for her own family. As J. M. Martin and Martin (1985) pointed out, most enslaved Africans had to adopt fictive kin in order to fill in the gaps left by blood relatives from whom they had been separated (pp. 22–23). Tubman was fortunate in that she had a large extended family consisting of her real, blood kin right there on the plantation or in the general vicinity. Both of her parents were intact and she had 10 brothers and sisters. Her deepest fear was that her own family members would be scattered around the country and never see one another again. When she was in her early years, she had already experienced her mother's grief at helplessly watching two of Tubman's sisters taken away to the "Deep South." To slaves closer to the North, as we saw in Henson's story, being sold to the Deep South was viewed as being sold to a sure hell, damnation, and death. Tubman believed that the only guarantee against her family being separated was to get them all to freedom.

With Tubman's "stubborn" attitude and contempt for slavery, she was the first member of her family that the master most wanted to sell. After finding out that her master was vigorously seeking someone who would buy her, Tubman prayed: "Oh, dear Lord change dat man's heart, and make him a Christian. Oh, Lord, convert old master" (Bradford, 1869/1971, pp. 23–24). But after seeing no change in her master's heart, she said:

> Then I changed my prayer, and I said, "Lord, if you ain't never going to change dat man's heart, kill him, Lord, and take him out of de way, so he won't do no more mischief." Next ting I heard old master was dead; and he died just as he had lived, a wicked, bad man. (Bradford, 1869/1971, pp. 23–24)

Tubman's new master had said that he was never going to sell any of his slaves out of state, but Tubman had had visions which told her "'Arise, flee for life!' and in the visions of the night she saw the horsemen coming, and heard the shrieks of women and children, as they were being torn from each other, and hurried off no one knew whither" (Bradford, 1869/1971, pp. 25–26). Unable to convince her husband, John Tubman, or any of her family members to flee with her, Tubman set out for freedom on her own by just simply walking off the plantation and following the paths her dreams and visions had mapped out for her.

On her way to freedom, Tubman made a vow. She said: "There are two things I've got a right to, and these are death or liberty. One or the other I mean to have. No one will take me back alive. I shall fight for my liberty and when the time comes for me to go, the Lord will let them take me" (Conrad, 1942, p. 13).

After taking her own freedom, Tubman was so steeped in her people's culture and values and so communally oriented and freedom-minded that she found that she could not help but mourn the plight of her loved ones still languishing under the yoke of slavery. She stated:

> I had crossed the line of which I had so long been dreaming. I was free; but there was no one to welcome me to the land of freedom, I was a stranger in a strange land, and my home after all was down in the old cabin quarter, with the old folks, and my brothers and sisters. But to this solemn resolution I came; I was free, and they should be free also; I would make a home for them in the North, and the Lord helping me, I would bring them all here. (Conrad, 1942, p. 11)

Seeking to bring all her family members and all the other enslaved Africans she could up North to freedom, Tubman made broad use of all her spiritual tools. Being a highly religious and spiritually sensitive person, Tubman found solace and inspiration in the spirituals that spoke of freedom, the power of God's love for the downtrodden, and God's hatred for oppression and injustice. Tubman particularly made extensive use of the spirituals as secret codes to instruct and inspire enslaved Africans to take their freedom and to have the courage to stick to the course after they had started. "Dead men tell no tales" is one of Tubman's most famous lines. The spirituals allowed Tubman to communicate to her Underground Railroad passengers without talking directly to them. The spirituals spoke a great deal about Moses leading his people out of bondage. Harriet would become the Moses of her people in slavery, going down into Pharoah's land. When Tubman was near her fellow fugitives, she would sing her favorite spiritual:

Hail, oh hail ye happy spirits
Death no more shall make you fear,
No grief nor sorrow, pain nor anger (anguish)
Shall no more distress you there. (Bradford, 1869/1971, p. 26)

This was a warning song to get the fugitives ready. After Tubman checked
to see that the coast was clear, she would come around again. If she sang the
following song, the hidden fugitives were to stay hidden and not to come out.

Moses go down in Egypt
Tell old pharo' let me go;
Hadn't been for Adam's fall,
Shouldn't have to die at all. (Bradford, 1869/1971, p. 26)

However, when she sang the following song, the fugitives knew that they
were to begin their journey bound for the promised land.

I'm sorry I'm going to leave you,
Farewell, oh farewell;
But I'll meet you in the mornin'
Farewell, oh farewell

I'll meet you in the mornin'
I'm bound for de promised land
On the other side of Jordan
Goin' for the promised land. (Bradford, 1869/1971, p. 18)

While on their way to the New Jerusalem, Tubman and her passengers
sang in spirited voices:

I'm on the way to Canada,
That cold and dreary land,
De sad effects of slavery,
I can't no longer stand;
I've served my master all my days,
without a dime reward,
and now I'm forced to run away,

to flee de lash, abroad;

farewell, ole master, don't think hard of me,

I'm traveling on to Canada, where all de

slaves are free. (Bradford, 1869/1971, p. 49)

Tubman's use of the spirituals was so creative and extensive that many spirituals such as "Mary, Don't You Weep," "Steal Away," "Wade in the Water," and "Follow the Drinking Gourd" became associated with the Underground Railroad. Certain other spirituals, such as "Go Down, Moses" and "Swing Low, Sweet Chariot" became personally associated with Harriet Tubman. She was known as "The Moses of Her People" and was often called "Old Chariot" because "Chariot" rhymes with Harriet and because Harriet had taken so many people on the ride to freedom.

Being so spiritually sensitive, Tubman believed that God was always with her, guiding her every step. She felt that she was so spiritually in tune with God and the spiritual universe that she always knew when danger was close by. She said that when danger was near her and her band of fugitives "it appears like my heart go flutter, flutter, and then they may say 'peace, peace,' as much as they like, I know its going to be war" (Bradford, 1869/1971, p. 80). God, prayers, visions, and dreams also told her where to go to get provisions for her little band of fugitives, and where to go for safety, money, food, and rest. Once, Tubman went to the house of one of her White friends and told him that God told her that he had money for her and gave him the amount God intended for him to give. Her friend told her that God must have been mistaken because he did not have the amount of money she was asking. Harriet said that God never lies and had never deceived her and that she would wait in the man's house until he did what God wanted him to do. "He went and scraped up the money" (Bradford, 1869/1971, pp. 51–52).

Tubman was so certain that God was on her side in her numerous ventures into the jaws of slavery and death that she believed she would never lose a passenger. When asked why she had continued to go back into slavery knowing that there was a $40,000 reward on her head, dead or alive, Tubman said that she always had God to lead her and to tell her what to do. She said "and he always did" (Bradford, 1869/1971, p. 35). Tubman, the most famous of all the Underground Railroad conductors, rescued more than 300 enslaved Africans, including her aging parents and practically all of her brothers and sisters and their spouses and children. She never lost a passenger.

Tubman's strong caregiving impulses did not diminish during the Civil War or after emancipation. During the Civil War, she served valiantly in the Union army as a nurse and a spy. General Rufus Saxon, writing on behalf of Tubman's request for a pension for her war services, stated: "I can bear witness to the value of her services in South Carolina and Florida. She was employed in the hospitals and as a spy. She made many a raid inside the enemy's lines, displaying remarkable courage, zeal, and fidelity. She was employed by General Hunter, and I think by Generals Stevens and Sherman, and is as deserving of a pension from the Government for her services as any other of its faithful servants" (Bradford, 1869/1971, p. 142). It took more than 30 years of battle before a petition to Congress finally awarded Tubman a pension of $30 a month. Tubman used her meager pension to establish the Harriet Tubman Home for Aged and Indigent Negroes in her home in Auburn, New York.

FREEDOM FROM THE RELIGIOUS CHAINS

As the lives of great Black caregivers such as Henson, Truth, Douglass, and Tubman suggest, enslaved Africans not only had to suffer in their physical chains but also had to free their minds from religious shackles. It was not enough for an enslaved African to be religious or to have undergone a life-shaking religious conversion. As long as they had swirling in their minds a representation of the White man as God and a belief in the racist myth ... alleging Black inferiority, they would always work against their own best interest. Ridding themselves of such notions was not an easy task because it appeared that the White master was all powerful, all knowing, and ever present. In that little universe called the slave plantation, the slave master had absolute control and authority. He was the absolute law and judge. He rewarded, he punished, and he doomed to earthly hell, fire, and damnation those who did not follow his stern commandments.

W. E. B. Du Bois (1903/1961) held that Africans saw their enslavement as a form of sorcery. He held that to the enslaved African, slavery "was to him the dark triumph of evil over him. All the hateful powers of the underworld were striving against him" (p. 146). Enslaved Africans believed that the White man had called up all the evil forces from the underworld and hurled them full force at them. To break this idolatrous form of sorcery or witchcraft, they had to develop a spiritual consciousness that transcended religion, at least the kind of religion their enslavers practiced and the kind that was instilled in them. This spirituality not only had to embrace old African concepts of community but also new concepts of race. Immersed in the servant-obey-your-masters religion and harboring notions of the White man as God, it was not possible for them to act fully in the interest of communal solidarity and welfare. Henson was known for his "spirit of sympathy" toward his enslaved companions and was trusted by them because of his many charitable acts (Henson, 1849/1962, p. 21). However, his own egotism, individualism, and obsessive desire for his master's praise and affection kept him from forming a bond with his fellow sufferers that would lead to freedom. Henson's egotism was the same kind of individualism that prompted some African kings and chiefs to sell their own people into bondage. Moreover, it was not possible for enslaved Africans to develop a positive concept of race as long as they believed in their souls that White men were gods. Without a sense of self-worth, dignity, and integrity drawn from a transcendental source higher and mightier than their enslavers and which even their all-powerful tormentors could not take away from them, enslaved Africans would never even feel they were worthy of freedom let alone have the courage to try to take it. The best they would be able to do was to always be on the level of intending to be free, yet never having enough confidence in themselves to take the risk of making actual steps in freedom's direction.

It was not easy for slaves to break the chains of racist religious mythomania. Henson was 50 years old before his racial and religious consciousness was provoked to the point that he could free himself from these religious shackles and become one with his people. And Truth was 48 years old when she stopped looking for a White man to be God. Douglass was fortunate in that he had two Black spiritual advisors, one a Christian and the other a traditional African practitioner, to guide his moral, religious, and spiritual choices. Tubman was also fortunate in that she was immersed in the folk culture of her people, which blended both Christianity and African spiritual practices and stressed communal caregiving. Regardless of how long it took and what method it took to free themselves from their religious chains, once they were free, a whole new world of possibilities opened up to them. After Henson freed his racial self from religious bondage, he said that his eyes not only opened to the present conditions of Black people but also to the early repressed traumatic events, which he said "had impressed themselves so deeply upon my childish soul" (Henson, 1849/1962, p. 58). After the racial self was free, these enslaved Africans could take freedom for themselves and others and be willing to die in the process. They could empathize with the past and the present as they saw more clearly visions of "a great gittin' up morning" and as they brought the past and the future into their present situation. With a spiritual self no longer fragmented or split, they could develop a more independent racial and gender identity that would allow them to reach maximum levels of caregiving and seek, like African people of old, to make their own personal mission and their people's destiny one. After Black freedom fighters such as Henson, Tubman, Douglass, and Truth, and thousands of other lesser known Black heroes and heroines had managed to free themselves from the slaveholder's religious shackles, they could truly sing in the words of the old slave spiritual:

> Slavery chain done broke at last,
> broke at last,
> broke at last,
> Slavery chain done broke at last
> Gonna praise God till I die.

F reedom fighters such as Tubman, Douglass, Henson, and Truth did not come out of bondage empty-handed. They brought with them a crusading spirit that had tremendous impact on caregiving in the free Black community. The great majority of former slaves seeking refuge in free Black communities had taken their own freedom by running away. Only a scant few had received their freedom through manumission (that is, through being freed by their owners). A few had purchased themselves and their families, but this road to freedom was a risky business. First, it was difficult for enslaved Africans to get their hands on cash; secondly, after saving for years what meager nickels and dimes they could, slaves seeking freedom via purchase were often the victims of unscrupulous slave masters who pocketed their money without granting them freedom. Most enslaved Africans coming into free Black communities were slaves on the run, fugitives seeking a haven from the vicious world they had left behind. Many fled from border states such as Maryland, Missouri, Kentucky, and Tennessee hoping to blend in with the free Black population in nonslave cities such as Cincinnati, New York, Philadelphia, and Boston and even slave cities with large free Black populations such as Baltimore, New Orleans, and Charleston (South Carolina). Whatever cities they found themselves in, it did not take the slave fugitives long before they began to make their mark on the free Black community.

First, enslaved African fugitives were not lacking in vision, hope, or ambition. The fact that they had defied bondage, punishment, and death to gain freedom showed that they were risk-takers. They had tasted slavery and they wanted more than anything to improve the quality of their lives. Many of the enslaved Africans seeking a fresh start in free Black communities had decidedly more ambition than free Black persons who were thoroughly demoralized and defeated by their wretched circumstances.

Second, many of the slave fugitives had skills and trades that were comparable to those of Black people born in freedom, and many were more advanced. On the plantation, Black people were allowed to do all kinds of work, including work requiring high levels of skill development and efficiency. This was not generally the case in the free Black community, where free Black people were relegated for the most part to unskilled manual labor.

Third, the living conditions of the average free Black person were not conspicuously above that of the average slave. A few Black people born in slavery were wealthy and enjoyed middle-class status, but the great majority of them languished in squalor. By no stretch of the imagination were so-called free Black people as free as White people. Racism was still an all-pervasive reality that free Black people could hardly forget. "How can I forget," one free Black person asked, when "I am sore from sole to crown"; when "it [racism] stood by the bedside of my mother when she bore me"; when "it has hindered every step I have taken in life"; when "it dims the sunshine of my days, and deepens the darkness of my nights"; when "it hampers me in every relation of life, in business, in politics, in religion, as a father or as a husband"; when "it came to the altar with my bride and now that my children are looking eagerly with their youthful eyes for a career, it stands by them and casts its infernal curse upon them" (Gerber, 1988, p. 173). Another free Black person (Crummell, 1875/1992) lamented: "Turn madman, and go into a lunatic asylum, and then, perchance, you may forget. The only place I know of in this land where you can 'forget you are colored' is in the grave." (p. 260)

Fourth, runaway slaves were free of much of the color complexes free Black people had toward one another. In the free Black community, many lighter skinned Black people had an air of superiority over darker skinned Black people. While lighter skinned Africans on the slave plantation often enjoyed special advantages, they also remembered that they were still slaves, made so by their own White fathers. They knew that it was their Black slave mothers who took care of them while their fathers' White wives often treated them with hostility and contempt. Lighter skinned slaves were as apt to flee the plantation as the darker skinned slaves; once in free society, it was difficult for them to entertain notions of superiority based on the White blood in their veins. In fact, many of the so-called "mulattoes" such as Frederick Douglass led the cause of abolition in which they sought the ultimate destruction of the world their White fathers had created.

The most important contribution slave fugitives brought to the free Black community was a new spirit of uplift and freedom. Free Black people such as Henson, Tubman, Truth, Douglass, and many others would not allow the free Black community to forget the slaves—their brothers and sisters in bondage. They even made free Black people more conscious of their own oppression and caste-like status. They helped to instill in free Black people a new faith in their ability to be the agency of their own destiny and inspired them to commit their lives to what Black people at that time called "inner work."

RACE WORK AND DESTINY

Specht and Courtney (1994) stated that the term "social work" started out in the late 19th century as "social works" and was used much in the same way as the religious term "good works" (p. 21). Long before the term "social work" was coined, "race work" had been the social work of 19th-century free Black people. Gilkes (1994) maintained that race work has "links to an unbroken tradition of community work or working for 'the race' that could be traced directly to antebellum communities, both slave and free" (p. 235). Carlton-LaNey (1996) held that "race work was essentially community service coupled with the constant struggle for social justice and racial equality" (p. 30). Race work was indeed community service; it was community work with a deep spiritual focus. It was based on the idea that Black people had a spiritual calling, mission, or duty to struggle for the freedom and uplift of Black people.

To some extent, free Black race workers had unconsciously blended the African concept of the destinal self with the Christian concept of predestination. Drake (1970) wrote:

> The slaves brought with them the belief that their lives were controlled by Fate or Destiny, but that an individual, within the broad outlines of his predestined Fate could determine specific courses of action by consulting "diviners" and could take responsibility for his own affairs, a concept not far distant from that of Calvinistic theories of predestination, except that the "will of God" in Africa was not ascertained by individual prayer and "waiting on the Lord." The belief in divine providence was grafted into this African belief. (p. 22)

Although West African spirituality and Protestant Christianity had concepts of destiny, the concepts were different in significant ways. The Christian concept of predestination entailed a notion of inherent individual sinfulness and the desire for individual perfectibility through following the path of Christ. To Europeans, this historically meant a notion of the rise and fall of civilizations. Economically, it meant a linear concept of destiny, of moving from poverty to wealth, from "rags to riches." Racially, it meant the notion that it was their "manifest destiny" to rule over the lands occupied by peoples of color. The West African concept of destiny did not involve inherent sinfulness, the rise and fall of nations, individualism, material progress, imperialism, and a linear concept of time. Race destiny among enslaved Africans in America came to mean answering a divine call to get Black people out of the mire of their present circumstances. Race work used the terms "agency," "architect," and "instrumentality" to indicate that in this sacred work, Black people were in partnership with God as they played an active role in fashioning their destiny as a people.

Race work activity among 19th-century Black people was unprecedented in Black American history. Moses (1978) wrote that "Racial uplift, Negro improvement, African Civilization, race progress, and African development were all ideas that made appearances in the rhetoric of Black leaders during the 19th century" (p. 20). Meier (1996) maintained that the 19th century, particularly the later years, "witnessed increasing emphasis on economic development, self-help, racial solidarity, and race pride" (p. 69). Clarke (1991) asserted that "the African American freedom struggles have their roots in the 19th century" (p. 54). Historians agree that the century was a "Golden Age" for "race work," for Black people engaging themselves in useful activity toward the uplift and liberation of Black people. Whether seeking to teach Black people to read or find them a permanent home in Africa; whether engaging in hiding fugitives or starting a Black relief society to give assistance to the aged, widows, and orphans; whether organizing women to raise funds to build churches or raising funds to buy the freedom of enslaved Africans, any work on behalf of the general well-being and uplift of Black people was deemed "race work." Given the spiritual nature of race work, it is no wonder that the chief caregiving race work institution in the free Black community was the Black church.

THE BLACK CHURCH:
THE LEADING RACE WORK INSTITUTION
African people fleeing slavery and seeking refuge in free Black communities definitely did not come lacking in spirituality and religiosity. These were

people who had long identified with the suffering and enslavement of the Hebrew people of the Holy Bible. These were people who had been inspired to leave slavery by stories of the Hebrew people fleeing bondage in Egypt. These were people who had managed to remember biblical stories by constantly repeating them in songs (called spirituals) and through finding in these stories parallels that mirrored their own lives. These were also people who had grown tired of attending churches with their slave masters, tired of White ministers who were adept in skirting around any thoughts of Christian brotherhood and careful not to draw any conclusions from scriptures that would favor any alteration in the master–slave relationship, tired of the segregated pews, and tired of the insults and indignities heaped on them every Sunday. It is no wonder then that the Black church, the most powerful institution in the free Black community, was founded for the most part by former slaves and not people born in freedom. Enslaved Africans, still bitter with memories of their experiences in White churches, were eager to create their own separate churches after they were on free soil. By seeking independent Black churches, free Black people wanted churches completely founded, funded, controlled, led, and operated by Black people. They wanted complete Black church autonomy.

For example, David George, a South Carolina slave, founded in 1775 one of the first, if not the first, independent Black Baptist churches in Silver Bluff, North Carolina. George Liele and Andrew Bryan, both of whom were slaves, were also pioneering Black Baptist church founders. Bryan created the first African Baptist Church of Savannah in 1788, while George Liele, who had converted Bryan and had preached in the Silver Bluff Church, sailed for Jamaica and created Black Baptist churches there. Richard Allen and Absalom Jones, also former slaves who had purchased their freedom, founded the African Methodist Episcopal Church in Philadelphia in 1787. Allen and Jones were irritated about the indignities Black people suffered in the St. George's Methodist Episcopal Church. When Black people were viciously snatched up by White ushers as they knelt in prayer and directed to the "nigger pews," that was all Allen and Jones could stomach. Their departure from the White church made Black people across the nation aware of the fact that they no longer had to suffer the indignity of segregation and the lack of opportunity for advancement in the White churches. Jones later went on to form the first Black Episcopal church in 1794, after breaking from Allen's A. M. E. church movement.

James Varick, another former slave, founded the African Methodist Episcopal Zion Church in New York City in 1796, again in response to the indignities suffered by Black people in White churches.

Because many of these Black church founders were former slave preachers, they not only were irritated at the treatment of Black people in White churches but also at their own treatment as slave preachers. White church denominations in the North licensed a few Black men to preach but often prohibited them from doing so, even from preaching to other Black people. This, of course, made it easier for Black preachers, eager for the opportunity to display their spiritual gifts, to break away from the White churches and form their own independent Black churches. Furthermore, these former slave preachers knew that their people were suffocating spiritually in the White churches; that Black people did not adapt well to the staid, ecclesiastical, liturgical, and sacramental atmosphere of many of the White churches; and that they were used to more lively and upbeat religious expressions. This explains why they were more attracted to the Methodist and Baptist denominations as opposed to the Anglican, Presbyterian, Catholic, and Episcopalian churches. They rebelled against the deep puritanical strains of the Calvinistic White churches and preferred what West (1999) referred to as their own "subversive joy." Also, the Methodist and Baptist denominations were not bogged down with notions of an elite who God favored above others. As long as people had the faith and the belief in the divinity of Jesus Christ, they would embrace and be embraced by the Methodist and the Baptist faiths. This meant that ministers in the Methodist and Baptist churches were "called" to preach. They did not have to have formal theological training or know how to read and write, a fact that suited many slave preachers very well because many were illiterate when they came out of slavery. Overall, former slave preachers could make the Black independent church an oppositional church, opposing slavery and the third-class citizenship of free Black people. They could never operate as an oppositional, subversive force while remaining in the clutches of White Christian domination.

THE RELIGIOUS BASIS OF SLAVE REBELLION

It was not easy for formerly enslaved Africans or free Black people to build their own independent Black churches. Southerners had come to associate Black independent religion with slave insurrection, especially given that the

Gabriel Prosser rebellion of 1800, the Denmark Vesey rebellion of 1822, and the Nat Turner rebellion of 1831 were slave uprisings led by deeply spiritual and religious men.

Gabriel Prosser sought to do for his people in Virginia what the great slave general Toussaint L'Ouverture had done for his people in Haiti. Prosser believed that God wanted him to be another Samson. The biblical Samson described in Judges 15:14-15 had "found a jawbone of an ass, and put forth his hand and took it, and slew a thousand men therewith" (Wilmore, 1998, p. 78). Bardolf (1959) wrote that Gabriel Prosser and his co-conspirator and brother, Martin Prosser, "won adherents by impressing them with testimony from the Bible that God would deliver them as he had delivered the Israelites" (p. 28). They laid out a military plan designed to slay thousands of White slaveholders. Vesey was fascinated by the biblical passage from Joshua 6:20-21 that speaks of Joshua and the trumpets and the walls of Jericho falling down. Vesey, a class leader in Charleston's African Methodist Church, was greatly given to drawing analogy between enslaved Africans and the Hebrew people of the Holy Bible. Vesey sought to sound the trumpet that would make slavery's wall come tumbling down.

Nat Turner was a religious zealot who confessed, "I was ordained for some great purpose in the hands of the Almighty" (Bardolf, 1959, p. 9). Turner said that his divine appointment was revealed to him by signs upon leaves and in the heavens and by voices he heard in the air (Aptheker, 1952, p. 296). After the Nat Turner rebellion in Virginia, American slavery was never the same. In fact, American slavery can be roughly divided into two major periods, before Nat Turner and after Nat Turner. Before Nat Turner, White enslavers had come to believe that their slaves harbored genuine love and affection for them and that their slaves were too happy-go-lucky, docile, and cowardly to rise up against them. After Nat Turner, White people could no longer entertain such illusions. After the Nat Turner revolt, which resulted in the death of more than 60 White slaveholders, White southern leaders imposed strict repressive measures, including holding any religious indoctrination of enslaved Africans as suspect and absolutely forbidding the building of Black churches. For example, John Floyd, who was governor of Virginia at the time, told the Virginia legislature that the "Yankee peddlers" among them were instilling "a spirit of insubordination" by "telling the Blacks, God was no respecter of persons—the Black man was as good as the White—that all men were born free and equal—that they cannot serve two masters—that the White people rebelled against England to obtain freedom, so have the Blacks a right to do" (Aptheker, 1952, p. 106). Governor Floyd also warned slaveholders that teaching enslaved Africans to read "so that the Bible's wonders might be opened to them" actually amounted to teaching them to "read the productions of David Walker and William Lloyd Garrison as well" (Aptheker, 1952, p. 107). Garrison was a White abolitionist who hurled strong invectives against slavery in his newspaper, *The Liberator*. Walker was the free Black Bostonian who wrote a scathing appeal calling for slaves to take up arms against slavery. Governor Floyd was convinced that instilling religion in slaves, teaching them to read, and "the urgings of the Negro preachers produced the Turner rebellion" (Aptheker, 1952, p. 107).

After the Prosser, Vesey, and Turner revolts, slaveholders severely muzzled the slave preacher and curtailed the movement of the local White plantation missionaries. They even believed that itinerant revivalists were having an undesirable influence on enslaved Africans. For example, Andrew Bryan and his followers were whipped and Bryan was jailed. It was only Bryan's stubborn refusal to give in and the intercession of his master (whom Bryan had converted to Christianity) that enabled his Savannah Baptist church to survive. Richard Allen was questioned by authorities after the Vesey revolt, and the Reverend Morris Brown and other Black ministers had to flee the South and transfer their labors to the North to avoid White persecution.

Born in a Southern atmosphere of repression, brutality, and terrorism, it is no wonder that the independent Black church in its early years took more solid roots in the North. The Black church overcame threats to its survival primarily because Black people demanded sacred space that would allow them to retain control over their spiritual lives. After the independent Black church gained a foothold and became a national movement, it was not long before it was second only to the Black extended family as the leading Black caregiving institution. Enslaved African runaways such as Henson, Tubman, Truth, and Douglass made sure that the Black church took the leadership role in the abolitionist cause. Black church doors were open generally for antislavery lectures and meetings and for anyone pleading the cause of oppressed Black people, when the door of public halls and theaters were closed to them. Furthermore, many Black preachers were in the Underground Railroad Movement and had been slave fugitives themselves; they not only became Underground Railroad agents but allowed their churches to become Underground Railroad stations hiding runaways and attending to their needs. Richard Allen's home, for example, was a haven for runaway slaves. Black preachers, whether literate or illiterate, whether they believed in insurrection or not, were not only convinced that God would eventually destroy the slave system in one way or another but also that the Bible did not support the position that Black men were cursed or inferior.

THE BLACK CHURCH, SOCIAL SERVICE, SOCIAL ACTION, AND SOCIAL CHANGE

Concerned about abolition and fighting for equal rights, Black ministers such as Richard Allen adamantly advocated that the independent Black church never relinquish its social service, social action, and social change function. Even under White control, the Black church had functioned primarily as three things:

1. a social center
2. a source of social therapy and social support
3. a form of social control.

Runaway slaves prompted the Black church to add a social service/social action/social change component to its other major social functions. Richard Allen, Absolom Jones, and other Black religious leaders were not content with a religion that did not address the day-to-day practical needs of the people, nor were they content with a Black church that did not challenge the status quo on behalf of oppressed Black people. They wanted the Black church to be more than a social center where Black people gathered in a nurturing familylike atmosphere around their religious bonds; more than a source of social therapy providing Black people with cathartic relief from the burdens of their oppressed status; and more than a form of social control chastising Black people for their sins and transgressions and urging them to lead morally upright and virtuous lives. They wanted the Black church to be in the forefront of improving the quality of Black life and of erecting God's kingdom on earth—in the "here-and-now," not just in the hereafter.

Because social action was the cornerstone of race work, 19th-century race men and race women particularly wanted the Black church to be an activist church. Allen, Jones, and other Black church leaders believed that taking personal responsibility for their own uplift made Black people copartners and colaborers with God in correcting injustice, oppression, and other human inequities. Crummell, the 19th-century Black preacher, stated, "We are not saved passively, in a state of effortless inertia. In order to become saintly, we must do something ourselves. The Holy Ghost will never carry us to heaven without our own wills, and our own holy actions. Even with the gift of divine aid, God has also thrown personal responsibility upon every man to achieve his own salvation" (cited in Moses, 1989, pp. 212–213). Maria Stewart chided that "talk, without effort, is nothing" (Lerner, 1972, p. 528). She pleaded, "O ye fearful ones, throw off your fearfulness and come forth, in the name of justice and make yourself useful and active members in society" (Lerner, 1972, p. 527). Militant leader David Walker (1839/1993) agreed, "Oh! My colored brethren, all over the world, when shall we rise from this death-like apathy? ... And be men!!!" (p. 81). Henry Highland Garnet cried out: "Let your motto be Resistance! Resistance! Resistance!" (Romero, 1978, p. 82). Frederick Douglass stated that Black people must, "Agitate, agitate, agitate!!!" Social activism, political struggle, and community organization were at the core of race work as the leaders demanded movement, action, and fighting back. Race workers of the 19th century were generally in agreement that Black people could not afford to wallow in fearfulness and "deathlike" apathy waiting idly for the coming of a better day.

THE FREE AFRICAN SOCIETY
Even as the Black church became the leading Black caregiving institution, the organization that set the tone for "race work" in the late 18th century and throughout the 19th century was the Free African Society. The Free African Society is significant in the Black helping tradition because it was the first Black mutual aid society. Du Bois (1899/1967) even went so far as to say that "it was the first wavering step of a people toward organized social life" (p. 19). The Free African Society was founded by Richard Allen and Absolon Jones in Philadelphia in 1787, before they teamed up to create America's first African Methodist Episcopal Church. Both Jones and Allen had hoped to create an organization that combined secular interests with a deeply spiritual relevance. Organized on a nondenominational basis, the Free African Society welcomed all Black men and women who led morally upright lives. The society's preamble read in part that:

it was proposed, after a serious communication of sentiments, that a society should be formed, without regard to religious tenets, provided the persons lived an orderly and sober life, in order to support one another in sickness, and for the benefit of their widows and fatherless children. (Wilmore, 1998, p. 106)

The Free African Society often held "prayer meetings," and its "religious meetings" were ecumenical, allowing for ministers of all denominations to be invited to conduct services. However, the chief function of the Free African Society was to provide social services. George (1973) wrote:

The guidelines clearly established the Society as a benevolent organization, concerned about the welfare of its members, their children, wives, and widows accordingly penalized, usually with a fine but sometimes with suspension. The dues that accumulated in the treasury were available to the widows and orphans of members, as well as others in need, at the rate of three shillings nine pence per week. (p. 53)

In regard to social service, the Free African Society did something that has shadowings of modern relief work. It appointed a "committee of monitors" to oversee the needs of free Black people. These monitors first conducted a survey of the free Black population in general. Then they made house calls to assess the needs of the society's members and to dispense funds to address those needs. Like modern relief workers, the monitors were also concerned with regulating the moral lives of their impoverished Black clients. The monitors paid strict attention to the morals of Black people and to their marriage and family life. They established strict injunctions against the use of alcohol, encouraged propriety and thrift, and took particular offense at marital infidelity. The monitors gathered data on the number of free Black people who were married and actually arranged marriages for unmarried couples who had been living together. They encouraged mothers and fathers to be responsible for their children and believed, overall, that stable Black families were key to building viable Black communities. While the monitors were committed to the uplift of the race, they often displayed a strong middle-class bias against lower class Black people. Monitors were often embarrassed by the alleged "loose" morals, sexual "licentiousness," and "boisterousness" of lower class Black people. They often chided lower class Black people for their propensity to frequent the pub, to sing "devil music," and to dance in "lustful" and bawdy" ways. Even

Richard Allen and Absolom Jones invited White people "to bring 'any complaints about our colour' to their attention so they could 'warn, rebuke, and exhort' the offenders" (Campbell, 1998, p. 28). Allen and Jones even went so far as to establish "a Committee for the Suppression of Vice and Immorality, aimed explicitly at curbing the perceived excesses of Philadelphia's Black lower class" (Campbell, p. 28).

Despite setting itself up as the guardian of Black manners and morals, Philadelphia's Free African Society gave birth to many other mutual aid societies in free Black communities from Baltimore to Boston. The Philadelphia Free African Society itself had grown so strong that it also reached out to White people in need. When Philadelphia suffered a yellow fever epidemic in 1793, Allen organized the Black community to nurse and dispense medicine to White people sick with the fever and to bury their dead. After the fever subsided, Allen and his people were condemned in the White press by White leaders who charged them with profiteering from the plunder of the sick and the dead. Allen and Jones, who were generally mild-mannered men, were prompted to write a lengthy and scathing response refuting those charges. The truth of the matter was that the Free African Society and other Black organizations engaged in this humanitarian act strained and exhausted their own financial resources, not to mention that they lost the lives of more than 300 Black people in this unprecedented desire to show the expansiveness of Black Christian humanity.

In some sense, the Free African societies that sprouted up everywhere were modeled after the White benevolent societies. White benevolent societies also sought to provide relief to orphans and widows and also to bury the dead. These Free African societies also emphasized puritanical, Victorian, bourgeoisie values and "character building." However, the most significant difference was that despite their bourgeoisie outlook, Free African societies were protest organizations operating in a Black oppositional culture. They were dissident societies, and societies of resistance. Therefore, the same monitors who chastised lower class Black people for the way they danced their dances, sang their songs, and sometimes acted in public, also organized lower class Black people to confront the White power structure for their citizenship rights.

To show their discontent, Free African societies throughout the northern states petitioned legislative bodies on the local, state, and national levels. For instance, in 1779 enslaved African members of Free African societies in

Connecticut sent the following appeal to the Connecticut General Assembly, which read in part:

> We perceive by our own reflection, that we are endowed with the same Faculties without masters, and there is nothing that leads us to a Belief, or Suspicion, that we are any more obliged to serve them, than they us, and the more we Consider of this matter, the more we are Convinced of Rights (by the laws of Nature and by the whole Tenor of the Christian religion, so far as we have been taught) to be free; we have endeavored rightly to understand what is our Right, and what is our Duty, and can never be convinced that we were made to be Slaves. (Wilmore, 1998, p. 58)

Free African societies were also the major driving force behind Negro National Conventions. The first Negro convention was organized by Richard Allen and the wealthy Philadelphia Black sailmaker, James Forten, in 1817. Other conventions followed throughout the antebellum years. The Negro conventions became the chief means for free Black people to air their grievances. These conventions allowed Blacks to rebuke the alleged inferiority of Black people, laud the achievements of Blacks, praise Black heroes and heroines, release pent-up emotions, train and showcase Black leaders, and reinforce their commitment to ending slavery and becoming first-class citizens.

Free African societies even spearheaded economic boycotts that struck at the heart and soul of slavery. Free Black people knew that the corn, cotton, cattle, pigs, tobacco, sugar cane, rice, and other products that slave labor had created made up a huge portion of the American market in both slave and nonslave states. By systematically refusing to purchase and use slave-made products, they hoped to put a huge dent in the slaveholders' pocketbooks. Richard Allen organized the Free Produce Society in 1830, which urged Black people and sympathetic White people to buy only items and foodstuffs produced by nonslave labor.

While Free African societies made extensive use of nonviolent protest strategies, their chief tool for Black uplifting was education. As early as 1804, Richard Allen led in the establishment of the Society of Free People of Color for Promoting the Instruction and School Education of Children of African Descent. Allen and other free Black leaders not only viewed education as the vehicle for gaining self-worth and respectability and for making a decent living, but they also believed that White oppression thrived off of the ignorance of Black people. Education, to them, was a political weapon. They believed that after Black people were literate and enlightened, no force on earth could keep them down. This unshakable faith in the power of education continued among Black people throughout the 19th century. They saw mental development as being just as important as moral development in the improvement of Black life and in the struggle for freedom, justice, and equality.

Overall, the Free African Society set the stage for the direction race work would take during the next 100 years. It established the paradigm for race work practice as it called for moral development, character building, protest, unity, and education to improve the quality of Black life and to challenge the subordination of Black people. Most importantly, as we indicated earlier, the Free African Society encouraged and prompted the Black church to add to its functions, the social service/social action/social change component.

ETHIOPIANISM

While race work operated largely out of Free African societies and within the context of the Black church, the dominant ideological thrust of race work was Ethiopianism. Ethiopianism was based on a simple biblical statement found in Psalm 68:31, which reads: "Princes shall come forth out of Egypt; Ethiopia shall soon stretch forth her hands unto God." No biblical saying captured the imagination of 19th-century Black people, enslaved and free, more than this one. It served as a religious myth, a dominant motivating force, an organizing ethos, and a Black tradition. Moses (1978) stated that "the Ethiopian tradition sprang from certain shared political and religious experiences of English-speaking Africans during the late 18th and early 19th centuries. It found expression in the slave narratives, in the exhortation of conspiratorial slave preachers, and in the songs and folklore of the slaves in the Old South and the peasants of the New South. On a more literary level, it appeared in the sermons and political tracts of the sophisticated urban elite" (p. 156). Wilmore (1998) wrote, "The great prophecy of Psalm 68:31 became a forecast of the ultimate fulfillment of the people's spiritual yearning. It is impossible to say how many sermons were preached from this text during the 19th century, but we know that Richard Allen, Prince Hall, Lott Carey, Henry Highland Garnet, Alexander Crummell, Edward W. Blyden, James T. Holley, and Bishop Henry M. Turner were all eloquent expositors of Psalm 68:31. They made it the cornerstone of missionary emigrationism both in the United States and Africa" (p. 148). Enslaved Africans found in the Bible "proof" that Ethiopians were powerful and respected when Europeans were still barbarians. To 19th-century Black people, Ethiopia came to represent all of Africa and to symbolize Africa's redemption. "Ethiopianism became an energizing myth in both the New World and in Africa itself" (Drake, 1970, p. 11). This myth was a comforting morale builder and pitted those Black people who believed it against those who assaulted their dignity and humanity on a daily basis. Although it was based on a biblical passage, it transcended all denominational and ideological ties and gave hope, purpose, and meaning to Black people across all class lines.

To 19th-century Black people, Ethiopianism was scriptural proof that God was operating in human history on the side of the oppressed. After they became aware that Egypt and Ethiopia were in Africa and were glorious civilizations built by Black people, they had heightened senses of African identity, group pride, and self-respect and began naming their churches, schools, and fraternal orders "African." Examples include the African Free Society and the African Methodist Episcopal Church. Ethiopianism afforded enslaved Africans with the opportunity to deal with matters of destiny and other eschatological issues within the context of their Christian beliefs. It helped Black people purge themselves of the religious feelings slaveholders had instilled in them. It freed them from believing that their degraded status was fixed and could not be changed.

Ethiopianism provided free Black people with a critical and oppositional stance against racist religious mythomania. The idea that "princes" and not slaves would come out of Egypt meant to Black people that soon they would rise to royal heights again. On the personal level, Ethiopianism assured free Black people that their good works would soon bear fruit and they need not despair. Ethiopianism gave them a forward-looking philosophy. It made them feel a personal sense of divine responsibility to develop their inner lives and to make themselves useful in the work of transforming the society. It helped them to define success and worth and dignity in terms of service and not solely in terms of economic wealth and political power. This meant that even the poorest, most wretched Black person engaging in race work could feel that he or she was carrying out the will of divine providence and speeding up the day when all Black people would stretch forth their hands to God.

ETHIOPIANISM AND RACE WORK IDEOLOGIES

All the major race work ideologies of the 19th century (accommodationism, civilizationism, assimilationism, abolitionism and insurrectionism) had an allegiance to the prophetic ethos of Ethiopianism.

To accommodationists who counseled Black people to be patient in their suffering and to concentrate on improving their spiritual lives in preparation for just rewards in the afterlife, Ethiopianism meant that God's hands were already working in history and that Black people need only to show patience, faith, and forbearance. For example, Reverend Daniel Alexander Payne, a bishop of the African Methodist Episcopal Church, believed that Black people could be patient because, "His Almighty arm is already stretched out against slavery, against every man, every constitution, and every union that upholds it" (Moses, 1978, p. 158).

To civilizationists, colonizationists, and emigrationists, Ethiopianism represented a prophecy that "soon" Africa's scattered children would return or "soon" Black people would find a refuge in America or someplace on this earth.

Civilizationism sought to bring to Africa and African people the so-called blessings of Western civilization while colonizationists hoped to establish a colony in Africa, the West Indies, or a place other than America, where people could realize the full benefits of their labor and govern themselves. The emigrationist sought some territory on the North American continent that would be amenable to oppressed Black people seeking their place in the sun. Assimilationism rejected any program designed to separate Black people from America. Assimilationist leaders, such as Frederick Douglass, believed that America was the home of Black people just as much as it was the home of any other people, that Black people had suffered and died to build this country, and that Black people must fight for all their rights and entitlements as American citizens.

Abolitionism supported the assimilationist view. It called for the emancipation of the slaves so that they could enjoy all the rights and privileges of American citizenship. To assimilationists and abolitionists, Ethiopianism meant that through moral suasion, agitation, and constant struggle, slavery days were numbered and a new day with Africa's hands stretched forth unto God was near. As the founder of Black Masonry in America, Prince Hall, admonished: "My Brethren, let us not be cast down under these and many other abuses we at present are laboring under, for the darkest hour is just before the break of day ... Thou doth Ethiopia stretch forth her hands from slavery, to freedom and equality" (Drake, 1970, p. 24).

To insurrectionists, the Ethiopian prophecy forewarned that the scourge upon Black humanity called slavery would soon be purged from the face of the earth through shedding blood. Walker (1839/1993) told Black people that, "the God of the Ethiopians, had been pleased to hear our moans in consequence of oppression and the day our redemption from abject wretchedness draweth near, when we shall be enabled in the most extended sense of the word, to stretch our hands to the Lord our God" (p. 20). Walker's appeal was considered by White slaveholders to be so incendiary that any Black person, slave or free, caught smuggling, distributing, reading, or even having it on his or her person or in his or her home could be hanged. The 19th-century Black poetess, Francis Ellen Watkins Harper, wrote:

Yes, Ethiopia yet shall stretch
Her bleeding hand forward;
Her cry of agony shall reach
Up to the throne of God. (quoted in Moses, 1978, p. 158)

RACE WORK VALUES AND ROLES
With Ethiopianism as the main ideological force behind race work, race work values represented an amalgam pieced together from various sources. Six of these race work values were:

1. old traditional African values of treating people right, practicing communalism and spirituality, building relationships, and living in harmony with nature, God, and the universe
2. Victorian values that stressed cleanliness, sobriety, hard work, thriftiness, and sexual chastity
3. educational values emphasizing faith in Black people's capabilities and a response to the racist myth boldly claiming that they were uneducable, incapable, evil children of Satan
4. protest or fighting back values that came from both their African warrior tradition, examples from the Holy Bible, and their own historical production of men such as Denmark Vesey, Gabriel Prosser, Nat Turner, and Toussaint L'Ouverture

5. accommodationist values of perseverance, patience, forbearance, and suffering that came out of the woes of their enslavement

6. most importantly, spiritual values that attested to their deeply felt need to put their trust and faith in a higher power.

The free Black community was saturated with this amalgam of race work values designed to improve the quality of free Black life and to free enslaved African people. As we intimated earlier, whenever free Black people began to move these values in an individualistic, bourgeoisie direction, they had an influx of fugitive slaves steadily coming into the free Black community to remind them of their obligations to the liberation of their brothers and sisters in bondage. Also, Black fugitives were so determined to shake off the oppressive dust of enslavement that they often surpassed free Black people in expressing values of self-improvement. These values informed, sanctioned, legitimized, and guided several key race work roles, such as the roles of the sacrificer.

THE MORAL DEVELOPER, THE MENTAL DEVELOPER, THE VINDICATOR, THE PROTESTOR, AND THE BUILDER

Playing the role of sacrificer gave the lives of many Black people a sense of meaning. To enslaved, abused, and downtrodden people, the idea that they would sacrifice themselves by enduring any hardship or deprivation so that another generation might know freedom and fulfillment was the only thing that gave them hope and the will to live. Many parents, guardians, mentors, and elders knew that their lives were not apt to improve markedly, so they lived for the sake of "making a way out of no way" for the younger generation.

Moral developers sought to curtail any criminal, immoral, disreputable, antisocial, divisive, sinful behavior that held Black people back from improving their lives and stretching forth their hands to God. Teachers, preachers, elders, and community leaders all felt a responsibility for moral development, which they termed "character building." Therefore, they created schools, temperance societies, churches, and so forth designed to improve the moral lives of Black people.

Mental developers saw education as the chief means Black people had at their disposal to improve their lives and to combat the racist propaganda that dubbed them ignorant and stupid. Many enslaved Africans had taken chilling risks to get a rudiment of education; free Black people often out-performed their White neighbors in building schools. They also created an unprecedented number of literary societies. Located mainly in the North, the Black literary societies wanted Black people to sharpen their intelligence so they could think seriously and reflect critically on the events affecting their day-to-day lives. Mental developers particularly emphasized that Black people should learn and reconnect themselves to their history. A major theme of Black churches, schools, and literary societies was Black history. It did not seem to matter to free Black people that their history was a tragic tale of pain and suffering. They believed that after they ploughed through all the misery and death, they would discover a Black heroic self, a self that had struggled against insurmountable odds to make its mark on the world. They believed that after they worked through their historical traumas, they would discover glories of their African past. Already, the Holy Bible had told them about two of the world's oldest civilizations, Ethiopia and Egypt. For exam-ple, H. Ford Douglass (1860/1998), a 19th-century Black leader, said that, "The men who justify slavery upon the assumed inferiority of the Negro are very slow to admit that the remains of ancient grandeur, which have been exhumed from beneath the accumulated dust of four centuries were wrought by the ingenuity and skill of the Negro, ere the Saxon was known in history" (p. 348). Free Black leaders believed that, "Europe has never reproduced and never will in our day bring forth a single human soul who cannot be matched and overmatched in every line of human endeavor by Asia and Africa" (Du Bois, 1907, p. 8).

As they immersed themselves in their history, it did not go unnoticed among 19th-century Black people that many of the greats among Black people were once former slaves, such as Crispus Attucks, Nat Turner, Toussaint L'Ouverture, Harriet Tubman, and Frederick Douglass. This served as an indication of what Black people were capable of doing through their own sheer will, determination, and power against overwhelming odds. The aim of Black mental developers, however, was not to authenticate the lives of exemplary Black historical figures but to cultivate race consciousness through collective identity and to give Black people a sense of generational continuity. Just as Africans in traditional Africa believed that ancestral con-nectedness was vital to self-discovery and group solidarity, Black mental developers believed that a sense of oneness with one's history was a vital first step toward sanity, stability, wholeness, and health.

Black history was also a major tool of vindicators seeking to wage cultural war against the pejorative stereotypes of Black people. Vindicators sought to redeem the race by proving Black people's capability to compete with White people and even outdo them in areas generally considered to be the exclusive domain of White people. Drake and Cayton (1945) stated that way into the 20th century, being "The Negro 'firsts' and 'onlies'," "catching up with the white folks," or "beating the man at his own game" became "a powerful motivation for achievement" (p. 391). 19th-century Black vindicators did not let any accomplishment of Black people, regardless of how small or insignificant it might have seemed in the eyes of White people, go without recognition. Even recognition of modest gains was important for Black people in their psychological struggle for self-respect (Cox, 1948, p. 7).

As we said earlier, Protestors sought to tear down the walls of Jericho and build upon its ruins a truly democratic society. The Black protest tradition was strong among 19th-century free Black people. They believed that character building, mental improvement, and historical immersion would strengthen Black people's inner lives in preparation of the racial self for social action.

Builders created schools, fraternal orders, abolitionist societies, temperance societies, literary societies, underground railroad stations, national Negro conventions, various businesses, and so forth. As we indicated earlier, the most important race work institution that 19th-century builders created was the Black church. Other key Black caregiving institutions, such as benevolent societies, fraternal orders, and schools, were usually under the auspices of the Black church.

Sacrificers, moral developers, mental developers, vindicators, protestors and builders were all race workers seeking a place where Black people could be free and treated like human beings. Whatever ideological stripes they wore or religious banners they served under, they wanted to become "a credit to their race," not a liability to its progress or a blight on its reputation.

CHAPTER SIX
Alexander Crummell, W. E. B. Du Bois, and the Transition of Race Work to Social Work

After the Civil War and the end of slavery, race work continued among Black Americans. They built churches and schools in numbers unprecedented in African American history. They made valiant attempts to bring into existing Black families the thousands of Black children who had been left scattered and homeless by the war. White Southerners who had been defeated in the war were taking thousands of Black children under so-called apprenticeship laws, which allowed children to be taken from families who allegedly could not take care of them. These children were being virtually used as slaves. Black people after emancipation also continued to fight for their citizenship rights amidst devastating political betrayals relegating them to a subordinate position—only a notch or two above the status of slaves. Most significantly, they had to struggle against bitter, vengeful, Southern Whites who put Black people under a systematic reign of terror. This period between the Civil War and the first few decades of the 20th century was the era of lynching, of what Patterson (1998) called the "feast of blood" (p. 169). Patterson (1998) wrote:

> there emerged in the post-Reconstruction South a neoslavery system into which religion, politics, and economics fused in the rituals of the lynch mob. In a substantial minority of lynchings, those rituals partook in a cult of human sacrifice, focused on the literal and symbolic castration of Afro-American males. The worshippers castrated and then immolated their victims alive, as burnt offerings to a Southern Christian God whom they felt they had to assuage and propitiate after their humiliating defeat in the Civil War and their traumas of losing a cherished way of life. (p. xiii)

This was the era of the Ku Klux Klan.

The Klan was as much a religion as a secular cult. Its icon of the burning cross was a powerful symbolic instrument that appealed directly to the religious impulses of its adherents. It was the KKK that formalized the cult of human sacrifice of Afro-American men that had spontaneously emerged in the lynching rituals of the post-Reconstruction South. (Patterson, 1998, p. xiv)

It was during this era that the Black helping tradition reached a peak level, but it was also a period of great frustration, disillusionment, and despair over having waited, prayed, and fought for emancipation and equality so long only to be faced with sharecropping, the chain gang, the Black codes, Jim Crow segregation, the lynch rope, and the KKK.

It was during this era of Black despair and gloom that Alexander Crummell and W. E. B. Du Bois sought to create a race work social philosophy that would allow Black people to carry the Black uplift thrust into the 20th century with the same fervor they had undertaken in the 19th century. By giving scholarly coherence to the philosophy and theology underlining race work, Crummell and Du Bois put race work on a sophisticated, theoretical, and intellectual plane that was attractive to early 20th century Black social workers and which had a tremendous impact on early Black social work thought. Essentially, what Crummell and Du Bois did was to spiritualize the concept of race not in the sense of proclaiming Black racial superiority but in the sense of instilling in Black people the idea that race was a sacred entity worth fighting for and worth advancing to the fullest heights of its God-given promise and potential. Such works as Crummell's *The Social Principle Among a People, and Its Bearing on Their Progress* (1875/1992) and *Civilization, the Primal Need of the Race* (1897/1995), and Du Bois's *The Conservation of Races* (1897/1995), *The Talented Tenth* (1903/1971), and especially *The Souls of Black Folk* (1903/1961) provided early Black social workers with a philosophical orientation and systematic race work framework. These works were to early Black social workers what Mary Richmond's *Social Diagnosis* (1917) was to the early social work profession in general. The most important contribution of Crummell and Du Bois is that they gave early Black social workers and other Black helping professionals a Black "strength perspective" centered around the concepts of destiny, mutuality, teleological optimism, divine gifts, and human agency. With this strength perspective Black social workers were able to continue the 19th-century race work that focused on building character, developing families, strengthening the Black church, and creating viable Black communities. With the strength perspective, they were able to help Black people to overcome their deep feelings of demoralization and disillusionment so that they could work together with enthusiasm to tackle the problems that faced them in the present and move toward their future with a positive outlook.

THE CRUMMELL-DU BOIS CONNECTION

Alexander Crummell might have remained in relative historical obscurity if W. E. B. Du Bois had not immortalized his name in his classic work, *The Souls of Black Folk* (1903/1961). Du Bois might not have become one of the greatest scholars the world has ever produced without the nurturing influence Crummell had on Du Bois's early thoughts. Both Crummell and Du Bois were quintessential race men who linked two different generations of race work scholarship. Essentially, the Crummell–Du Bois connection represented the proverbial changing of the guards because the late 19th century spelled the ending of Crummell's career as the leading scholar and race man and the beginning of Du Bois's career as the leading scholar and race man of the 20th century. Crummell, born in the first half of the 19th century (1819), graduated in 1851 from Cambridge in London, England, and spent 20 years in Liberia, West Africa, as an Episcopal minister, political leader, and agent of the American Colonization Society. After his return to North America in 1873, he became a major figure in the uplift cause of Black America. During one of the gloomiest and most pessimistic moments in African American history, the period known as the Reconstruction Era, Crummell preached an optimistic, forward-looking philosophy designed to inspire confidence and to circumvent the rise of alienation and despair among Black people. This inspiring worldview challenged feelings of Black inferiority and the racist ideology that justified Black subordination. Crummell's forward-looking, optimistic worldview appealed to the idealism, race consciousness, and intellectual enthusiasm of the young Du Bois. Du Bois, who was born after the Civil War (1867), was completing his doctoral dissertation at Harvard University when he met Crummell in 1895. He said upon first meeting Crummell that, "instinctively I bowed before this man, as one bows before the prophets of the world" (Du Bois, 1939, pp. 157–158). Together these two great intellectual giants would create a highly distinctive race work social philosophy and strength perspective centered around the concepts of destiny, mutuality, teleological optimism, divine gifts, human agency, and social debt.

DESTINY

The core of the race work social philosophy created by Crummell and Du Bois rested upon the idea that races were sacred creations of God and that God gave each race a divine destiny to fulfill. Throughout Crummell's ministry in Africa, he propagated the idea that, "We see everywhere God's hand in history—ordering, controlling, directing the footsteps of men, of families, and of races" (Crummell, 1891/1969, p. 415). Believing that God never allows evil to run unchecked, Crummell taught that God was working in history on the side of oppressed Black people. After returning to America, he preached this message with even more fervor, enthusiasm, and urgency. Crummell (1897) told a distressed Black audience that when God does not destroy a people but, on the contrary, trains and disciplines them by bringing them "through a wilderness of disasters, you may take as a sure and undoubted fact that God presides, with sovereign care, over such a people, and will surely preserve, educate, and build them up" (p. 204). Crummell reminded the Black audience that nation after nation and tribe after tribe had fallen because they had incurred the wrath of God, but not Black people. He told them which God was interested in their plight and was carrying grace among them. He assured them that they need not entertain the shadow of a doubt that the work that God was carrying on "is for the elevation and success of the Negro" (Crummell, 1877, p. 204).

Twenty years later, Du Bois (1897/1970) would utter similar sentiments regarding race destiny in less theological and more historical terms. Instead of emphasizing a God-ordained mission for Black people to fulfill, Du Bois propagated the idea that history was demanding that Black people as a race make a contribution to civilization and humanity that "no other race can make" (Du Bois, 1897/1970, p. 261) Du Bois (1897/1970) told a group of Black scholars that "the fact remains that the full, complete Negro message of the whole Negro race has not yet been given to the world" (p. 255). He said that Black people must nurture and protect their historical mission by making sure their destiny is not an absorption of White American interest but "a stalwart originality which shall unswervingly follow Negro ideals" (Du Bois, 1897/1970, p. 256). He believed that after Black people have been organized around and inspired by their own race ideals, harnessing their full power and potential as a race, that there is no power under God's heaven that can stop the advancement of millions of "honest, earnest, inspired and united people" (Du Bois, 1897/1970, p. 258).

Although Crummell and Du Bois were not alone among 19th-century race men and race women who believed in providential design and historical destiny, these two intellectual giants gave scholarly focus and shape to the old race work ideas. This came at a distressing time when many Black people were beginning to waiver in their belief that Black people would ever attain the elusive freedom and equality they had sought for more than 200 years. The idea that God was on the side of the oppressed had inspired Black people from Harriet Tubman to Nat Turner, from Sojourner Truth to Frederick Douglass, and Crummell and Du Bois were hoping to inspire another generation of Black people with this old, time-worn race work idea.

MUTUALITY

Race unity, race organization, race pride, and race identity, Crummell and Du Bois believed, were the keys to Black people fulfilling their divine destiny and bringing their historical message to the world. Therefore, both race men eschewed individualism and extolled the development of the racial and communal self. The cornerstone of Crummell's thought in this regard was expressed in his work "The Social Principle Among a People" referenced earlier. In this work, Crummell (1875/1992) stated that, "No man stands up entirely alone, self-sufficient in the circle of human needs" and that Black uplift and race destiny cannot be done in the confined sphere of individual, personal effort (p. 258). Crummell stated that history records no imposing scheme and no great and notable occurrence that was accomplished by a single, isolated individual. It was only through the social principle of "mutuality," Crummell maintained, that Black people could develop "the reciprocal tendencies" that would join them together for specific purposes and strivings along the line of race (Crummell, 1875/1992, p. 258). In an address to students at Hampton Institute, Crummell (1896/1995) asked, "Are we to live simply for ourselves? Are we to be absorbed only in our own interests? Are the forecastings of the human soul to pertain mostly to selfish, personal ends?" (pp. 189-190). He answered, "No, my friends, the provisions of human souls, are to reach out from the limitations of our personal being to larger circuits and wider circumferences than our own individualism" (pp. 187–190). He told the students that care and interest in their race makes them coworkers with God for some noble purpose in the future.

Du Bois (1897/1970) also believed that "the history of the world is the history, not of individuals ... but of races" (p. 252). He stated that it is not as individuals but as a race working together, suffering together, and fighting for a better life together that Black people can advance. He wrote that only "Negroes inspired by one vast ideal, can work out in its fullness the great message we have for humanity" (Du Bois, 1897/1979, p. 256). Later, Du Bois stated that Black people should emulate the communalism displayed in the traditional African village. In 1930 he wrote: "The African village socialized the individual completely, and yet because the village was small this socialization did not submerge and kill individuality" (Du Bois, 1930/1970, p. 376). Du Bois believed that through inner tenacity and strength of tradition, the African village was able to do on a small scale what the modern world has continually attempted on a wider scale and never satisfactorily accomplished. Through individualism, Du Bois maintained that Black people were in danger of becoming a soulless, divisive, antagonistic, atomized self. Du Bois held that it was the individualism of some African leaders that made them participate in the enslavement of their own people.

TELEOLOGICAL OPTIMISM

During the Reconstruction period, Black people were disappointed that the freedom for which they had prayed for so long and dreamed about so often had eluded them. The Civil War had been fought and Black soldiers had died alongside White soldiers. The emancipation of enslaved Africans was granted and guaranteed by the 13th Amendment to the Constitution of the United States of America, but Black people were not granted full, first-class American citizenship. Vengeful and vindictive forces in the southern community were seeking to strip Black people of the few citizenship rights they had gained. Relegated to a semislavery existence as sharecroppers, they were free, but poverty, ignorance, disease, and all the ominous shadows of the plantation still haunted their lives. They were free, but justice was totally blind to harassments, intimidations, and the outright killing of Black people.

Crummell, starkly aware of the sense of gloom hanging over Black people, preached that the status of Black people was no more fixed than the so-called curse of Ham. Crummell taught Black people that despite their current circumstances, they should move forward and denounce any notion that they could never rise any higher than their allegedly defective, genetic makeup would allow. Crummell (1895/1995) told an audience of young Black people, "don't you listen, for a moment, to the delusive dictum of finality." He asked them, "In what cell of the Negro's brain has Almighty God dropped the stagnant atom of finality" (p. 182)? Crummell reminded them that Black people had already risen from slavery to partial freedom and were making strides towards full freedom and self-respect. In 1895, Crummell told them that there was no spell that had fallen upon Black people that confined their capacity "to narrow and contracted grooves" (p. 182). He said that no race had a monopoly on the world of art, science, philosophy, and letters and that there are no bounds to what an active, energetic, hopeful, and ambitious race could accomplish.

Moses (1998) held that, "as a rule, antebellum African American writers shared Crummell's progressive teleology ... and took comfort from a worldview in which the cycles of history would always follow in the direction indicated by the arrow of truth. One need only be on the right side of God to guarantee a permanently favored place in the progression of history" (p. 103). Du Bois (1897/1970), inspired by his mentor's optimistic outlook, also believed that Black people had the intellectual and cultural capacity and spiritual strength to overcome all obstacles against them knowing that both history and God were on their side. Du Bois warned Black people that people who do not believe in their great destiny, who do not trust in their ability and worth, who laugh at and ridicule themselves, and who wish to God to be anything but themselves will never write their name in history. He held that Black people "must be inspired with the divine faith of our Black mothers, that out of the blood and dust of battle will march a victorious host, a mighty nation, a peculiar people, to speak to the nations of earth Divine Truth that shall make them free" (Du Bois, 1879/1970, p. 259).

DIVINE GIFTS

Crummell, Du Bois and other race work scholars at the closing of the 19th century believed that Black people should be optimistic about their future prospects not only because God and history were on their side but also because they had inherent and acquired "gifts." The idea was that if Black people developed their gifts, the vital qualities inherent in the race, they would have solid reasons for being optimistic. Frederick Douglass (1869/1998) explained that, "the theory that each race has some faculty, some peculiar gift or quality of mind or heart needed to the perfection and happiness of the whole is a broad and beneficent theory, and besides its beneficence, has in its support, the voice of experience" (pp. 499–500).

Nineteenth-century Black race work leaders were in general agreement that Black people must use their gifts for altruistic ends. Frances Ellen Watkins Harper (1875/1998), the Black poet, feminist, novelist, and abolitionist, held that, "if you have ampler gifts, hold them as larger opportunities with which you can benefit others" (p. 567). Nineteenth-century Black race work leaders also generally agreed that the consequences were dire for Black people who did not develop their divine gifts. Crummell (1877/1992) maintained that history has shown that any people who have "perverted the gifts of God, and brought imbecility upon their being, they perish" (p. 199). It was their divine gifts, 19th-century race workers believed, that made Black people unique, special, and blessed, and which distinguished them from other races or peoples.

Nineteenth-century race workers spoke of "gifts" in the same way social workers today use the word "strengths." Although the Black sociologists Andrew Billingsley (1968) and Robert Hill (1971) created the contemporary strength perspective in their work on Black families, they are given little credit or recognition in social work literature. Actually, Billingsley and Hill were following a rich tradition in the Black helping experience since scholars such as Crummell and Du Bois advanced the strength perspective well over 100 years ago.

As early as 1877, in his work *The Destined Superiority of the Negro*, Crummell (1877/1992) was identifying Black strengths that he called divine gifts. He recognized plasticity, receptivity, and imitation as inherent qualities in Black people that have made for their survival, vitality, strength, and resiliency. Crummell (1877/1992) explained that, "The Negro, with a mobile and plastic nature, with a strong receptive faculty, seizes upon and makes over to himself, by imitation, the best qualities of others" (p. 201). Crummell observed that by a strong assimilative tendency, Black people duplicate themselves through culturally borrowing from other races among whom they dwell while retaining their own unique characteristics and peculiarities. They are, according to Crummell, able to adapt to different social circumstances while maintaining their own identity and sense of mission. Crummell recognized other gifts in his 1895 sermon entitled, "Incidents of Hope for the Negro Race in America" (Crummell, 1895/1995, pp. 174-184). Gifts include perseverance, desire for mental stimulation, moral and spiritual perception, and courage. Regarding these strengths, he stated that despite the murderous invasion of slave traders, the horrors of the middle passage, the sufferings of slavery, persistent poverty, bitter disillusionment, and political powerlessness, Black people have persevered. Crummell (1895/1995) held that, "the Negro lives and grows because vitality, in his case, springs from internal sources" (p. 176). He stated that despite the laws and penalties seeking to forbid Black people to learn and to keep them in abject ignorance, Black people have "groped, and stumbled, and plodded on; struggling to emerge from the darkness of ignorance, to attain, if possible, the ability to read, and the illumination of letters" (p. 177). Despite the attempt to present Black people as morally depraved and spiritually deprived, even in their "pagan state the spiritual instinct always has had the ascendancy" (p. 180). Crummell (1895/1995) said that he did not "pretend angelic qualities for our race," but he believed that because of Africans' sociable, humane, obliging, and hospitable nature, plus their tenderness toward their parents and great respect for the aged, Black people's aboriginal qualities made them amply fitted for Christianity. Crummell (1895/1995) warned that people should not read into Black religiosity, morality, and spirituality that passivity is the normal, aboriginal quality of the race. He wrote that, "The Negro ... is brave as well as gentle; courageous as well as amiable; a gallant soldier as well as a patient sufferer and an enduring martyr" (p. 180). Overall, Crummell believed that God had given Black people the constructive capacity to direct their inner, invisible, intellectual, and spiritual nature toward the work of building up the human soul.

Du Bois also believed that Black people were endowed with the gift or capacity for constructiveness. He was of the belief that the gifts of Black people would not only save them but also save White America. He wrote:

We are the first fruits of this new nation, the harbinger of that Black tomorrow which is yet destined to soften the whiteness of the teutonic to-day. We are the people whose subtle sense of song has given America its only American music, its only American fairy tales, its only touch of pathos and humor amid its mad money-getting plutocracy. As such, it is our duty to conserve our physical powers, our intellectual endowments, our spiritual ideals (Du Bois, 1897/1970, p. 258).

Nearly 30 years later, Du Bois (1922) delineated in more detail the gifts he believed Black people had given to America in a book simply entitled *The Gifts of Black Folk*. He first highlighted the contribution African people have made to America in their role as explorers, laborers, and soldiers. Then he emphasized the contributions Black people have made to America in their struggles for freedom, democracy, and the emancipation of women. Next, Du Bois addressed the contribution Black people have made to America in the areas of music, art, and literature. Finally, he examined what both he and Crummell believed was the greatest gift of Black people to White America, the gift of the spirit. Du Bois (1922) wrote:

> Behind the half childish theology of formal religion there has run in the heart of Black folk the greatest of human achievements, love and sympathy, even for their enemies, for those who despised them and hurt them and did them nameless ill. They have nursed the sick and closed the staring eyes of the dead. They have given friendship to the friendless, they have shared pittance of their poverty with the outcast and nameless; ... and in this lies the real grandeur of their simple religion, the mightiest gift of Black to White America (p. 337).

AGENCY

Spirituality, resilience, courage, vitality, a will to live, perseverance, and a dogged determination to survive and be free were among the gifts that many 19th-century race workers recognized, cultivated, and tried to pass down through the generations. Believing that God's unseen hand sits in history through the dark, secret counsels of the human mind, 19th-century race workers believed that it is through human agents that God works His will. Crummell (1891/1969) believed that although people are not mere machines, even in God's hand, "they nevertheless act either consciously or unconsciously as the agents of God" (p. 414). He believed that even when people do evil deeds, God distracts their evil counsels and directs them to the ends God proposes. With these beliefs in mind, Crummell asked who were God's human agents to be in helping the masses of illiterate, downtrodden Black people to cultivate their gifts? Who were to be God's human agents in guiding the Black masses toward the fulfillment of their destiny? "Who," Crummell (1897/1993) asked, "are the agents to lift up this people of ours to the great plane of civilization" (p. 198)? Crummell believed that this divine vanguard work was "to be done by the scholars and thinkers ... For to transform and stimulate the souls of a race or a people is a work of intelligence" (p. 198).

Du Bois also believed that the educated, talented Black leaders must step to the forefront and help the masses cultivate their strength and exert their power. He proposed the creation of a "Talented Tenth" of professional Black people to serve as the agency of uplift for the 90 percent of Black people still submerged in poverty, ignorance, and disease. Du Bois (1903/1971) wrote:

> The Negro race, like all races, is going to be saved by its exceptional men. The problem of education, then, among Negroes must first of all deal with the Talented Tenth; it is the problem of developing the Best of this race that may guide the Mass away from the contamination and death of the Worst, in their own and other races (p. 34).

Du Bois (1903/1961) believed it was imperative that "trained Negro leaders of character and intelligence, men of skill ... college-bred men, Black captains of industry, and missionaries of culture; men who thoroughly comprehend and know modern civilization ... can take hold of Negro communities and raise and train them by force of precept and example, deep sympathy and the inspiration of common blood and ideas" (p. 129).

SOCIAL DEBT

To Black professionals of the early 20th century, Du Bois's call for the emergence of a Talented Tenth was a call for them to find meaning and purpose in their lives by being of service to their race. Many Black people became social workers in response to Du Bois's call, but it was also a call for them to repay a social debt. Both Du Bois and Crummell sharpened the old race work philosophy that believed that all Black people owed a debt to ancestors for the sacrifices they had made on their behalf. They believed that the way for Black people to repay their debt was to dedicate their lives to the uplifting of Black people. They believed that talented, educated Black people not only owed a debt to the ancestors but also to God. God had seen fit to have them rise above the status that suppressed the strivings of the Black masses. To whom much is given, much is expected. They expected the educated, talented Black people to show their thankfulness and gratefulness for God's blessings to them by helping other Black people to be so blessed as well.

HIGHER EDUCATION

Seeking a Black elite to serve as the agency of Black uplift, Du Bois and Crummell advocated liberal education to train the Talented Tenth. In this respect, they were in opposition to Booker T. Washington, who had amassed considerable power and influence as an advocate of the industrial training of Black people. As early as 1897 in his address entitled "Civilization, the Primal Need of the Race" Crummell (1897/1995) expressed unease over Washington's espousal of industrial education. He stated that the special need of Black people "is the force and application of the highest arts not mere mechanism; not mere machinery; not mere handicraft; not the mere grasp on material things; not mere temporal ambitions" (Crummell, 1897/1995, p. 196). Du Bois wrote that "Mr. Washington represents in Negro thought the old attitude of adjustment and submission" (1903/1961, p. 48). Du Bois said, "The question comes: Is it possible, and probable, that 9 million men can make effective progress in economic lines if they are deprived of political rights, made a servile caste, and allowed only the most meager chances for developing their exceptional men? If history and reason give any distinct answer to those questions, it is an emphatic NO" (1903/1961, p. 49).

In essence, both Du Bois and Crummell were idealists opposing Washington's materialism. They wanted young Black people to guide their lives by grand, noble ideas of excellence, to be principled men and women dedicated to uplifting Black people and to relieving suffering in the world instead of being overly preoccupied with making money and accumulating things. Du Bois asked what would happen if young Black people abandoned the traditional Black struggle for a better and more just world in pursuit of "golden apples" laid before them (1903/1961, p. 69)? What, he asked, "if the people be wooed from a strife for righteousness, from a love of knowing to regard dollars as the be-all and end-all of life?" (Du Bois, 1903/1961, p. 69). And what happens to the future of Black people if the ancient Black struggles for goodness, beauty, truth, and freedom "degenerate into a dusty quest of gold" (Du Bois, 1903/1961, p. 69)? Crummell (1897/1995) wrote that young Black people must be taught that property, official position, money, and lineage are not the root sources of power and progress, that none of these "are fixed factors, in so large a thing as the destiny of man" (p. 197). Crummell maintained that education should teach young Black people that a people's greatness springs from their ability to grasp the grand conceptions of being and that it is the "large majestic and abiding things which lifts them to the skies" (1897/1995, p. 197).

CHARACTER BUILDING AND FAMILY DEVELOPMENT

After exceptional race men and race women were developed, both Crummell and Du Bois believed that their chief role was to build character and to develop the Black family. In 1885 Crummell stated, "Nothing, next to religion, can compare with the work which is to be done in this sphere" (Crummell, 1885/1995, p. 127). Crummell maintained that for individuals, societies, races, and nations, advancement is not possible without the development of character. Crummell believed that without strong character Black people would not only be susceptible to vice, decadence, sin, and ruin but would also be without the mental and moral toughness to face adversity and without the principles to maintain a steady course toward their destiny. Character building, he believed, would make new men and women out of Black people and transform them from passive, apathetic, hopeless beings into active, fighting instruments that would carry out the will of God.

As for family, Crummell and Du Bois advocated "family preservation" more than 100 years before it became a popular theme of social work. Crummell practically worshipped both character and family development. Crummell believed that Black people must first and foremost emphasize character building as evidenced in high moral and intellectual attainment and strengthening the family as the basis of all human progress and civilization. He entreated Black people to look into their Bibles and see how God has set great works upon the family and how He sees it as the greatest of all human institutions. Crummell wrote, "the family; parentage; motherhood; the birth of children; the ordering, the love, and the thrift of households; reverence and obedience of the young; the fear of God; those are the foundation-stones of all human society" (Crummell, 1879/1995, p. 217). Crummell believed that strengthening the family and building character were life and death matters for Black people. In 1879 he wrote, "if we don't inspire, everywhere, family allegiance, family devotedness, family reverence and obedience; we shall be a lost people in this land" (p. 217).

Du Bois, following in the footsteps of his mentor, was also a strong advocate of character development and family development. Regarding the former, he particularly believed that Black people must wage war on the street ideology that was corrupting and criminalizing Black life. Du Bois believed that the first step toward solving the race problem lay in the correction of the immorality, crime, and idleness among Black people themselves. He wrote that Black people must become "united to keep Black boys from loafing, gambling and crime; united to guard the purity of Black women and to reduce that vast army of Black prostitutes that is today marching to hell ... Unless we conquer or prevent vices they will conquer us" (Du Bois,

1897/1970, pp. 259-260). As late as 1947, when character building was no longer in vogue, Du Bois (1947) still believed that Black people "must not forget the attempts at character-building in the 19th century" (p. 440). Du Bois also saw the Black family as a focal point of analysis, study, and intervention. His book, *The Negro American Family* (1908) was considered to be the first scientific study of Black family life. In that work, Du Bois traced the Black family from traditional Africa, through slavery and emancipation, to the turn of the 20th century. He wanted to see how far Black people had progressed in the 20th century with respect to their family life and concluded that they had made tremendous progress in America but still had far to go in strengthening their moral and sexual lives.

THE BLACK CHURCH
Because the responsibility for character development and family development was put largely in the hands of the Black church, both Crummell and Du Bois believed that the Black church should be a race-oriented church working for the social betterment of Black people. Crummell, an Episcopal minister, naturally believed that for the Black church to be successful in character building, family development, and shaping the destiny of Black people, it needed to develop a race-conscious, race-work ministry that was molded and prepared by Black teachers and professors. In an undated piece, titled "The Work of the Black Priest," Crummell wrote that the Black church should focus on uplifting the Black family and that it needed to teach every righteous soul that the Kingdom of heaven "is now at hand ... right here ... in the family; in the relations of husband and wife; in the rearing of children in the duties of citizenship; in the circles of society! That no man need to die to realize heaven" (Crummell, n.d./1992, p. 139). Crummell (1887) believed that the great need of the Black race, in their present state of freedom, is a new religion (p. 158). This meant to Crummell that the Black church must not only concern itself with matters of the soul but also with social, economic, and political concerns. Churches should sponsor schools, industrial education, hospitals, and other services, Crummell advocated, to attend to needs of both the body and the soul.

Du Bois also believed that the church had vital race work to perform in preparing Black people for the demands of the 20th century and for ushering in "The New Negro." In his book *The Philadelphia Negro* (1899/1967), heralded as the first social science study of the Black community, Du Bois wrote that "all movement for social betterment" such as beneficial societies, secret societies, cooperative and building associations, employment agencies, charitable and relief work, and youth work "are apt to centre in the churches" (p. 207). He believed that the Black church needed to continue its social betterment function.

PROTEST

If Du Bois and Crummell had any areas of differences, it was around the function of protest in the Black struggle. Crummell was not convinced that protest and agitation would lead to the breakdown of racial prejudice and oppression. Crummell's (1875/1992) idea was that character, not agitation or protest, "is the grand, effective instrument which we are to use for the destruction of caste" (p. 264). He believed that after Black people gained superiority in character, prejudice was sure to decline. Crummell believed that the primary responsibility of Black people was to get their own moral, educational, economic, social, and family life together and to leave the responsibility for extirpating racial prejudice to White people. He maintained that White people were responsible for upholding racial exploitation and that it was also their responsibility to root it out of their souls and destroy it. Black people, he maintained, had enough on their hands lifting the race up to such grand heights that no one in the land will associate Negroes of culture, refinement, and character with inferiority and degradation. He said that Black people should be so busy working toward their own uplift that they left no room for waging war with racial oppression and, thus, inviting their own extermination.

When it came to the need for protest, Du Bois was more in tune with Frederick Douglass than was his mentor, Crummell. As indicated earlier, Du Bois was also a strong advocate of character building. However, his idea of strengthening Black people's character was for them to be so strong, principled, prepared, and ready from within that they would be able to hold together psychologically as they went into battle against powerful and deadly odds. Du Bois wanted Black people to be so spiritually, morally, and intellectually tough and resilient that they would be able to stand up emotionally, physically, and intellectually to the inevitable forces of reaction. Du Bois went on to become a leading advocate of Black political protest. One of his charges against Booker T. Washington was that Washington played down the need of Black people to protest for their political rights and entitlements.

Later, he would break from Crummell's American Negro Academy and form the Niagara Movement in 1909, which was the precursor to another protest organization of which Du Bois was a founding official, the National Association for the Advancement of Colored People (NAACP), which was formed in 1910. The chief objective of the Niagara Movement and the NAACP was to protest the condition of Black people and become the leading organs for social change.

THE PAST AND THE FUTURE

Du Bois and Crummell also had different views about the role of time. Both Crummell and Du Bois had a keen sense of history and the role that both God and human agency played in it. However, Crummell believed that Black people, Black youths in particular, should take on an attitude of looking forward instead of looking backward. In an 1896 address to students at Hampton Institute, Crummell (1896/1995) told young Black people, "it is the rarest of instances wherein one finds any advantage in ruminating upon the past" (p. 187). Crummell reminded these young people that they were "the inheritors of sorrow and disasters," the heirs of a people who had known the horrors of the Middle Passage and more than 200 years of crushing enslavement on the blood-stained soil of America. He asked what all these memories of the agonies and wrongs of their ancestors could yield "but bitterness, melancholy and despair." He told them that looking backward could bring them "neither health, nor strength, nor life," that they should "let the dead past bury its past" and look forward (Crummell, 1896/1995, p. 188).

Crummell (1891/1969) had come to the belief that, "Man is a creature so formed and fashioned that besides his grasp upon the present, he has a power of historic life, which sends forward his influence far beyond his own times, and makes him an agent of might and even of responsibility in other generations." He said, "human life is a stream, which springs up, and flows over at its fountain head; and likewise flows onward forever towards the ocean! So we, too, go onward in vital power, creative influence, and plastic energy, generations after our bodies have been laid in the tomb" (Crummell, 1891/1969, p. 142). It is by this principle that binds the present to the future under a sense of duty and responsibility to the future generations that young Black people, he believed, should conduct their lives. Crummell (1896/1995) believed that, "Human beings are born of destiny! Their lives are given them in order to stretch out, beyond their times, above and beyond

Spirituality and the Black Helping Tradition in Social Work

both selfish and transitory things" (p. 189). Crummell (1896/1995) believed that young Black people should look forward to truth, beauty, and spiritual excellence; look forward to learning and the opportunities for useful work; look forward to rearing strong families and building stable communities; look forward to uplifting the race, to a regenerated America and the reign of peace upon the earth; and, beyond all, look forward to "that ineffable peace, and that endless light which are promised believers, in the kingdom of grace and glory above" (Crummell, 1896/1995, p. 192).

Du Bois also believed that Black people should look to the future. However, siding with his other mentor, Frederick Douglass, he also believed that Black people would never have a sense of the future without a thorough knowledge and deep interest in their past. Du Bois believed that by probing their past, Black people would find sorrows, horrors, and disasters, but he also believed that beneath the pain, suffering, and hardships they would also find courage, strength, beauty, regality, victory, and truth. Du Bois saw the connectedness of the present generation to their ancestors as indispensable to building a future and leaving a legacy for the future generations. Du Bois stated, "Negro history must be taught for many critical years by parents, in clubs by lecture courses, by a New Negro literature which Negroes must write and buy. This must be done systematically for the whole Negro race in the United States and elsewhere" (Du Bois, 1960/1973, p. 152). Du Bois went on to become the leading historian and the leading sociologist in Black American history. His book, *The Negro* (1915), was the first scholarly treatise linking Black Americans and other Black people in the diaspora to their West African heritage. In an expanded version, he would give that book the title *Black Folk Then and Now: An Essay in the History and Sociology of the Negro Race* (1939) to contrast the condition of Black people as leaders of West African empires and North African dynasties to their current status in the Americas and the Caribbeans. Du Bois believed that people without a strong knowledge and feelings of their connectedness to the past were like historical amnesiacs groping their way to the future without the force of historical precedent to guide and direct them.

THE TRANSITION OF RACE WORK TO SOCIAL WORK

Despite differences with his mentor regarding protest and the role of history, Du Bois carried Crummell's race work philosophy into the 20th century and influenced early generations of 20th-century Black professionals. Bardolf (1959) wrote:

In the age of accommodation, 1865-1900, any kind of distinction, be it only the attainment of a college degree, thrust a Negro into the role of race leader, but the maturing Negro community in 1900–1936 concentrated responsibility for race work in the professionals of the NAACP, the Urban League, the institutional church, the press, the interracial commissions .... The Talented Tenth were in fact the principal reliance of those organizations. (p. 135)

Early 20th-century Black social workers were among the Talented Tenth who led the race work in the Urban League, the institutional church, the interracial commissions, and the NAACP. For example, in 1968 Du Bois wrote that among the people attending the conference leading to the founding of the NAACP were an impressive number of scientists and social workers (p. 254). Du Bois (1968) also said that "the social workers were ready to take up a new task of abolition" and added that few were "followers of Booker T. Washington" (p. 254). Most early Black social workers were firmly in the Du Bois camp and not the Washingtonian camp because Du Bois gave them an intellectual framework to guide their practice with Black people, linked them to the Black race work tradition, and, along with Crummell, inspired them to see social work and helping others not just as a career but as a spiritual calling.

Overall, by giving race work scholarly coherence and focus, Crummell and Du Bois gave early Black social workers and other Black helping professionals a positive, hopeful, forward-looking, spiritual outlook at a time of peonage, chain gangs, political disenfranchisement, de facto and de jure segregation, and lynching. They gave them a positive concept of race and Blackness. They gave them a sense of race mission at a time when White scholars were predicting that the Black race, now free from White plantation paternalism, was doomed to extinction. They helped them to see communalism as a key to Black race survival and uplift and to see the dangers of individualism and egotism. Crummell and Du Bois provided early Black social workers with an optimistic view of Black people's prospects that helped them to overcome the immobilizing, pessimistic sociopolitical realities confronting Black life. They helped them to develop a strength perspective of Black life, to concentrate their attention on cultivating Black gifts instead of being overly preoccupied with Black pathologies. Crummell and Du Bois gave early Black social workers a sense that helping was a divine calling, a spiritual mission, and a debt they owed to the ancestors and to God. They made early

Black social workers value higher education and the liberal arts as opposed to the industrial education popularized during that time by Booker T. Washington. They helped early Black social workers to concentrate less on global racial concerns and focus more of their attention on character building through mental and moral improvement, family preservation through viewing the family as a sacred institution, and community development by trying to create a modern version of the communalistic African tribal village. They helped them to see the Black church as an instrument of social, economic, and political uplift, not just as an institution for saving souls. They helped early Black social workers to concentrate on cleaning themselves up morally, intellectually, and emotionally so that they could be mentally tough enough to meet the challenges of protesting their condition and fighting for both internal and external change. They helped them to develop a keen sense of the beauty, victories, and inspiration to be found in a history of suffering and oppression. They provided them with a keen sense of leading their lives not only for the sake of their own generation but also for the sake of the Black unborn. They made them believe that even as they departed the earth, their good works would live on, inspiring future generations to rise up and be free.

In 1959 Bardolf noted that because Du Bois and Crummell gave race work an intellectual appeal, "race work, became more than ever the task of professionals" (p. 240). Bardolf stated that "while the business of 'race work' gravitated to full-time professionals, other 'leading Negroes' became instead more simply the race's foremost church, education, or business leaders; or artists, writers, scientific or technical experts" (p. 239). In other words, race work, which used to be the province of anybody interested in the uplift of Black people, was steadily becoming the specialization of Black social workers and other Black professional social reformers whom Du Bois and Crummell had called on to become the leading force for Black social betterment. Race work had also become a specialization in terms of its social problem focus. In the past, its chief concern was the liberation of the race on the whole from slavery and racial oppression. Du Bois and Crummell had given it more specific, manageable, and realizable objectives—the building of character, the strengthening of Black families, and the stabilization of Black communities. This area of specialization and objectives put race work particularly in the purview of the budding profession called social work.

In fact, if any one person is said to be the founding father of Black social work, it would have to be W. E. B. Du Bois.

Du Bois and Crummell gave to early Black social workers a race work paradigm that was more refined than the old race work paradigm (which took a defensive position against racist religious mythmaking). As Table 1 shows, Crummell and Du Bois had turned the old race work paradigm into an offensive, forward-looking, transforming, and transcending social philosophy.

Table 1: The Race Work Paradigm vis-à-vis the Racist Mythmaking Paradigm		
	The Racist Mythmaking Paradigm	*The Race Work Paradigm*
Providential Intervention	God anointed White people as the elect to rule over the darker people of the world.	God is a just God active in human history on behalf of the oppressed.
Agency	Black people were made to serve White people and are too childlike and dependent to determine their own destiny.	Black people are the instrument of their own liberation and co-partners with God to rid the world of evil, injustice, and oppression.
Divine Gifts	God made Black people incredibly stupid and depraved and gave them few gifts except maybe to be singers, dancers, clowns, and buffoons.	Black people are endowed by God with divine gifts, the greatest of which is their ability to care.
Destiny	Black people are destined to be servants and slaves at the bottom of society forever.	Black people are destined to play a leading role in freeing themselves and ushering in God's Kingdom on earth.
Race Relations	The status of race relations is fixed in superordination and subordination molds, and Black people are only suited to serve in a subordinate role.	White people are not superhumans, not Gods, only humans, and Black people should cooperate with those who love justice and freedom on the basis of their spiritual, religious, and communal values.
Change	The status of Black people is fixed with God and they are to remain at the bottom of society while White people remain at the top forever. Therefore, there will be no change in Black-White relations.	God has already intervened in history and in the personal lives of Black people, and with God working through them, and for them, positive change in their lives is inevitable.
Hope	There is no hope for Black people for they are cursed and doomed.	There is hope for Black people as long as they believe in God and in themselves.

DU BOIS AND EARLY BLACK SOCIAL WORK

Du Bois did not just give early Black social workers a refined race work paradigm to guide their practice, and he did not just motivate pioneering Black social workers with his Talented Tenth concept. He also helped to lay the groundwork for the professional social work training of Black people. As the leading Black social scientist in America and a professor of economics and history at Atlanta University from 1897–1910, Du Bois's pioneering, sociological studies on "economic cooperation" among Black people (1907) and "social betterment" (1909) called on Black people to think about helping in a more systematic way. He believed that they should use the latest scientific knowledge of the day to guide their helping practices instead of always relying on good feelings or intuitive intentions. Du Bois's courses on "social reform" and other areas pertaining to Black social welfare required students to study various methods of reform designed to improve the social and economic conditions of oppressed people. These courses required students to engage in "social experiments," to use the urban environment as a sociological laboratory, and to do fieldwork in settlement houses and other social betterment organizations, such as Lugenia Burns Hope's Neighborhood Union. Du Bois believed it was imperative to bring Black students in contact with the Black masses, not to dictate to them but to learn from them and, most importantly, to avoid allowing their higher level of education and social status to alienate them from the Black masses. Black students in Du Bois's department had to go among the Black people and work in social service institutions located in the heart of even the poorest Black communities. Du Bois wanted the students to feel that they were one with the Black masses and to feel that they were agents in a divine cause. He wanted them to be able to mourn with their people like race men and race women of the days of old.

CHAPTER SEVEN

Early Black Male Social Workers and the
Integration of Spirituality and Science

The call of W. E. B. Du Bois for the development of an educated Black elite to shoulder the burdens of the race had particular appeal to Black male social workers. Du Bois's call for service to the race gave Black males a rationale to take up caregiving with no threat to their masculinity. With the exception of the dominance of Black males as preachers, Black females (not Black males) had been the leading caregivers in the Black community. With Du Bois's call for Black males to devote themselves to social service, Black males could reject notions that helping people was primarily women's work and that social work was a woman's profession.

This chapter focuses on four of the major Black male social work pioneers—Reverdy C. Ransom, Richard R. Wright, Jr., George Edmund Haynes, and Monroe N. Work—who took up Du Bois's call and, like race men of old, sought the cohesion of the spiritual, racial, communal, and destinal selves. Before we discuss how these pioneering Black male social workers sought to integrate spirituality and social work, we wish to establish the setting by saying a few words on the spiritual life of Black people at the turn of the 20th century.

HISTORICAL SETTING

What we found in the first two decades of the 20th century is that the most prominent early Black male social workers were men of God who primarily sought to use social work to strengthen the social service component of the Black church. The social service function of the Black church had become weakened with the rural-to-urban, south-to-north migration of thousands of Black people between the late 19th century and the 1930s. Large urban centers saw a proliferation of Black churches of every variety, description, and denomination, not just the Baptist and Methodist churches prevalent in Black communities during the 19th century. Holiness and Pentecostal churches particularly sprang up during the era of the Great Black Migration and enjoyed wide appeal to lower class Black migrants.

The more established Black Methodist and Baptist churches were calling for a learned priesthood and far more emotionally restrained church services. The Holiness and Pentecostal churches still allowed for the fullest expression of feeling the Holy Ghost, including making a joyful noise through singing, spirit possession, and even speaking in tongues. These churches, which were small storefront churches for the most part, were taking therapeutic and social support functions away from the larger Black churches. The larger Black churches found themselves not only competing for members with other large Black churches of different denominations but also with these small fundamentalist Black churches that connected the Black masses to a style of worship with roots in slavery and indeed with ties to their African past.

If the Holiness and Pentecostal churches were presenting a problem to the more established Black Baptist and Methodist churches, fraternal orders such as the Masons, Elks, and Odd Fellows, as well as fraternities and sororities at Black colleges, were beginning to cut into the Black church's function as a social center and a system of mutual aid (Wilmore, 1998, p. 192). These lodges, sororities, and fraternities provided Black people with a social and emotional outlet and with mutual aid in times of crises. They gave them an enhanced sense of social status and identity. Furthermore, they freed thousands of Black people from the moralism and tight control of "old line preachers" (Wilmore, 1998, p. 193).

During the first three decades of the 20th century, Black women's clubs, which saw a phenomenal rise during the last decade of the 19th century, were outperforming the Black church in the area of social services. Black women had continued to use the extended family paradigm forged out of the fictive kinship support systems of Black women in the kitchens, cabins, and fields during slavery. They became the leading "race women" seeking to carry on the race work tradition in the Black community. The more established historic Black church denominations were plagued by intense rivalry between denominations and congregations, and elite ministers often vied with one another for the most desirable pulpits and preferments, for powerful national offices, and for bishoprics. Wilmore wrote that as they engaged in this "ecclesiastical gamesmanship," energies and money were diverted from self-help and community welfare concerns (Wilmore, 1998, p. 191). Black women's clubs stepped in to fill the gap. Secular Black civil rights and social service organizations, such as the NAACP and the National Urban League, also challenged the Black church's social service and social change functions. While the primary objectives of early Black male social workers was to strengthen the social service and social change functions of the Black church, they also sought to meet other objectives by integrating spirituality and social work.

SPIRITUAL OBJECTIVES

In a nutshell, early Black male social workers sought to integrate spirituality and social work to meet several major objectives:

- To carry on the race work tradition of the historic Black church. Black churches at the turn of the 20th century seemed ill-equipped to deal with the massive social problems the rural, Southern Black peasantry brought to the urban North. Early Black social workers were convinced that the new helping profession called social work could help Black churches reach the level of racial uplift activity they had achieved during the 19th century.

- To advocate the race work idea of agency, destiny, and social debt. Early Black social workers believed that social workers were the chief agency for the uplift of Black people during the 20th century. Some Black social workers, as we pointed out in an earlier work (E. P. Martin & Martin, 1995) believed that social workers should usurp the social service function from the Black church altogether, while others (such as the people we highlight in this chapter) believed that social work should play a complementary or supplementary role to the Black church. Whatever the case may be, early Black social workers also sought to carry on the old race work idea of social debt. As we stated earlier, this idea advocated that better-off Black people, in particular, owed it to their ancestors for the sacrifices made on their behalf and owed it to God for being so good to them to shoulder the responsibility of helping the Black masses to rise. This was considered to be their God-given destiny.

- To assess the contradictions between White America's Christian beliefs and its brutal racist practices. This was an early race work tool for social change. This tool was used in all of the efforts to gain freedom and first-class citizenship.

- To promote cultural diversity and interracial cooperation. Despite seeking to heal racial wounds through more genuine practices of Christianity, early Black male social workers believed it was of the utmost importance to promote a program of cultural diversity and interracial cooperation. They did not hold to the view that White people were inherently evil any more than they believed that Black people were inherently stupid. They knew that throughout Black people's sojourn in America there had always been White people who had played an active role and taken extreme risks to go against the powerful racist tide of the dominant White society. They wanted to encourage and maximize White people's struggles against racism by cooperating with them in a fight for freedom, democracy, justice, and equality. They believed that the best method for respecting cultural differences and promoting interracial cooperation was by appealing to the spiritual strivings Black people had in common with people of other races and nationalities. The early Black minister–social worker R. R. Wright, Jr., (January 21, 1926) wrote:

White people are humans, just like Black people .... And it will be a sad day for the Negro when all our eggs are in the basket of protest .... The great highway of sympathy of friendship is still open. And the Christian religion ... is still the greatest method yet known to man for the solution of our social problems. So let's give a little study to the ways of friendship between our racial groups. (p. 1)

• To help Black people develop an awareness of and to realize their God-given talents and gifts. This was also a carryover from the strength perspective of race work. Early Black social workers, we will see later, discussed what race workers called divine gifts in more secular, social work terms. In respect to inspiring Black people to build upon their strengths, they made use of the old Black preacher's tool of inspiration. They wanted Black people to have a larger, more advanced vision of their capabilities, and to help Black people overcome feelings of inferiority and believe in themselves.

SPIRITUALITY AND EARLY BLACK MALE SOCIAL WORKERS
Ransom, Wright, Haynes, and Work are unique in that they had studied to be ministers and, with the exception of Haynes, each became an ordained minister in the African Methodist Episcopal Church. It was during their studies as seminary students and their church work that they began to believe that the Black church was not living up to its Black uplift mission. The idea that

the Black church needed to concentrate more on social service and "practical Christianity" led them into the social work field. These men were not only influenced by a race work tradition that had called on the church to be the leading Black caregiving institution, but they were also influenced by the social gospel movement, the social settlement movement, and even Christian socialism, which were popular at the turn of the 20th century.

Because Ransom, Wright, Haynes, and Work started out pursuing a career in the ministry, the social gospel movement had a particular appeal to them. The social gospel movement reinforced the old race work idea that the Black church should play a larger role in the earthly, day-to-day affairs of Black people by seeking solutions to the myriad social ills confronting them. Ransom, Wright, Haynes, and Work also were influenced by the settlement movement brought to the nation's attention through the work of Jane Addams's Hull House Settlement in Chicago. Moreover, these early Black male social workers were influenced (some more than others) by socialism, not so much by Marxian socialism calling for the violent overthrow of capitalism as by Christian socialism, which called for a peaceable, reformist approach that appealed to their religious inclinations. Foner wrote that "The Christian Socialist Movement was short-lived and fleeting but it left a deeper mark on Black Americans than did any of the other organized groups seeking to achieve socialism" (1983, p. 4). Another powerful influence on early Black male social workers was sociology. Wright and Work became the first Black students to earn sociology degrees from the University of Chicago. Wright went on to become the first Black person to receive a PhD in sociology from the University of Pennsylvania, while Work received a PhD in sociology from the University of Chicago. Haynes also studied sociology as he pursued a PhD in economics from Columbia University. While Ransom did not receive any degrees in sociology, his biographer, Morris (1990) wrote:

> Ransom was closely associated with four Blacks trained in sociology research: Richard R. Wright, Monroe N. Work, George E. Haynes and W. E. B. Du Bois. Wright and Work were young ministerial assistants to Ransom during his pastorate at Chicago's Institutional Church and Social Settlement (1900–1904) ... George E. Haynes ... worked with Ransom during the latter's editorship of the *A.M.E. Review* ... Despite the excellent contributions of Ransom's younger colleagues, his

fellow militant, W. E. B. Du Bois, with whom he participated in the Afro-American Council, the Niagara Movement and the NAACP, was the unquestioned elder statesman of Black sociology. (pp. 83–84)

Early Black social workers not only were deeply religious men trained for the ministry but also were among the first Black scholars conducting sociological studies of Black life. In the early days of Black social work, the ministry, social work, and sociology were inseparable; and, as a brief examination of the social work careers of Ransom, Wright, Haynes, and Work will show, these early Black social workers had the task of reconciling spirituality, social service, and social science. These early Black male social workers also had to make spirituality, social work, and sociology fit into their race work paradigm. Not only were these pioneering social workers seeking to uplift Black people but also, as we indicated earlier, to make their divine race work mission that of promoting interracial cooperation and saving the souls of White people.

REVERDY C. RANSOM, THE BLACK CHURCH, AND SOCIAL SETTLEMENT

Reverdy C. Ransom had already gained a reputation as a Black militant when he was kicked out of Oberlin College in 1882 for leading a protest against segregation, when he hid his heretical, socialistic views from the faculty at Wilberforce University for fear he would also be expelled from there, and when he sought to use his early ministry in the African Methodist Episcopal Church to trailblaze in social service, the social gospel, and the settlement movement.

As an A.M.E. minister, Ransom had nothing but praise for the historic role the Black church had played in the uplift of Black people. He believed that the Black church had served as the "chief center" of Black people's social life, that "every religious service, whether on Sunday or through the week, is also a family reunion" (Ransom, 1935, p. 25). Ransom's concern was that the Black church was falling short in the areas of social service, social justice, and erecting a Kingdom of God on Earth. He not only believed that the Black church should follow the lead of the Social Gospel Movement but also that of Christian socialism. In 1897 he wrote, "socialism, like the inspired carpenter of Nazareth, places more value upon man than it does upon riches. It believes that … the only sacred thing on earth is a human being" (Ransom, 1897/1983, p. 287).

During his ministry in Allegheny City, Pennsylvania, Ransom had observed the wretched tenements and witnessed the abject poverty among the people who lived on the river. He said it was there that he received his "vision of the need for social service" (Morris, 1990, p. 103). When he became pastor in 1896 of the Bethel A.M.E. Church in Chicago, his vision had materialized. Ransom could see that the Black ministers were bewildered by the hordes of Southern Black migrants coming to Chicago and were "unprepared by training, experience and vision, to cope with the moral, social and economic conditions so suddenly thrust upon them" (Morris, 1990, p. 82). In 1949 Ransom wrote, "I soon realized that the old stereotype form of church services practiced in all Negro churches fell far short of meeting the religious, moral, and social conditions that confronted them" (p. 82).

In Chicago, Ransom counted among his personal friends some of the leading White social workers and social reformers of the time, people such as Jane Addams, Clarence Darrow, Robert Ingersoll, Mary McDowell, and Graham Taylor. He also befriended such Black leaders as the anti-lynching crusader Ida B. Wells Barnett and the noted Women's Club leader, Fannie Barrier Williams. Inspired by these friends and by Du Bois, Ransom organized the Men's Sunday Club, obligating more than 500 of Chicago's most prominent Black men to align themselves with the needs of the impoverished Black masses. Ransom believed that somehow Black people who were well off and Black people who were less fortunate must be brought together until the race on the whole stood free, equal, and uplifted. Also, seeking to promote interracial cooperation and Christian brotherhood, Ransom opened his church to the Manassa Society, an organization of 700 men and women in biracial marriages, who were having difficulty finding a home in any church, Black or White, because they were "shut out from social intercourse with [W]hite people and in most cases received a cold welcome even among colored people" (Ransom, 1949, p. 92).

In 1900, Ransom quit Bethel to build his "church of the future," the Institutional Church and Social Settlement where he hoped to blend social work and Black spirituality to meet the multileveled needs of Black people. With this move he had the active sympathy and cooperation of Jane Addams of Hull House, Graham Taylor of Chicago Commons, and Mary McDowell of the Chicago University Settlement. Ransom, who had no formal training in social work, received private lessons and personal experience in social work under the tutelage of these famed pioneering White social workers.

Jane Addams particularly took an interest in passing on her vast knowledge about social settlements to Ransom. Morris (1990) wrote:

> Ransom considered Addams to be one of the "finest personalities" he had ever known, and he called on her for advice and assistance during the formative period of the Institutional Church and Social Settlement which he founded in Chicago in 1900. It was due in part to Addams' influence that Ransom received significant financial support for the Institutional Church and Social Settlement from Chicago's [W]hite elite leaders ... Jane Addams' relationship with Ransom is significant because she is one of the key persons, along with Graham Taylor, who indirectly provided Ransom with a format and structure that was useful in his Institutional Church. (pp. 78–79)

Addams, Graham, and McDowell, all leaders of their own social settlements, helped Ransom to integrate social work technique with race work as he sought to make his Institutional Church and Social Settlement a helping model that Black communities across the country could duplicate. It was partly because of the interracial cooperation Ransom received among leading White social workers that he opened his Institutional Church and Social Settlement to all people, regardless of class or color. He felt that in the area of social services, the Black church should reach across denominational lines and give help to nonmembers as well as members. Although Ransom's Institutional Church and Social Settlement was open to all people regardless of class, color, or denomination, he wanted it to focus particularly on the needs of the Black migrants who were steadily coming into Chicago in search of the promised land. Ransom's social experiment sought to provide a wide array of social services. "It opened in a building with an auditorium seating 1,200, a dining room, a kitchen, a gymnasium, and eight other large rooms. Its activities included a men's forum, a women's club, a nursery, a kindergarten, clubs for boys and girls, a print shop, and an employment bureau. It offered concerts, classes in sewing, cooking, music, and lectures by leading Black and White speakers. Ransom hired the University of Chicago seminarians, Monroe N. Work and Richard R. Wright, Jr., to assist him with the boy's club" (Luker, 1991, p. 174).

Ransom also sought to use his Institutional Church and Social Settlement to attack the street denizens who preyed on naive, unsophisticated Black migrants. Like Du Bois and Crummell, the old race work leaders, he was concerned with the deleterious effect the street ideology was having on the moral character of Black people, especially Black youths. Ransom was determined that he would match the saloons and drinking halls in keeping his church open seven days a week. Ransom's Institutional Church and Social Settlement so aroused the ire of policy numbers racketeers that his church was dynamited. The explosion blew out the rear of the building where Ransom's office was located but no one was hurt. However, it was not the street racketeers that led to the demise of Ransom's social experiment. Ransom's effort was broadly supported by the Black masses and the progressive elite, Black and White. His problem was with conservative Black ministers within his own A.M.E. church denomination. Ransom said that his church and social settlement was entirely beyond their conception of what a church should be. He wrote, "Their only appeal was preaching, praying, singing, shouting, baptizing and holy communion, but going out into the street and highways, bearing a message of social, moral, economic and civic salvation they did not believe to be the function of the church" (quoted in Morris, 1990, p. 112).

Because Ransom's Institutional Church and Social Settlement was still under the auspices of the A.M.E. church and Ransom was still an A.M.E. minister, his conservative colleagues accused him of bringing socialism into the church, managed to get him transferred to Boston, and ordered his replacement to make the Institutional Church and Social Settlement "a regular A.M.E. church, to cut out the social foolishness, and bring religion back" (Wright, 1965, p. 148).

Ransom carried his ideas of social service to his new assignment in Boston, where his race work ideas became more pronounced than ever as he came in contact with such militant Black leaders as Boston's Monroe Trotter and became the editor of *The A.M.E. Review*, the chief news organ and journal of the A.M.E. church. Ransom advocated a militant racial Christianity that concerned itself with the "here-and-now" needs of Black people. He wrote that as Christians:

> we shall concern ourselves, not less about Israel in Egypt, but more about the Negro in America; not less about the Hebrews in the "fiery furnace," but more about Negroes burnt at the stake; not less about the daughters of Jerusalem by the rivers of Babylon, but more about our own

daughters on the banks of the Mississippi; not less about Paul in the Phillipian jail or his appeal to Caesar, but more about the prison pens and peonage camps of the South and our own appeal for political and social justice in the United States (Ransom, 1949, p. 72).

Like race workers including Crummell and Du Bois, Ransom believed that Black people's most profound God-given gift was their deep spirituality. He believed that having a profound spiritual and emotional gift meant that Black people had a unique message to give to the world and were destined not only to rise themselves but also to soften the aggressive, avaricious, arrogant, exploitative, and imperialistic behavior of racist and money-grubbing White people. He advocated that with their unique, rich, spiritual gifts, Black people are "the last spiritual reserve of Christianity," the last hope to "prophecy to the dry bones of our civilization" until it is "clothed with the flesh" of "our common human brotherhood" (Ransom, 1949, p. 7). Their deep spiritual gift, Ransom (1935) wrote, gave Black people the potential for "spiritual leadership" that could both "lead America to achieve that brotherhood which transforms the children of men into the spirit and likeness of the children of God" (p. 98) and have an impact on a spiritually barren and bankrupt Christian world. In 1935, Ransom prophesized, "if Americans of African descent can survive the social, economic and political inferno through which they are passing," they could "take the moral and spiritual leadership of the Black race throughout the world to rescue the Cross of Christ from infidel Christianity" (p. 2).

Ransom went on to become a bishop of the A.M.E. Church but remained one of its staunchest advocates of social work and race work across denominational lines. He set the standard for other early Black social workers as they sought to integrate spirituality with social work practice.

RICHARD R. WRIGHT, JR. AND SOCIAL SERVICE IN THE CHURCH

Although Ransom's settlement work in Chicago was short-lived, lasting only four years from 1900 to 1904, people from around the country and from abroad came to Chicago to study this social service experiment under the auspices of the Black church. It also launched the career of Richard R. Wright, Jr., who was to carry Ransom's mixture of race work and social work forward. Ransom had hired Wright and Monroe N. Work as ministerial assistants to run the Boy's Club in his Institutional Church and Social Settlement when both were seminarians at the University of Chicago. Wright's interest in social work began at the University of Chicago when his seminary studies threw him in the midst of the social gospel and where "he found in the social gospel a more satisfying meaning and purpose for Christianity than ever before." Wright (1965) wrote: "For me there was little else for the church to do than to make practical its belief in God and brotherhood, and to help build a Christian society on Earth" (p. 149). After his work among Chicago's poor as a minister at the Trinity Mission, Wright said that he shifted his interest "from the theological to the sociological point of view." He said that even though he had gotten a bachelor's degree in Biblical Theology, he "saw plainly that the church must devote more time to the social without of course neglecting the theological"(Wright, 1965, p. 114).

At Ransom's Institutional Church and Social Settlement, Wright's beliefs in "applied sociology" and "practical Christianity" were reinforced and his tutelage under Ransom and his contacts with prominent White social workers such as Jane Addams and Mary McDowell helped him to become well-grounded in social work. Wright (1965) wrote that by the time he received a bachelor's and a master's degree in Theology from the University of Chicago and was ready to leave Chicago to work on his PhD in sociology at the University of Pennsylvania, "I considered myself a professional man, having many years of training and experience in social work among colored people" (p. 161).

In Philadelphia, Wright continued his social work and race work practice by becoming a community organizer for the Philadelphia Armstrong Association. His major work there was to organize Black mechanics and to strengthen the Colored Mechanic Association, a Black labor union that sought to bring recognition, respect, and integration into the broader labor community. While working on his PhD, Wright also got the opportunity to conduct research with his old colleague Monroe N. Wright and with his idol, W. E. B. Du Bois. Together these three scholars, who were to become the leading sociologists of the early 20th century (Du Bois had already received that distinction) were doing research on the peonage system in Lowndes County, Alabama. Wright was so moved by wretchedness and semi-slavery conditions that he joined the board of the Society of the Abolition of Slavery, which was founded by Benjamin Franklin in 1775. Although this organization was all but defunct by the time Wright joined it in 1907, Wright was determined to breathe new life into it and once again enlist it in the Black uplift and liberation cause.

While Wright was conducting research for his PhD dissertation on "The Negro in Philadelphia," in 1965 he recounted that he found little material in public records about Black Americans "except those on the pathological side" (p. 153). He also wrote that most of the public records showed "C" for colored, "B" for Black when it came to arrests, jails, penitentiaries, almshouses, hospitals, and vital statistics, which encouraged investigators to write about pathological conditions among colored people, especially those concerning crime (Wright, 1965, p. 153). Wright said that he was concerned that the Black child who reads nothing in his textbooks but the inferiority of his or her race, who never sees a picture of Black people except as criminals, whose attention is never called to the progress of his or her people, who knows nothing of history but what he gets from American textbooks, could never feel that he or she "had all the biological qualifications of equality" (1965, p. 323). Wright was of the belief that no people can rise higher than their heroes; if a race does not appreciate its heroes, they must degenerate. Wright felt it was a function of the minister and the social worker to magnify the deed, exploits, and achievements of its heroes so that the young people would be inspired to develop advanced notions of their own promise and potentialities.

After receiving his PhD in sociology, Wright's research, social work, and sermons probed the positive, constructive side of Black life with "a sociological slant." He said that as a social worker and as a minister, his major sermon was that Negro-Americans must believe in the divinity of their personalities, that they are the children of God, the source of all power, and put no limitations on the possibilities of their achievement. In 1965 Wright stated, "Negro-Americans must believe this, teach it, preach it, sing it, and hardest of all, live it" (p. 327).

To Wright, social service and Christianity went hand-in-hand because Christianity cannot be practiced without social service. Wright's social work in the church was based on the idea that "Jesus preaches but little about heaven and hell but much about service" (Wright, 1922, p. 19). Wright defined social service as "social justice" that gives all people the best opportunities to develop into the highest kind of personhood and to make the very best of their existence on earth (Wright, 1922, p. 14). He maintained that the whole teaching of Jesus is to give dignity to human existence and to awaken divinity in every human life. Wright moved away from his old race work mentor,

Ransom, when he made a distinction between social service and social work. To Wright, "Social Service is spiritual and altruistic, while socialism is materialistic and selfish. Social Service grows out of religious needs of the soul, socialism out of the material needs of the body." Wright (1922) also said that "Socialism has much truth in it and can teach the social worker much, yet Socialism is not identical with Social Service, which covers a much greater field" (p. 28). Wright's critics wrote that his views regarding socialism were misleading and misguided and motivated by the fact that he and his father, Richard R. Wright, Sr., were capitalists who owned a Black bank in Philadelphia. However, Wright (1965) countered that "we looked upon our bank not only as a mere business, but as a social service not just to make money, but to try to lay a firm financial foundation for our people" (p. 194). He wrote that money is not the root of all evil, but the love of money and the willingness to do wrong and to sacrifice principle to get it is. He believed that money was the root of much that was good, and that it was an absolute necessity if the Black church was to thrive and if Black people were to rise.

While Wright and Ransom had different views concerning capitalism and socialism, they were in total agreement about using spirituality to promote interracial cooperation. Like Ransom, Wright was strongly convinced that racial prejudice is the greatest stumbling block, next to personal ignorance, in the progress of humankind. Both Ransom and Wright were appalled that racism was like a malignant growth on the body of the White American church. Wright (1965) wrote, "I attacked religion in America as un-Christian because of the attitude of churches toward Negro-Americans" (p. 117). He stated:

Nineteen hundred years from now our posterity will wonder how we of the 20th century could harbor so much race prejudice; how we could preach the Gospel to men and women and yet deny them education as we do the Blacks in America; how we can preach Christian manhood and yet condone the systematic exploitation of Black women and children; how we can even invite "all who truly repent and are heartily" sorry and yet if the penitent is Black deny him the communion of the Lord's supper. (Wright, 1925a, p. 1)

Wright (1965) said, "While I still thought it was necessary for the church to do a great deal of 'social work,' I thought of the church as creating the atmosphere of brotherhood in all the operation of life, and that 'spiritual job' was the church's greatest value to mankind" (p. 117). In both his social work and in his ministry, Wright (1965) "put extra emphasis on the Holy Spirit permeating not only the individual human heart, but the social life, the national conscience, and all humanity" (p. 116). Like Crummell, Ransom, and other race workers, Wright had come to believe that "the Anglo-Saxon and Teuton" lacked the religious temperament to give the world a rejuvenated Christianity that would lead to universal brotherhood and the establishment of God's Kingdom on earth. Like Crummell and Ransom, Wright believed that Black people, endowed with the rich gift of spirituality, had a duty to teach universal brotherhood to a cold, un-Christian White world that sorely needed it. He wrote:

God put the Negro here to test America's sincerity. Are the great moral principles we preach here of Christianity, Democracy, Opportunity, Equality, Feminine Emancipation, all as sounding brass or a tinkling symbol? Are not Americans merely worshippers of themselves? Can they apply these principles to others? The Negro is the test. And as the Negro becomes more and more intelligent, this test for America will be harder. American ideals will either break down or be proved by the Negro. (Wright, 1925c, pp. 1, 4)

Wright (1916) believed that, "if European and American Christianity is to get back to Jesus, it will be because those people who understand the temperament of Jesus take it back" (p. 4). Fullwinder (1969) believed that Wright was so convinced of the sterility of White Christianity and the spiritual gifts of Black people that he wrote, "Wright had pushed God into the background and had given the mission of saving mankind to the colored race" (p. 41). However, Wright, Ransom, and other ministers/ social workers essentially were simply following an old race work tradition that upheld the idea that White people had much to teach Black people in terms of industrialism, business, science, and technology but so little to teach them in regard to manners and morals, religion, and spirituality as long as they believed that they were chosen by God to rule colored humanity.

While Wright was adamant in his stand that White America for the most part had taken the brotherhood and sisterhood out of Christianity, he was just as critical of the A.M.E. Church as he advocated national reform in its accounting system, fought for larger participation of laymen in decision making, called for the equal rights of women, sought better training for preachers and more rigid requirements for admission to the ministry, sought more interchurch cooperation, and cited the need for a stronger moral and spiritual leadership. Most significantly, Wright advocated throughout his life that the A.M.E. Black church should never give up its social service/social change function and never lose its concern for community welfare and liberation that was utmost in the minds of the founding fathers of African Methodism. Despite pockets of hostility to Wright's persistent call for progressive reform in the A.M.E. Church, he had enough broad support to be elected an A.M.E. bishop in 1936.

GEORGE EDMUND HAYNES AND INTERRACIAL CHRISTIAN COOPERATION

George Edmund Haynes had more success in the work of interracial cooperation than Richard R. Wright, Jr., because he was less strident in his criticism of the White church. After becoming the first Black person to graduate from New York University's School of Philanthropy (which later became the Columbia School of Social Work), the first to earn a PhD in sociology and economics from Columbia University, and the first to establish an undergraduate social work program at a Black college, Fisk University, Haynes went on to become cofounder and the first executive director of the National Urban League, the leading Black social service agency in the nation. Like most Black social workers of his time, Haynes was influenced by the race work ideas propagated by both W. E. B. Du Bois and Booker T. Washington. Carlton-LaNey (1996) wrote that the type of community work in which both George Edmund Haynes and his sister Birdye Haynes engaged can best be described as "race work" which, she said was such an integral part of their lives and careers that "it formed the foundation upon which they worked and served to endear them to their people" (p. 32). Birdye Haynes was the first African American to graduate from the Chicago School of Civics and Philanthropy. She became an administrator of New York's Lincoln House Settlement from 1915 to 1922, but her career in social work was short-lived because of her untimely death in 1922.

In his race work efforts, George Haynes became the chief promoter of social work education among Black Americans. His idea was to train a cadre of Black social workers to meet the needs of Black Southerners migrating to big cities in the North. Also, as the head of the National Urban League, Haynes also directed the League toward serving the Black migrants.

After receiving a master's degree in sociology from Yale University in 1904, Haynes entered the Yale Divinity School with the dream of becoming a minister, but dropped out to attend to the failing health of his mother. However, the conviction that religion is best expressed through social service remained with him throughout his life. He developed this conviction in his first professional work in the Colored Department of the International Committee of the Young Men's Christian Association (the YMCA). While doing his postgraduate studies, Haynes accepted an offer from none other than Reverdy C. Ransom to serve as the editor of the Department of Social Science of the *A.M.E. Church Review*. Morris (1990), Ransom's biographer, wrote:

> Haynes' professional and academic activities and associations placed him, in many respects, within the Social Gospel Movement. Like Ransom, Haynes believed that religion had to be relevant and thus practically applicable to the current condition of the world. On this and many other issues, Ransom and Haynes shared similar viewpoints. Neither Ransom nor Haynes was content with the traditional religious practices of their numerous associates. (p. 90)

For example, in one of his *A.M.E. Church Review* articles entitled "The Church and Social Science," Haynes urged the church to free itself from the old social apathy and to dedicate itself "to the settlement of race problems, to the betterment of living conditions in city and country, and to the abolition of every form of social injustice" (Morris, 1990, p. 92). When Haynes organized the social work program at Fisk University, the curriculum included such courses as "The Social Ideals of the Bible," "The History and Principles of Religious Education," and other courses addressing religion and spirituality (Weiss, 1974, p. 75). Because Fisk University's Social Work Program served as a model, other Black social work programs across the nation had no problem integrating social work with religion. For example, the Social Work Program at Talladega College offered a year-long course covering "General Principles, Biblical Teaching and Practical Sociology" (Weiss, 1974, p. 76). The Atlanta University School of Social Service at

Morehouse College instituted a curriculum that was identical to the social work curriculum at Fisk University (Parris & Brock, 1971, p. 192).

Similar to most race workers/social workers of his day, Haynes felt that the greatest gift Black people had acquired was the gift of spirituality, which he said, received its highest expression through their churches. In 1922 he wrote, "The Negro takes his religion as the dominating fact and factor of his life and pours all his love, enthusiasm, money, and energy into the Black church because other avenues of group expression are closed to them" (Haynes, 1922, p. 57). Haynes believed that it was the spiritual self of Black people that informed their communal and racial selves. The gift of spirituality led to the gift of perseverance, he wrote, as the enslaved African kept faith "that the God to whom he cried in moaning and longing ... would someday, somehow bring liberty and opportunity" (Haynes, 1922, p. 77). The gift of spirituality, Haynes believed, also leads to the gift of communalism. Although racial prejudice and racial persecution "have left their mark in Negro life," Haynes wrote, "the soul of this people vibrates with its pristine fervor of fellow-feeling ... which love alone lavishes and which money cannot buy." Haynes stated that the strong sense of fellow-feeling among Black people causes them to value "personal relations ... above property associations" (Haynes, 1922, p. 79), and he hoped that before "fixed differences of class arise among Negroes" based upon associations of capital, property, and class, the Black "business and professional classes may develop their present sense of responsibility to the wage-earning classes and spread a group solidarity, a feeling of social responsibility, throughout the whole people" (Haynes, 1922, p. 89).

Haynes (1922) believed that the growing sense of fellow feelings and a growing awareness of their own self-worth gave Black people a keen sense of fair play and justice (p. 79). Despite their suffering in the hands of others, he wrote in 1922 that there is no historical evidence of Black people seeking to dominate, oppress, or treat any other people unjustly and unfairly. Haynes believed that Black people's gift of fair play, sense of justice, and spirituality could be adjusted to accommodate all Americans.

Throughout Haynes's academic and professional life he had strong support systems among White people. Distinguished White social workers such as Edward T. Devine, Ruth Standish Baldwin, and Frances Keller were major influences in helping Haynes to launch the National Urban League. Haynes had always had an interest in interracial relations and, after leaving the National Urban League to serve as the Director of Negro Economics for the

United States Department of Labor (from 1918 to 1921), he took a position in 1921 as the Executive Secretary of the Department of Race Relations of the Federal Council of Churches. Haynes (1922) hoped that through inter-racial cooperation, "The idea that the American Negro is a person and an end in himself will ... gradually ... replace the idea of the Negro only as a servant" (p. 156). He hoped that adjustment would be formed "on the basis of brotherhood rather than brute force" (p. 6). Haynes was of the opinion that if Black people and White people could not unite on the basis of common human needs, they should be able to cooperate on the basis of their common spiritual strivings. Haynes remained optimistic concerning interra-cial cooperation and held his post at the Federal Council of Churches until his retirement in 1947.

MONROE N. WORK AND THE SOCIOLOGICAL ANALYSIS OF THE FACTS

Even before joining Richard R. Wright, Jr. to pursue a divinity degree from the Chicago Theological Seminary and before joining Ransom at the Institutional Church and Social Settlement, Monroe N. Work had already become an ordained minister in the African Methodist Episcopal Church. However, after he and Wright became the first Black people to enroll as soci-ology students at the University of Chicago in 1898, Work said that he came to realize that a theological education was limited in providing the informa-tion he believed he needed to serve Black people. He believed that because no group had suffered more from a lack of knowledge concerning themselves than Black people, "sociological research could provide a great service to Blacks through the compilation of factual data." Work said, "it was then that I dedicated my life to the gathering of information, the compilation of exact knowledge concerning the Negro" (McMurry, 1985, p. 28).

By the time Work took on his first academic job at Savannah State University in 1903, he had given up the ministry to pursue his idea of "the impact of facts." He continued his interest in social work and carried Ransom's idea of a Men's Sunday Club to Savannah not only to mobilize Black public opinion for social improvement, but also so that he could disseminate the vast information he was beginning to compile on Black life, history, and culture. While working to become the first Black person to receive a PhD in sociology at the University of Chicago, he accepted an offer by Booker T. Washington in 1908 to become the Director of Records and

Research at Tuskegee Institute. Work's acceptance of the job at Tuskegee indicated that he was not caught up in the split between the warring Du Bois and Washington camps. Work had become involved as a researcher with the Atlanta University studies conducted by Du Bois and even joined Du Bois's Niagara Movement, which was in direct opposition to the accommodationist politics of Booker T. Washington. On the other hand, Work believed that Washington's industrial approach to improving the economic conditions of a people only a few generations removed from slavery was appropriate as well.

Work's main interest was in using the facts as a basis for social reform. He believed that the scientific, empirical presentation of factual data could do much to eradicate prejudice among White people, stamp out feelings of inferiority among Black people, and serve as a guide for shaping social welfare policy. Work's research projects at Tuskegee earned him the reputation as the nation's foremost collector and disseminator of social science data pertaining to Black Americans. His signature achievement was editing and publishing *The Negro Year Book: Annual Encyclopedia of the Negro* which became the most comprehensive study of Black people ever compiled. In *The Negro Year Book*, Work covered practically every conceivable area of Black life, classifying information into 98 different categories. Starting in 1912, Work edited nine editions of *The Negro Year Book*. Its bibliography was so extensive that Work started publishing a separate *Bibliography of the Negro in Africa and America* in 1928. Researchers, policy makers, educators, scholars, social workers, and social reformers from all over the world made extensive use of the copious information Work provided.

Black lay persons, as Work intended, also found much to be inspired by in *The Negro Year Book*. Work had long been of the opinion that the historical facts of Black life, history, and culture would do far more to help average Black people to overcome feelings of inferiority, self-hatred, and low self-esteem than any racial propaganda or revival-type sermons appealing to emotionalism. Work continued to see his research as race work designed overall to improve the quality of Black life. As Work's biographer, McMurry (1985) stated, "Like many Black scholars of his time, Work was forced by current conditions to become a 'race man' and to devote his energies to defending and trying to uplift his fellow Blacks" (p. 10). Like many race workers of his time, Work continued to express "a faith in Black potential and a dream of a truly biracial America" and was "actively engaged in projects to bring to fruition his hopes for his race and his country" (McMurry,

1985, p. 110). Work took a special interest in Black health care. Ever since becoming a social worker during his days in Chicago, he had been appalled by the health conditions of poor people, Black and White. He became convinced that good health was certainly a precondition for progressive achievement. Work created the *Health Week Bulletin* and promoted Negro Health Week, making it a national campaign. Not only did he compile copious data on the status of Black health nationwide, but he also kept meticulous records of lynchings. He considered the lynching of Black people as the number one threat to Black health. Work's *Annual Lynching Report* was amply used by social workers, social reformers, policymakers, and social activists nationwide seeking the passage of a national antilynching bill.

In pursuing race work and interracial cooperation, Work (like his colleagues Ransom, Wright, and Haynes) also took a strength perspective. He strongly believed that Black people had special gifts or strengths and believed "that Negroes should not despise the rock from which they were hewn" (Work, 1916/1969, p. 326). Work (1923) believed that few people have been able to "bear up under most grievous burdens" that Black people have (p. 43). He wrote that "no other group of people give so large a percentage of their earnings for religious work" (Work, 1923, p. 44). He also wrote, "No people in the history of the world have sacrificed so much to secure an education" (Work, 1923, p. 44). Work believed, like Ransom, Wright and Haynes, that the greatest gift of Black people was their strong spirituality. Work said that the richness of their spirituality is indicated by the spirituals. He wrote that, "the spirituals developed by slaves in the United States represent a contribution in the field of religious literature comparable in some respects to the Psalms of the Bible" (Work, 1923, p. 43). To Work, the strength of Black spirituality was verified completely by the fact that never in the history of America had Black people tried to prevent any other group from having and enjoying all the privileges and rights of a free and full life. In 1923 Work wrote that, "in none of the literature put out by the Negro since his emancipation is there an instance of their urging that any rights and privileges be taken away from the [W]hite man" (p. 45). Work believed that showing solid historical evidence of the gifts of Black people was more powerful and convincing than claiming that these gifts were God-given and fixed forever in the genetic makeup of Black people, leaving little room for the development of other strengths to meet the demands of new environmental circumstances and cultural challenges.

Although Work's research was "scientific," empirical, and secular, he continued to be spiritual in his race work endeavors. His spirituality remained an internalized domain assumption that was never expressed or made explicit for the sake of value neutrality, objectivity, and empiricism in sociological research. Work still sought to tie his research interest to the theological concerns he had developed while he was a theology student and a social worker. He continued to believe that Black people had a unique spiritual contribution to make to the world. Therefore, behind his desire to be a detached social scientist concerned primarily with an objective presentation of the facts, Work continued to hold on to the idea that, "the lives of Black people are a living example of the words of Paul when he speaks of the 'love that believeth all things, hopeth all things, endureth all things" (Work, 1923, p. 45). This love, Work (1923) stated, "is an interpretation of the Christ-Spirit and is a contribution to the establishing of God's Kingdom on earth" (p. 45). Even as a prominent sociologist with a reputation for his meticulous fact-finding, Work could not give up the dream that such a kingdom on earth is possible.

THE SECULARIZATION OF SOCIAL WORK

The extensive research of Monroe N. Work shows the transition from spirituality in race work to the secularization of social work in the Black helping tradition. Race work scholars and leaders had helped transform race work from a reactive helping framework that responded largely to racist religious mythmaking into a proactive caregiving framework, giving Black people greater assurance of themselves in being the architects of their own survival and advancement. With this proactive approach, early Black social workers were able to take the offensive in putting White America on the defensive. Instead of viewing themselves as sick, deviant, inferior creatures, the race work philosophy of Crummell and Du Bois provided them the basis for seeing White society as deviant and pathological in terms of its inability to live up to its own most cherished values and ideas. As the Black sociologist, Cox (1948) wrote:

The basic ideological problem of [W]hites in their relationship with Negroes, then, is that of reconciling two standards of morality. The powerful democratic Christian beliefs developed in Western society are on the side of the Negro; the racially articulate [W]hites must shoulder the task of demonstrating that these beliefs do not include colored people. Thus they strive to see democracy as implying equal opportunity among [W]hites in their exploitation of Negroes. But such an interpretation must be constantly reinforced, for it rests insecurely on the broader worldview. (p. 434)

It was by taking a positive, proactive race work approach to race relations that early Black social workers were able to criticize the White church and challenge it to do more to promote interracial cooperation. It was also this proactive race work approach that allowed early Black social workers to carry the strength perspective of race work over into social work. As Figure 2 illustrates, pioneering Black social workers all adopted the race work concept that Black people were endowed with special gifts.

Figure 2: Race Work "Gifts" and Black Social Work "Strengths"

Race Work Gifts

Crummell   Mutuality; vitality; capacity to endure; moral perception; deep religious sense; spiritual perception; capacity to adjust; improvisation; receptivity, mental capacity; family feelings; forward-looking attitude; capacity for constructiveness; courage

Du Bois   Exploration; labor that helped build America; persistent struggle for democracy; military defense of America; contribution to American literature and art; Black folklore; sense of humor; ingenious musical ability; spirituality; religious hopes, tolerance, and faith; African communalism; intellectual capacity

ALEXANDER CRUMMELL
(1819-1898)

*Source: Reprinted with permission from Prints & Photographs Department
Moorland-Springarn Research Center, Howard University.*

FREDERICK DOUGLASS
(1818-1895)

W. E. B. DU BOIS
(1868–1963)

THYRA J. EDWARDS
(1897–1953)

Source: Reprinted with permission from Prints & Photographs Department Moorland-Springarn Research Center, Howard University.

JOSIAH HENSON
(1789–1883)

Source: Reprinted with permission from Prints & Photographs Department
Moorland-Springarn Research Center, Howard University.

SOJOURNER TRUTH
(1797-1883)

MONROE N. WORK
(1866-1945)

RICHARD R. WRIGHT, JR.
(1878–1967)

*Source: Reprinted with permission from Prints & Photographs Department
Moorland-Springarn Research Center, Howard University.*

Black Social Work Strengths

Ransom   Deep spirituality; deep emotionality; racial tolerance; concern about here-and-now; social salvation over personal salvation; love of true democracy; race consciousness; radicalism; class consciousness; sense of fair play

Wright, Jr.   Deep spirituality; deep emotionality; capacity for caring; racial tolerance; interracial cooperation; capacity for service

Haynes   Deep spirituality; race consciousness; patience under pressure; optimism under pressure; racial tolerance; personal relations valued above property associations; deep sense of fair play and justice; interracial cooperation

Work   Cheerfulness despite burdens; perseverance; spirituality; caring ability; racial cooperation; racial consciousness; desire for education; interracial cooperation; literary ability; sense of history; sense of justice and fair play for others

One can see from Figure 2 that spirituality figured prominently in both the race work "gifts" and the Black social work "strengths." The major difference between race work "gifts" and Black social work "strengths" was that early Black social workers tended to speak of Black strengths in terms of "ability," "capacity," "propensity," and "potentiality," and to maintain that these strengths are socially acquired and culturally determined products of history instead of the sacred endowments of divine intervention. As Table 2 shows, early Black social workers also adopted the race work concept of human agency but had come to see human agency less as a copartner with God that would work out the destiny of Black people and more in terms of a Black vanguard that would raise Black people's consciousness to their fullest human potential and promise. It shows that with early Black social workers, hope was placed not so much on bringing God's Kingdom upon the earth but on improving the social, economic, and political condition of Black people and establishing interracial harmony in America and the world.

Table 2: The Secularization of the Race Work Paradigm		
	Race Work	*Black Social Work*
Providential Intervention	God is on Black people's side	History is on Black people's side
Agency	Black people in copartnership with God are the agency of change	Black people in cooperation with freedom-loving White people are the agency of change
Gifts	A God-given endowment and divine inheritance	Socially acquired skills, traits, abilities, capacities, and potentiality
Destiny	A divine plan	A historical promise and potentiality
Hope	God's promise of the coming of the Kingdom of God on Earth	Instilling in the younger generation the need to continue the struggle for full first-class American citizenship and interracial cooperation

Spirituality and the Black Helping Tradition in Social Work

Although many Black ministers/race workers/social workers remained spiritual and religious persons and held on to private, inner-psychic spiritual assumptions to guide their race work/social work practice, they publicly expressed only secular views. By the turn of the 20th century, the old magical thinking of the conjurer or the voodoo man had waned in influence and popularity in the Black community, and those claiming to have the power to manipulate nature were seen basically as fakers and frauds, as objects of amusement, curiosity, and contempt appealing only to the most ignorant, superstitious, and gullible of the race. Even religion was coming into question by the new secular helping profession called social work. Freudian notions that religion was an illusion, a narcotic, and an obsessional neurosis were slowly creeping into social work thinking. Many Black social workers were also heavily influenced by Max Weber's sociological dogma that called for an "objective," value-free sociology. This value-neutral sociology rejected the expression of religious, moral, spiritual, political, or ethical values and viewpoints. Social workers/sociologists such as E. Franklin Frazier, who was an atheist, could easily reconcile his spiritual nonbelief with a secular sociological orientation, but it was difficult for those Black social workers such as Ransom, Wright, Haynes, and Work who were either ministers or had studied for the ministry. Wright (1925b) admonished, "Let no one believe that the religion of Jesus can be overthrown by 'reasoning,' by logic or by science" (p. 4). To keep from suffering profound incongruence between their personal spiritual values and the calls for secularity and value neutrality in their professional lives, Wright, Ransom, Haynes, and Work generally used secular tools of gathering knowledge to pursue their spiritual interests.

Race work social philosophers such as W. E. B. Du Bois and Crummell were also faced with the issue of spirituality and science. Crummell, a minister, saw no distinction between the two, seeing both as the work of God. Also knowing that Black people were a deeply religious and spiritual people, Crummell would have thought it was insane to ignore or to downplay this significant reality of Black life in the name of ascertaining the "facts." As for Du Bois, earlier in his career he too had come to believe that it was time for Black people to rely less on spiritual intuition and emotionalism in determining reality and more on an objective appraisal of the facts. However, one day as he was walking the streets of Atlanta he saw on display in the window of a downtown grocery store the knuckles of a

Black lynching victim and he had a change of mind. In 1968 Du Bois wrote in his autobiography, "one could not be a calm, cool and detached scientist while Negroes were lynched, murdered and starved" (p. 222).

CHAPTER EIGHT
Early Black Female Social Workers, Spirituality, and Fictive Kinship

Early Black female social workers, like their male counterparts, came on the historical scene in the era of the "New Negro." Alain Locke (1925), the chief spokesperson, said that the New Negro resented "being spoken of as a social ward or minor, ... as a chronic patient for the sociological clinic, the sick man of American democracy" (p. 11). The New Negro, he said, was no longer "something to be argued about, condemned or defended, to be 'kept down,' or 'in his place,' or patronized, a social bogey or a social burden" (Locke, 1925, p. 3). The turn of the 20th century was not just the era of the New Negro in general but also a long-awaited hour of the New Negro woman. Early Black female social workers no longer wanted to be patronized and kept down. They wanted to make their own place in the world.

Historically, Black women had always been in the forefront of Black caregiving and the uplift cause. They almost single-handedly undertook the burden of caring for the sick, the elderly, the infirm, the orphaned, the mentally ill, the children, the men, the entire Black community, and a great portion of the White community as well. Being largely responsible for holding individuals, families, and communities together, they, more than anybody else, suffered the shocks, strains, and traumas of separation and loss from both natural and human causes. They, more than anybody else, felt a need to dig deep into the spiritual reservoir of their heritage, to call forth sacred powers within to deal with the hardships and the uncertainties of being Black women in a society that subordinated women and hated Black people. They, more than anybody, believed that they could call on other Black women for nurturing, strength, understanding, support, and confirmation when they could call on nobody else. They could reach out to each other in the cabins, the fields, the kitchens, the churches, and all the other sacred spaces in which Black women carried out the work of mourning and administered the work of healing.

Black female social workers were given Black middle-class status because they emerged during the New Negro Era typically better educated than the masses of Black women and they had professional roles. However, these women were not concerned with middle-class lives devoted to individualistic pursuits, conspicuous consumption, and putting as much social distance between themselves and the masses as possible. According to Locke, they were also even more radical and race conscious than the old race work leaders. They were influenced not so much by the Social Gospel Movement, the Social Settlement Movement, and Christian Socialism as their male counterparts were. Rather, their influences were the Harlem Renaissance Movement, the Garvey Movement, Pan Africanism, and radical Marxism, which were gaining in popularity during the time. Locke (1925) wrote:

> Some of the recognized Negro leaders and a powerful section of [W]hite opinion identified with "race work" of the older order have indeed attempted to discount this feeling as a "passing phase," an attack of "race nerves" so to speak, an "aftermath of the war," and the like. It has not abated, however, if we are to gauge by … those of the independent, popular, and often radical type who are unmistakable symptoms of a new order … the American mind must reckon with a fundamentally changed Negro. (p. 8)

The New Negro female social workers were on a mission to reach across class and status lines. They did not want to form a "Talented Tenth" seeking to lift up less fortunate Black women. They wanted to form fictive kinship ties with them and organize them around their common interests, with the objective of breaking down barriers that thwarted their full development as women.

In our previous work on the Black helping tradition, we defined fictive kinship as "the caregiving and mutual-aid relationship among non-related Blacks that exists because of their common ancestry, history, and social plight" (J. M. Martin & Martin, 1985, p. 5). We saw fictive kinship as the primary device for enlarging social relationships among Black people. Early Black female social workers also wanted to form fictive kinship with other Black women on the basis of spiritual bonds. It was not just common history and common suffering that brought New Negro female social workers in contact with their sisters only a generation or so removed from slavery. It was also common spiritual strivings to break from old oppressive gender barriers and become a mass, potent, radical force for communal action and social change. The fictive kinship bonds they forged as they sought to move an entire people forward represented the highest expression of the spiritual, racial, and communal selves.

The focus of this chapter is on four Black female social workers who came into prominence during the era of the New Negro (roughly 1900–1935) and carried social work from The Great Depression to the end of World War II. These pioneering Black female social workers were S. Willie Layten, Maymie De Mena, Eva Bowles, and Thyra J. Edwards. All of these women, with the exception of De Mena, had professional training in social work and all, with the exception of Edwards, sought to blend spirituality, race work, and social work. Layten, like Ransom, Wright, Jr., Haynes, and Work—her male counterparts—wanted to use spirituality and social work to expand the Black church's social service/social change function. However, unlike her male counterparts, a chief problem confronting her in the Black church was Black male patriarchy, which enjoyed a long history of relegating Black women to the fringes of influence or closing the door to female power altogether. Bowles, like these early Black male social workers, wanted to use spirituality and social work to promote cultural diversity and interracial cooperation. However, unlike them, the biggest obstacles to achieving these objectives were White Christian women who used their power to keep Black women subordinated. De Mena had to struggle with Black male chauvinism in the world's largest Black organization, Marcus Garvey's Universal Negro Improvement Association (UNIA). No Black organization before or since carried Ethiopianism further than the UNIA. De Mena blended social work techniques with Ethiopianism to empower Black women and to keep a virtually bankrupt UNIA alive during the Great Depression. Edwards somewhat represented a departure from both spirituality and race work. Although there is no indication that she relinquished the spiritual influences of her upbringing, the dominant influence on her social work practice was socialism. She sought basically to organize and empower Black women not so much on the basis of racial affinity but on the basis of their class interest with working-class women of the world, regardless of color.

None of these early Black female social workers were mainstream social workers. Each stood on the fringes of mainstream social work practice of the time. For example, although these Black female social workers all were willing to work with and even within the National Urban League, the leading mainstream Black social work agency during the New Negro Era, none of them elected to move in its Black bourgeoisie direction. Mainstream Black social work was holding the notion that the race problem would be solved after Black people threw off the yoke of servility, took on bourgeoisie mannerisms, treaded through the baptismal waters of Victorian morality, and trained for industrial employment and inclusion. Layten, De Mena, Bowles, and Edwards were militant Black barrier breakers seeking to merge the spiritual, communal, racial, and destinal selves. These pioneering Black female social work activists sought to blend spirituality, race work, social work, and the new radicalism of their time in an attempt to work with Black women as sisters in finding a sense of place and space in the religious, racial, interracial, and international community. They did not want to become a social burden or be defended. Instead, they wanted to organize as a power base along spiritual lines so they could defend themselves and be a social asset to their families and communities.

SARAH WILLIE LAYTEN AND THE RELIGIOUS COMMUNITY

S. Willie Layten was "born in the Church," as Black people used to say. Her father, William H. Phillips, was a prominent Black Baptist minister, and Layten became active in the church at an early age. Born in Memphis, Tennessee, in 1863, Layten graduated from Lemoyne College in Memphis in 1881. Being very close to her family, she followed them from Tennessee to Arkansas where she got married. In 1882, she and her husband moved to Los Angeles, California, where Layten taught in the public schools and became active in the Black women's club movement. She also began work with Black Baptist women that sought to advance their status in the Black Baptist Church. In 1894, Layten left her husband in California and she and her daughter followed Layten's parents to Philadelphia, Pennsylvania. In Philadelphia, she decided to pursue her interest in integrating social work with church work. There, she took courses in social work at the University of Pennsylvania and graduate courses in sociology at Temple University. Layten had already gained a prominent reputation as an effective leader with great organizational skills. When she was elected as the first president of the Woman's Convention (WC), she was already noted for her work that advanced Black women in a church hierarchy dominated by Black male ministers and deacons. The Woman's Convention was formed in 1900 as a woman's auxiliary of the powerful National Baptist Convention.

With Layten in charge, the Woman's Convention gave itself the task of making an entrenched Black male patriarchy more receptive to the needs of Black women and more responsive to Black women's demands for expanded leadership roles and equality in the Black Baptist church community. To fulfill this grand quest to challenge Black male hegemony and to empower Black women, Layten formed fictive kinship ties with some of the most talented Black women of her day. She shared leadership responsibilities with such strong Black females as Virginia Broughton, a progressive Black activist, Mary Cook, a feminist theologian, and Nannie Helen Burroughs, a radical womanist educator. Layten and these women also formed fictive kinship with Black female ancestors such as Maria Stewart, Jarena Lee, Julia Foote, and many other Black women in the 19th century who took the Black church to task for seeking to relegate Black women to singing, praying, and preparing Sunday dinners while denying them the right to teach, preach, vote, and otherwise have a voice in determining the direction of the Black Baptist church.

Broughton, a graduate from Fisk University in May 1875, had encountered the conservative, anti-feminist Black Baptist church hierarchy long before becoming the recording secretary of the Woman's Convention. In 1907, she called this hierarchy the "cruel warfare" that was waged against Black women who sought empowerment and leadership in the male-dominated Black Baptist church (Broughton, 1907, p. 31). Broughton (1907) wrote in her autobiography that "the large majority of men really believed the [woman's] work unlawful and forbidden by the Scriptures" (p. 29). She said that Black ministers, deacons, laymen, and even husbands were jealous of the popularity of the woman's work in the church and disdainful and insensitive to any criticism that came from a woman. Broughton (1907) said, "as if there was some cause of alarm for the safety of their own positions of power and honor, all rose up in their churches, with all the influence and power of speech they could summon to oppose the woman's work and break it up if possible" (pp. 34–35).

Cook, who had graduated in 1887 as valedictorian of her class from the State University in Louisville, challenged any religious instructions that sought to justify the subordination of Black women in the church on biblical grounds. In 1887, Cook asked, "Should woman be silent in this busy, restless world of missions and vast church enterprises?" (Cook, 1887/1998, p. 676). Her answer was a resounding "No!" Cook was of the belief that "all good causes owe their success to the push of women. Therefore,

Cook (1887/1998) believed that the woman's place was "in all places where human souls are found," including in the pulpit (Foner & Branham, 1998).

Burroughs, the corresponding secretary of the Woman's Convention, was one of its most powerful and eloquent spokespersons. She waged a relentless, scathing attack on Black male patriarchy. She believed that ministers who sought to keep women from being equal partners in the church's destiny and ministers who maintained a parasitical rather than a helping relationship with the struggling Black masses should not be allowed to stay in the Black community. In 1927 she told Black audiences that they needed to "chloroform" their Uncle Toms, "whether they are in the church as preacher, in the school as the teacher, in the ward as politician" (Lerner, 1972). She worked indefatigably for the Woman's Convention. Burroughs said that in her first year in office she "labored 365 days, traveled 22,125 miles, delivered 215 speeches, organized 12 societies, wrote 9,235 letters, and received 4,820 letters" on behalf of the Woman's Convention (Higginbotham, 1993, p. 158). In 1909, Burrough's workload for the Woman's Convention increased as she founded and headed the Woman Convention's National Training School of Women and Girls, located in Washington, DC.

Layten, Broughton, Cook, Burroughs, and other Black women formed such a tight-knit spiritual sisterhood with such a fervent belief in the divinity of their mission that it was virtually impossible for Black male opposition in the Black Baptist church to divide and conquer them. While they were under the auspices of the National Baptist Convention and supported its programs, they demanded a high degree of autonomy and self-determination. These women demanded autonomy, including the rights to exclusive control over their own finances and programs. Despite minor differences among themselves, they stood as one in the face of opposition and in respect to major decisions. So strong were their loyalties to one another and so enduring was their commitment to a common cause that 20 years after the Woman's Convention came into existence, it still had its same leaders guiding it with Layten still as vice president, Sylvia Bryant still as first vice president-at-large, Broughton still the recording secretary, and Burroughs still the corresponding secretary (Higginbotham, 1993, p. 157).

Inspired by the motto "The World for Christ. Women Arise. He Calleth Thee," Woman's Convention leadership headed by Layten worked with zeal to recruit members, and their hard work and relentless dedication bore fruit. The Woman's Convention sought to organize Black women around their needs, to help them to become activists, participants, and doers in regard to their own well-being. The Woman's Convention undertook the task of recruiting thousands of unknown, unmotivated Black women who were lacking in confidence and race consciousness and transforming them into agents of social change, forces to be reckoned with in their own local communities. Therefore, the Woman's Convention tackled practically every conceivable problem and issue imaginable pertaining to the Black woman, her family, and her community. It specialized in Black health care, child welfare, prison reform, recreation, housing, nutrition, and education. Seven years after its inception, the Woman's Convention represented nearly 1.5 million Black women, with branches and membership in every state in the Union. Even the most recalcitrant Black minister had to be pleased with the number of new members these women were bringing into the Black Baptist church denomination.

The Woman's Convention leaders called on the promising but newly formed profession called social work to help them fulfill their mission and to give a scientific basis for their church work. Layten and other leaders of the Woman's Convention advocated "practical Christianity" and, like Black male social workers such as Ransom, Wright, Haynes, and Work, strongly believed that the Black church needed to broaden its social service function. Higginbotham (1993) stated that the Woman's Convention leadership strongly denounced "churches that refused to include social salvation in the program of saving souls" (p. 178). Under Layten's leadership, the Woman's Convention encouraged Black women to get professional training in social work and to pursue social work as a profession. Under her leadership, the Woman's Convention used every opportunity to expose its members to social work practice by bringing in social workers, Black and White, to lecture and conduct seminars at its annual conferences. The Woman's Convention created its own settlement house in Washington, DC, and placed it under the direction of M. Helen Adams, a trained professional social worker. It established its own Social Science Department that was designed to gather information and vital statistics on infant mortality rates, the prevalence of sexually transmitted disease, the extent of housing over-crowdedness, nutritional needs, and other social welfare concerns of Black people.

The Woman's Convention also worked closely with outside secular social service organizations. Layten took a personal interest in working with the White social worker, Florence Kellor, in Kellor's National League for the

Protection of Colored Women (NLPCW). This organization sought to carry on the work started in the late 19th century by Victoria Earle Matthews, the cofounder in 1896 of the National Association of Colored Women. Matthews had sought to wage war against the vicious employment agents who waited at piers, bus stations, and train depots to prey on Black Southern migrant girls, promising these girls room, board, and employment while in actuality feeding them to big-city prostitution rings. In 1897 Matthews established a settlement house called the White Rose Mission to provide lodging, social services, job training, and employment for the Black girls who had migrated from the South to New York City. Layten and Kellor sought to do on a national level what Matthews had done in the New York City area. Layten's Woman's Convention members met these girls in New York, Philadelphia, Baltimore, Boston, Memphis, Norfolk, Richmond, and Washington, DC. In their work with these girls, Layten and the Woman's Convention made a distinction between "rescue" and "prevention" social work. "Rescue social work" was designed to aid people already in distress, while the much-preferred "prevention social work" was geared toward striking at the root structural cause of social problems so as to prevent them before they became symptomatic and malignant (Higginbotham, 1993, p. 176). In 1911, the National League for the Protection of Colored Women joined with the Committee on Urban Conditions and the Committee for Improving the Industrial Conditions of Negroes in New York to form the National League on Urban Conditions Among Negroes (NLUCAN). This organization would later become the National Urban League. Layten was one of the founders of the National Urban League and served as one of its first field secretaries.

Layten and the Woman's Convention gave priority to social work concerns but also sought political reform. Layten wanted the Black church to mobilize the Black migrants for political action. Layten herself was appointed during the 1920s by the National Republican Committee of Pennsylvania to organize Black women in her state, and Burroughs became head of the National League of Republican Colored Women (Higginbotham, 1993, p. 227). In 1913, the Woman's Convention issued its own seven-point political manifesto calling for decent housing, the right to vote, the end of lynching, and other citizenship rights.

Higginbotham (1993) stated that the preoccupation of Layten and other Woman's Convention members with secular social work and political reform should not distort the fact that spirituality was still the preeminent factor in these women's lives. Burroughs (1927/1972) spoke the sentiment of her sisters in struggle when she said that it is "the internals and eternals, rather than the externals" that are important and that "what the race needs are mental and spiritual giants who are aflame with a purpose … for a conquest not of things, but of spirit." Burroughs, Layten, and other leaders of the Woman's Convention, like race work leaders of the 19th century, believed that the greatest gift Black people had was the gift of the spirit. Taking a stance held by Ransom, Wright, Haynes, and other race work male social workers, Burroughs, as spokesperson of the Woman's Convention in 1927 wrote that, "it will profit the Negro nothing if he enters into ungodly competition for material possessions when he has gifts of greater value. The most valuable contribution which he can make to American civilization must be made out of his spiritual endowment …. I believe it is the Negro's sacred duty to spiritualize American life" (Burroughs, 1927/1972, p. 551). Such beliefs were the dominant motivating force behind the race work of Layten as she led the Woman's Convention.

Seeking to create a glorified Black womanhood and believing that Black people must develop their spiritual gifts, Layten and her Woman's Convention members openly and freely expressed their religious fervor. Higginbotham said that their meetings were filled with praying, testifying, singing spirituals, and shouting even as they took care of secular concerns around the material well-being of Black people (Higginbotham, 1993, p. 277). Just as in traditional Africa, these Black women believed that one's spiritual life and material well-being should go hand-in-hand, that the sacred and the profane worlds were inseparable.

EVA DEL VAKIO BOWLES AND THE
INTERRACIAL CHRISTIAN COMMUNITY

While S. Willie Layten fought against Black male chauvinism within the Black church to give Black women a sense of community, Eva Bowles, born in Ohio in 1875, worked to give Black women a greater sense of place and space within the segregated Young Women's Christian Association (YWCA). Bowles had taken an interest in YWCA work through her friendship with Addie Hynton, the wife of William A. Hynton, who was a Black social worker hired in 1889 as the first Black secretary of the Young Men's Christian Association (YMCA). While working on a degree in social work at the Columbia University School of Philanthropy, Bowles began work in 1905 as the secretary of Colored Young Women's Christian Associations in New York City. With this position she became the first Black YWCA secretary. Under her leadership, the Colored Branch of the YWCA located in Harlem became the largest Black YWCA branch in America. After leaving her YWCA post in New York to serve as the first Black caseworker for the Associated Charities in Columbia, Ohio, Bowles was asked to return to New York to become the National Secretary of the Bureau of Colored Work for the National Board of the YWCA. This position put Bowles in charge of all of the YWCA's Black girls and Black women on a national level. Bowles sought to use her position to make the YWCA a pioneer in interracial experimentation. In 1920, Bowles stated: "I believe that the YWCA has a great share in proving that democracy is not a failure and that Christianity is not a mockery" (p. 484). Bowles was concerned about the extent of the racism within the YWCA in regard to the "colored" branches. These branches were controlled and governed by local White officials of segregated YWCAs. While Black women could not join YWCAs with White members, they also were forbidden to form independent branches without the permission of White women at field headquarters. White women selected the leader of the colored YWCA branches and directed their activities. Black women were not given decision-making authority within the YWCA leadership hierarchy, and independent Black branches suffered an inequality of resources. Moreover, in the national annual meetings of YWCA officials and members, White women, particularly those in the South, refused to meet with Black officials and members. Bowles believed there was no way for these White women to have an understanding of Black women and their problems, given the social distance between the two races, and that therefore there was no way for them to appreciate Black womanhood and to demonstrate a sincere commitment to advancing their interests. In 1920, Bowles asked, "Is this fair—is this Christian? Is this as Christ would have it?" (p. 482).

Bowles believed that her mission was to put more Black women in positions of authority, to create more independent Black YWCA branches with Black women in full charge, and to promote interracial cooperation. It was only when Black women operated with White women on an equal basis that such cooperation between the races could become a reality. Bowles acknowledged that to some extent her quest to form more independent

Black YWĆA branches and her desire to promote interracial cooperation were contradictory. She knew that the colored branches of the YWCA were created in the first place to keep Black women from seeking membership in White YWCAs. She believed that if the Black, segregated branches were to exist, Black women should at least direct and control them without first having to consult with "their [W]hite overseers associated with the [W]hite branches" (Bowles, 1920, p. 424). She also believed that colored people were their own best interpreters and could best articulate their own needs. Overall, Bowles thought that her best strategy for accomplishing the goal of interracial cooperation was to form fictive kinship ties with other Black women around the country and build a Black woman's power group within the YWCA, whose voice would be too strong to be silenced or ignored. In 1920, Bowles stated, "I am, with faith in God and my colored women, willing to help bring about the real association spirit in action as well as words" (Bowles, 1920, p. 480).

Through Bowles's tireless effort, effective leadership, and fictive kinship ties to Black women, she was able to open up independent, largely Black-controlled YWCA branches across America. She fought bitterly with the National Board of the YWCA to have the colored branches report directly to the National Bureau of Colored Work, her office in New York, instead of reporting to the local White YWCA officials who tended to treat Black women with White paternalism, disrespect, and outright racist contempt. Bowles was so successful in working with her Black sisters around the country that in 1917 she was appointed the Director of the Colored Work Committee of the YWCA's War Work Council. The Colored War Work Council was appropriated $200,000 to improve the recreational opportunities of Black girls entering the war industry for the first time and to provide places of recreation and entertainment for Black World War I troops. To accomplish this vast undertaking, Bowles employed a number of impressive locally and nationally recognized Black club women. Together these Black women under Bowles's leadership established 16 hostess houses in various Army camps across the nation to entertain Black troops and set up recreational and industrial training centers in 45 cities. Also, working with Black women across the nation, Bowles was able to increase colored branches from 16 in 1915 to 49 in 1920, to increase the paid local Black YWCA staff from nine to 86, and to increase the national YWCA from one national secretary to 12. President Theodore Roosevelt was so impressed with the magnitude and quality of Bowles's war work that he designated $4,000 of his Nobel Peace Prize award to the colored work of the YWCA to be disbursed as she pleased.

After the war ended, Bowles used the strength of Black YWCA membership to press for more equitable representation in YWCA local and national wards and communities and to tackle the sensitive issue of interracial cooperation. Bowles believed that Black women and White women in the YWCA had to find ways to come together to work on common projects. She was successful in orchestrating group discussions among Black women and White women in the North, but in the South, even after the war had been fought allegedly to preserve freedom and democracy, "race fraternization" was illegal in the Southern states and in some cases was a lynching offense. Black women and White women in the YWCA could not even sit together in conventions, stay in the same hotels, or ride in the same box cars.

In trying to break down the segregated practices of southern YWCAs, Bowles worked closely with her friend, Lugenia Burns Hope, a Black social worker who had created Atlanta's Neighborhood Union. In their correspondence with one another, Bowles and Hope would often trade war stories about their fight for interracial cooperation in the YWCA movement and the price both of them were paying psychologically in this war. For example, in 1920, Bowles had written Hope that, "our colored secretaries from headquarters must no longer be excluded from Southern soil. We have no desire of pushing things any faster than communities will allow but we do have resources and knowledge of things that will be helpful and that are necessary to ideal growth. We have no fair way of being interpreted unless the women themselves know us" (Bowles, 1920, p. 480). In one letter to Eva Bowles, Hope expressed the amount of hostility she had had to endure for suggesting that White women, as long as they were prejudiced toward Black people, could not possibly be fully committed to the highest development of Black girls. Hope wrote:

I am just as much interested as ever in YWCA work for colored girls and women and if you should not find me working in the cause it would be either because some people would not permit me or I could not accept some obviously unChristian and retarding ways of doing things.... The downright unGodly way in which they sought to carry their point and discredit an unselfish colored woman [myself, I mean]. (cited in Rose, 1989, p. 106)

Bowles never could accept the reality that people calling themselves Christians could so easily take on the arrogant myth of White superiority. The constant battle with White YWCA officials began to take a toll on her physical and emotional health. She said, "Few people can realize what it means to live a racial life and at the same time to be 'forevermore' realizing you are an interracial problem" (Bowles, 1920, p. 487). In 1931, the YWCA struck another blow to her emotional health when it summarily dismantled the Council of Colored Work as an administrative entity. Bowles and her supporters first hailed this as a major victory, a giant step toward including Black women in all areas of YWCA leadership and policy making on a nonsegregated basis. However, in 1932, when the YWCA national board presented its reorganization plan, Bowles could see clearly that this plan would not make White and Black women partners and equals in working together to secure a future for women and girls of all colors. The reorganization plan instead would diminish "the participation of Negroes in policy-making" and leadership roles. Seeing the erosion of gains she had painstakingly devoted her life to achieving, Bowles resigned her post in protest after having served the YWCA for years. After her resignation, Bowles became a political organizer and the executive director of the National Colored Merchants Association. On June 14, 1943, she died of cancer without having seen her dream fulfilled of an interracial community truly working in the name of Jesus Christ.

MAYMIE LEONA TURPEAU DE MENA AND THE RACIAL COMMUNITY

Maymie De Mena (also known as Madame De Mena) was born in 1891 in San Carlos, Nicaragua. She joined Marcus Garvey's Universal Negro Improvement Association (UNIA) in 1925 when it was in disarray because of the incarceration of its leader earlier that year and an internal struggle for power. In his heyday between 1914 and 1921, Garvey had organized an estimated 4 million Black people worldwide under the banner of "One God, One Aim, One Destiny." By the time De Mena became a member, the UNIA had more than 800 chapters in 40 countries. Garvey appealed to the deep need in Black people for race pride, group solidarity, African identity, and a sense of community. Based on the ideology of Ethiopianism, a call for Black economic self-sufficiency, and a cry for the liberation and redemption of Africa, the Garvey Movement took center stage on four continents. By the time De Mena came on board as a lecturer and organizer, Garvey followers were badly splintered, disillusioned, and dispirited. Garvey was serving time in the Atlanta penitentiary for mail fraud, and a petite Black bourgeoisie who had joined the UNIA for pecuniary gains was trying to take over the finances and holdings of the organization and take control from Garvey. Garvey, impressed by De Mena's intelligence, zeal, and bilingual skills, appointed her an organizer with the chief duty of traveling around the country as an assistant to Garvey's wife, Amy Jacques Garvey, who was desperately trying to keep her husband's dream of a redeemed Africa alive.

De Mena and Amy Jacques Garvey formed a tight-knit fictive kinship bond. De Mena also made sure that her daughter, Berniza De Mena, was part of the Garvey fictive extended family. Traveling with Amy Jacques Garvey, De Mena was tutored in the trials, tribulations, pride, and glory of the Garvey Movement. With the incarceration of her husband, Amy Jacques Garvey had come from under the shadow of her husband and was adopting a stance calling for the inclusion of women that the patriarchal authority of Garvey would never sanction. Although Marcus Garvey had placed Henrietta Vinton Davis, Amy Jacques Garvey, and a few other women in leadership positions, he basically believed that women operated best when under male authority, leadership, and guidance. Amy Jacques Garvey had believed all along that, "The Negro woman is the backbone of the race" (cited in Adler, 1996, p. 20). She had been a personal witness to all the work women had done in the Universal Negro Improvement Association as they served in the Black Cross Nurse Corp and other women's auxiliaries responsible for launching numerous social and recreational programs for the organization. She had also been a witness to the fact that the labors of women in the UNIA had largely gone unrewarded, unrecognized, and unappreciated.

With Marcus Garvey incarcerated, Amy Jacques Garvey began to express more openly her criticism of Black men, charging that, "The doom of the race lies in the lethargy of its men." Amy Jacques Garvey warned Black men to "be honest enough to admit your laziness" and to stop "your whinings and 'can't be done moans.'" She had come to believe that one day women will rule men and "that the world will then be a better place in which to live" (cited in Adler, 1996, p. 21). She believed that because women in their maternal roles were self-sacrificing and well-trained to serve others and to subordinate their own feelings for the common good, they have "a purifying effect on politics" (cited in Adler, 1996, p. 18). With Garvey's imprisonment, Amy Jacques Garvey wrote: "We serve notice on our men that Negro women will demand equal opportunity to fill any position in the Universal Negro Improvement Association or anywhere else without discrimination because of sex." She said to UNIA men that "we are very sorry if it hurts your old-fashioned tyrannical feelings," but warned that "we not only make the demand but we intend to enforce it" (Garvey, cited in White, 1999, p. 138). Amy Jacques Garvey was charged with the responsibility of keeping the Garvey Movement together during its most turbulent hours.

De Mena first came into contact with the UNIA when she served as a Spanish translator aboard Garvey's SS General Coathals when the ship was on its ill-fated Caribbean tour. Although many Black people believed that Garvey and his organization had come to an end, De Mena became an ardent believer in Garvey and his doctrine and came to America to see what she could do to save him and the UNIA. Although Garvey had given De Mena the duty of traveling around the country as an assistant to Amy Jacques Garvey, so much talk was made of this "small woman, about ninety pounds, with a voice of thunder" who was said to have "electrified" audiences in Chicago, Detroit, Cleveland, Richmond, and Washington, DC, that Garvey sent her out on her own to infuse life into his moribund organization (Smith-Irvin, 1989, p. 60). She also proved effective as a fund-raiser. Garvey appointed her to be an assistant international organizer and sent her on a tour of Central America and the Caribbean to rally his troops and to consolidate his power abroad. Her pay was $25 a week.

After Garvey was released in 1927 and deported to Jamaica, De Mena became the driving force behind organizing the 1919 UNIA Convention held in Kingston. She herself created quite a storm when she led the parade on horseback, brandishing a sword as if she were a Black Joan of Arc. During the convention, De Mena became the mastermind behind changing the name of the organization to the Universal Negro Improvement Association of the World. This move freed Garvey from many of the lawsuits against the Universal Negro Improvement Association in the United States and left his opponents to fight one another over what flesh had not already been picked from its bones. Garvey rewarded De Mena for her service to the cause by appointing her as the Officer-in-Charge of the American field which meant he was literally putting her at the head of all his branches in the United States. As Officer-in-Charge, De Mena decided to follow the lead of Amy Jacques Garvey and seek to organize the UNIA women into a positive force for change. Her position was not an enviable one because the UNIA divisions in the United States were in a state of disarray and she was literally sent by Garvey to save his organization with the Great Depression coming. Also, she was literally on her own because Amy Jacques Garvey, her mentor, had followed her husband to Jamaica and would later follow him to England. De Mena believed that it was only by working with the UNIA women that she could salvage what was left of the UNIA in the United States. She knew that women formed a large percentage of the membership of the UNIA and believed it was time for them to take charge. She said, "For seven years we have been lauding our men through the press, on the platform, and, in fact from every angle while in reality the backbone and sinew of the Universal Negro Improvement Association has been and is the real women of the organization." De Mena wrote, "There are scores of women workers, full of zeal, courage and initiative scattered throughout ... who are capable of rendering greater service to the race if placed in higher positions" (cited in White, 1999, p. 137). She warned men that doors that were once closed against women in the UNIA would be open and that under her leadership there would be "election and appointment of more women to the executive offices than heretofore" (cited in White, 1999, p. 138). By calling for the empowerment and leadership of Black women, De Mena and Amy Jacques Garvey were, in effect, calling for revolutionary changes within the organization that Marcus Garvey at the height of his power would not have approved.

De Mena knew that many of the Black women in the UNIA had not simply joined the organization to pursue abstract ideas and principles calling for Africa's rebirth. They joined because the UNIA was like a social center, an extended family, a place where they could develop fictive kinship ties with Black women, establish intimate bonds with men, and have a place to bring their children. Most importantly, the UNIA was a deeply religious and spiritual organization. It operated around the biblical statement in Psalms 68:31: "Princes shall come forth from Egypt; Ethiopia shall soon stretch forth her hands to God." Garvey himself wrote that "we believe in the God of Ethiopia" (cited in Burkett, 1978, p. 34).

Although it claimed to be basically a secular, international organization which had among its goals to administer and assist the needy and to conduct a worldwide commercial enterprise and intercourse for the good of Black people everywhere on the globe, some scholars believed that Garveyism was essentially a religious movement. Burkett (1978) made a case that Garvey's main goal was to create and institutionalize "a civil religion" and that Garveyism was able to strike deep roots in Black communities primarily because it was firmly grounded in Afro-American religious tradition. Frazier (1926) wrote, "Garvey who was well-acquainted with the tremendous influence of religion in the life of the Negro proved himself matchless in assimilating his own program to the religious experience of the Negro" (p. 148). James Weldon Johnson (1968) wrote that "the movement became more than a movement, it became a religion. Its members became zealots" (p. 255).

Whether a religious organization or not, the UNIA was operated much like a Black church with sacred music, prayers, testimonies, and with Garvey himself often using the vocabulary of Black religion and confessing that "I wish I could convert the world of Negroes overnight to the tremendous possibilities of the Universal Negro Improvement Association .... I have contributed my bit to preaching this doctrine" (cited in Burkett, 1978, p. 24). As one Garvey member said:

My mother carried all of the girls into the UNIA so I was a member at a very young age. I grew up in the organization. We had to go whether we wanted to or not .... Instead of going to church on Sunday, we would get up early and go to the Detroit division of the UNIA, diligently every Sunday. (Smith-Irvin, 1989, p. 59)

Garvey's "church" preached that it was sound mental health for Black people to believe in a Black God. Also, like race men and race women of the 19th century, Garvey sought to organize Black people around the idea of divine mission or providential design. Moses (1989) wrote:

The idea of institutionalizing the Kingdom of Christ within the context of a worldly empire was certainly not a new idea to Black Americans. Garvey's brand of Christian imperialism made it possible for Blacks, who had always felt somewhat threatened by the mainstream concept of Manifest Destiny, to participate in one of the most virile of American traditions. Every Garveyite could be a Christian soldier, assured of the righteousness of his cause and of his leadership in a specially favored race.

The idea that Africans were a specially favored race had, of course, been well-developed in the writings of 19th century Black religious thinking. (p. 138)

De Mena, faced with saving a moribund organization in the face of the nation's worst economic depression, put a softer touch on the idea of divine mission to redeem Africa. Her chief concern was with organizing Garvey's chaotic, antagonistic, and scattered forces. She mixed religion and race pride with the aim of rallying Garvey's badly battered troops. In 1931, she said, "We should religiously emulate the gift of God through his son Jesus ... by helping those among us who are less fortunate; by measuring the lives of others intelligently and generously—then we can exemplify the fatherhood of God and the brotherhood of man (cited in Barbour & Strong, 1981). De Mena preached to Black people that they should demonstrate Black love through unity and service. She said, "Without love the world is a very dreary place to live in, thus the security of a nation, individual or race is the full consciousness of his service to his neighbor" (cited in Barbour & Strong, 1981). Garvey had had visions of Black people becoming millionaires and acquiring royal status in a glorious African empire. De Mena was seeking to get Garvey's followers to define their worth and status in terms of race coop-eration and of being of service to others instead of in terms of financial wealth or royal status. She was faced with the same problem many race work leaders were confronted with during the dreary years of so-called recon-struction—how to keep hope alive in a people when the objective reality shows no reason to hope. De Mena sought to fight the skepticism that was keeping Black people from cooperating in the service of one another. She wrote "It is true that there are many of us whose minds are still small; it is true that we are very skeptical, because of living in an age of skepticism, but the time has come when we must spring this big surprise on the world, and this can be done by our wholehearted cooperation in the future (cited in Barbour & Strong, 1981).

De Mena understood that in organizing women for leadership, empow-erment, and change, she would have to concentrate her energies on meet-ing the day-to-day practical needs of UNIA members and focus less on global concerns. Therefore, De Mena relied heavily on social work as a tool to bring more social service programs into the UNIA to help its members overcome the Great Depression. De Mena fashioned herself into a social worker and she was one in every sense of the word. However, her area of social work specialization was not Freudian psychology, which many social workers were utilizing. After feeling overwhelmed by the Great Depression, many social workers, Black and White, had retreated from social reform and social action and started entertaining notions not of freeing people collectively suffering oppression but of freeing individuals one at a time from their neuroses. De Mena's area of specialization was community organization, which would not take solid root in social work until the 1960s. In seeking to organize Black people into a racial community, to give them a sense of belonging and purpose during an economically dreary period in history, De Mena often differed from Garvey. Garvey had favored the petite bourgeoisie over the proletarian class, believing that the masses needed the guidance of a Black aristocracy. De Mena sought to organize the rank-and-file members; she believed the foot soldiers of the UNIA were capable of uplifting themselves after they became conscious of their own worth and power. Although Garvey had had a magnetic effect on his followers, he tended to be autocratic and aloof. Garvey believed in a hierarchical chain-of-command, proper protocol, and deference to authority. One of his followers said that "whenever he asked something of you, you automatically found yourself saying 'yes sir!'" (Smith-Irvin, 1989, p. 69). Another said, "I never made personal contact with Mr. Garvey .... He could not talk to anybody unless he was strictly business" (Smith-Irvin, 1989, p. 60).

De Mena sought to meet as many UNIA members as she could on a face-to-face, informal basis to show them that the UNIA leadership took a personal interest in them and their needs. As she traveled around the country, De Mena formed fictive kinship ties with Ruth Smith, who became her travel companion. Smith had been in the Garvey Movement since she was a child. Although she had never held any administrative or leadership position in the Garvey Movement, De Mena hired Smith as her driver and secretary as she traveled around the country to resolve conflicts in the UNIA divisions. Smith said: "It was always a struggle for power. In those days, men would come into the UNIA to obstruct us. They were looking for money" (Smith-Irvin, 1989, p. 60). Despite the opposition and even the threats on her life, De Mena became very adept at resolving tension within UNIA divisions and was often lauded for her achievements in this area. For example, the following report from the Detroit division, one of the largest and most potentially explosive divisions in the UNIA of the World, is typical of the praise De Mena received for her organizational ability and conflict resolution skills:

Last Sunday, November 22, another soul-stripping meeting was held and there is not the least doubt that Madame De Mena has got all the factions together …. This getting together required a great deal of diplomacy and tact, not to mention hard work, on the part of Madame De Mena. She had her work cut out, but this fearless woman, despite the many threats to get her if she ever came to Detroit, not only came but she has got the people together, all difficulties straightened out so far, and a new organization erected on the old. (Barbour & Strong, 1981, p. 1)

The report further stated that:

Under God and Garvey; under the diplomacy and headwork of De Mena plus the active support of the membership it won't be long before the colors of the Red, Black and Green of the UNIA of the World will again take their rightful place in the sun. (Barbour & Strong, 1981, p. 1)

Not only was De Mena adept in resolving conflict and kicking "the self-seekers" out of the organization, but she was also skilled in forming new divisions. For example, one report announced:

The New Orleans Division and the South in general has had a reawakening in the UNIA on the occasion of the visit of the international organizer, Madame M.L.T. De Mena. During her visit many members have come into the organization. Forty-two have been added to the New Orleans Division, while the divisions visited by her—Alabama, Louisiana, Mississippi, and Texas—have equally been blessed. The people have very little or no money at all, but their spirit of loyalty to Hon. Marcus Garvey and the UNIA have not wavered. (Muse, 1931, p. 3)

De Mena proved to be such an adept leader, she was being heralded as "The Voice of Garvey." She was also respected because she was receptive to the economic troubles UNIA members were suffering. Although she saw to it that the divisions paid their dues to the national headquarters, she allowed whatever other money the divisions raised to be used to meet their own needs. In the glory days of the UNIA, Garvey had made sure that all his leaders and workers on the UNIA payroll were well paid. He had hoped that decent salaries would reduce the temptation to steal from the organization's coffers. The division leaders under De Mena worked largely without pay. As for De Mena herself, Smith said, "Madame De Mena and I were paid a subsistence for what we did, and if we were in a place and they could not raise enough money to send us to another place, we had to wait until they raised the money" (Smith-Irvin, 1989, p. 60).

Working closely with the women in the organization, De Mena knew that she was working with the most skilled Black caregivers and organizers in the Black community. By forming fictive kinship bonds with Black women, De Mena managed to keep new UNIA of the World divisions sprouting up everywhere despite severe economic hardship. De Mena had not only managed to stir the Garvey Movement through the Great Depression, but in fact helped it to grow. She wrote in a 1932 editorial to *The New World*, the UNIA's chief news organ:

> Through the fightings within and without, we have surmounted the many difficulties that faced us when we took charge of the field in June, 1930. Many new divisions have been added to our number; many sleeping ones have been awakened, and notwithstanding the terrible financial depression in our country at this time. (De Mena, 1932, p. 1)

De Mena sought to consolidate her hard-fought gains by encouraging members to hold on to the principles and dignity of the organization, to stay in the fight, and to endure to the end. Despite economic hardship, she managed to raise enough money to create Liberty University to prepare the future leadership of the UNIA of the World. She believed that the future of the UNIA of the World would be ensured by preparing a strong, race-conscious, communally oriented, young Black leadership that worked on the basis of gender equality.

After guiding the UNIA safely through the Great Depression years, seeing its membership and divisions grow, empowering its women, and making sure she had prepared future leaders to take it over, De Mena during the latter part of the 1930s followed her husband, Percival Aiken, also an active Garveyite, to his home in Kingston, Jamaica. While she was in Jamaica she continued her work as a social worker and was active in local charities, women's groups, and political organizations. She became the owner-editor of *The Ethiopian World* and with a few other prominent Jamaican women formed the Women's Liberal Club, once again forming fictive kinship ties with her sisters for the purpose of being agents of social change. Ford-Smith (1991) wrote:

> The Women's Liberal Club was to become the feminist organization which had the most impact on the lives of Black women of the middle strata. It could not have done so without the organizational experience of the UNIA .... Madame De Mena's experience as an orator and as an elegant, well-known example of the gracious, beautiful Garveyite woman was an essential element in attracting to the women's movement the approval of those who had supported the work of the UNIA. (p. 81)

While in Jamaica, De Mena continued her activity in the Harmony Division of the UNIA in Kingston. Even after Garvey's death in 1940, she remained active in the UNIA until her own death in 1953.

THYRA J. EDWARDS AND THE INTERNATIONAL COMMUNITY

Thyra J. Edwards, born in 1897, sought to find places for Black women in the international community. After receiving training in social work at the Chicago School of Civics and Philanthropy, Edwards pursued her interest in child welfare and took various social work positions working with children, culminating in the founding of her own children's home. Edwards also pursued her interest in labor relations by taking courses at Brockwood Labor College in New Jersey. Becoming increasingly disillusioned with how child welfare was handled in America, Edwards, through the help of A. Philip Randolph, the leader of the Brotherhood of Sleeping Car Porters, received a fellowship in 1931 from the American Federation of Labor (AFL) to study child welfare legislation, industrial relations, and other areas for six months at the International People's College in Elsinore, Denmark. After completing her courses, Edwards spent an additional six months touring England, Sweden, Finland, Russia, Austria, Germany, and France. Edwards took a lifelong interest in the plight of oppressed working-class people of the world and would spend the rest of her professional life integrating social work and international affairs.

Edwards was particularly interested in the plight of the darker people of the world and believed that Black Americans needed to develop a global outlook so they could see what they had in common with other oppressed people of color. While abroad, Edwards further developed a global perspective of child welfare and the plight of women. She could see how the feminization of poverty, the vicious exploitation of women as workers, and the general abuse and neglect of women affected the welfare of the world's children. She was aware that the general abuse and neglect of women under the patriarchal hegemony occurred globally while men prepared for war and sought even greater dominion over the earth. Edwards returned to America with a burning desire to mobilize Black women and to link their struggle in America to the progressive struggles of oppressed women of the world.

She became a labor organizer for the International Ladies Garment Workers Union, an affiliate of the American Federation of Labor. As a labor organizer, Edwards led the struggle to unionize the largest employer of Black women in the garment industry in Chicago, the Ben J. Sopkins Apron Factory. Edwards wrote that she was appalled at how easily Mr. Ben J. Sopkins was able to bring an Uncle Tom Black leadership in to convince the garment workers that they should be loyal and thankful to Mr. Sopkins and to show not even the slightest sign of protest over their low wages and working conditions. In 1935 Edwards said that "caught between the nether stones of unscrupulous employers and uninformed and unscrupulous race leaders," it was difficult to organize "the great uniformed mass of unskilled labor" (p. 82). However, she believed that if Black people did not become a part of the labor movement, they would always be subordinate.

During the Great Depression, Edwards combined her work as a labor organizer with relief work, serving as an assistant district administrator of the Chicago Relief Association. She believed that the areas that impacted most on the quality of women's and children's lives were their employment and economic circumstances. She urged social workers who were down in the trenches with the poor to combat the stereotypes fanned by right-wing politicians that held that Black people would rather seek a handout and live off the public dole than work (Edwards, 1936, p. 214). She urged social workers to become advocates for the poor and fight for equity and fairness in the allocation and disbursement of funds for direct and work relief in Chicago and other Black communities. She also advocated that social workers themselves should become unionized and should even rank close with communist and other leftist groups leading the fight for unionism and the struggle against the eviction of poor tenants who were unable to pay rent.

When Edwards became a social worker and live-in resident of the Abraham Lincoln Centre, a Black progressive settlement house, she had the freedom to fulfill her mission of raising the global consciousness of Black people, especially Black women. She organized what she called "travel seminars," taking Black groups of college students, teachers, social workers, labor union members, ministers, and so forth on tours of France, Italy, Belgium, Denmark, Austria, Germany, Russia, Switzerland, Sweden, Finland, and England. The main purpose of her tours was to expose African Americans to the most progressive, militant, left-wing scholars, political activists, students, women, and leaders of the world so they would have some understanding of the international connection of the Black struggle in America. Edwards's tours became so popular that she added Mexico, working with her fictive sister, Doris Wooten Wesley. She believed that Black people in America should have close political ties to Mexico, Haiti, the Virgin Islands, Hawaii, the Philippines, and Puerto Rico because people in these countries were all the oppressed colonial subjects of the United States of America.

While conducting travel seminars, Edwards also worked as a foreign correspondent. She was a good friend of Claude Barnett, the founder of the Associated Negro Press, and most of her articles were sent to him. Being one of the most traveled women in America, Black or White, she also wrote stories for *The Chicago Defender, The Soviet Russia Today, The Women Today* (a U.S. trade union magazine), and The Federated Press (the news service bureau for American labor). During her travels, Edwards was deeply disturbed by the rise of fascism and the evil portends it had for the colored people of the world, and her stories to the international press reflected this concern.

Edwards got her chance to personally fight against fascism when the Civil War broke out in Spain in 1936. She and other progressive Black leaders such as Paul Robeson, Mary McLeod Bethune, A. Philip Randolph, Richard Wright, Adam Clayton Powell, Sr., Langston Hughes, William Pickens, and others started a fund-raising drive in America to purchase a fully equipped ambulance to be donated to the Spanish Republic Army locked in deadly conflict with the fascist Spanish forces led by Franco. With the untiring work of Edwards and the Black nurse, Salaria Lee, not only was the group able to raise the money but Edwards, Lee, and Constance Kyle, a White Chicago social worker, personally delivered the ambulance to Spain under the auspices of the Social Worker's Committee to Aid Spanish Democracy. Edwards was driven by the belief that whenever and wherever Black people fought against oppression in the world they were advancing their own freedom. Amid the air raids, the bombings, and the constant shelling, Edwards, Kyle, and Lee stayed in Spain. Lee set up a nursing unit and Edwards worked tirelessly setting up homes and relief stations for the thousands of homeless children in the colonies. She also set up psychiatric units to deal with the psychological and emotional effects of war on children, probably making her one of the first social workers to treat war trauma in children.

After the bitter, bloody, Spanish Civil War ended and the fascist forces were victorious, Edwards shifted battle grounds to another front. She went to Mexico and used her contacts there to set up the Spanish Relief Campaign, which helped more than 40,000 Spanish refugees gain political asylum and resettle in Mexico.

Once back on American soil, she continued her work on behalf of women and children. She became the chairperson of the women's section of the left-wing National Negro Congress and the executive director of the Congress of American Women, an interracial women's organization. Edwards also managed to maintain a grueling schedule lecturing and conducting seminars around the country for the Foundation of Religion and Labor, an organization calling for religion and labor to close ranks in the proletarian class struggle for equality, social justice, and democracy.

Edwards's work for the Foundation of Religion and Labor indicates that she was comfortable with blending her religious faith and her militant left-wing ideas. Although she herself was brought up in the Wesleyan Methodist tradition, she maintained associations with radical left-wing groups throughout her adult life. Moses (1982) stated that even radical Black Marxists (which Edwards denied she was when questioned by a committee of the House on Un-American Activities) often "made use of Christian rhetoric and preacherly style in their efforts to mobilize popular support" (p. 13). He said that the "Marxist concept of history" and the "Christian concepts of providence" have particular appeal to many leftist-oriented Black people because "both envision a millennium in which the righteous, clean-living faithful will triumph over the sybaritic denizens of Babylon" (Moses, 1982, p. 13). For example, Paul Robeson, who was brutally hounded for his leftist leanings, sang the spirituals all over the world, including communist countries such as Russia, to inspire workers of all colors to keep up their fight against capitalist exploitation and imperialist domination. Edwards's exposure to different brands of leftist political thought—social democracy in Sweden, Fabian socialism in Great Britain, fascism in Germany, and communism in Russia—pushed her deeper into the radical, leftist, socialist camp. Within the purview of both her religious upbringing and her role as a leftist fellow traveler, her great interest was in forming solidarity with the women of the world. She was strongly of the belief that class-conscious women were more concerned with the plight of the world's children than were fascist-minded men, and that the welfare of women and the welfare of children were interrelated. She not only saw the proletarian class as the vanguard for bringing about the worldwide socialist revolution but saw Black women, most of whom were highly religious, as playing a special role in this regard.

At the end of World War II, Edwards served on an international committee that investigated postwar conditions of women and children in Germany. In 1945, she married Murray Gitlin, an official of the United Jewish Appeal, and followed him to Rome in the late 1940s after he became director of the Italian branch of the American Joint Distribution Committee. While in Italy, Edwards organized the first Jewish child care program in Rome to assist Jewish children who had been victims of the Holocaust (Ades, 1953). Being a Black American woman dealing with children suffering from war trauma in Spain and working with young survivors of the Holocaust in Italy was consistent with her work as a pioneer and founder of international social work practice.

CONCLUSION

Layten, Bowles, De Mena, and Edwards sought to harness the spiritual energies of Black women and make them a potent force for social change. Their strong sense of commitment, their high level of energy and vitality, their indefatigable work habits, their strong belief in Black people, and their faith in a higher calling made them women who were truly on a mission. In pursuing their mission, these Black women became social work pioneers, using social work as a tool to work out their visions of a better world. Layten was combating male patriarchy and asserting feminist rights at a time when women social workers more or less were taking male hegemony and women's subordination for granted. Bowles was fighting for cultural diversity, multiculturalism, and interracial cooperation at a time when these areas were anathematized by social work practice. De Mena was shaping community organization skills decades before community organizing was seen as a legitimate social work role. International social work was largely pioneered by Edwards's efforts.

These social work pioneers were not without opposition. Collectively, they were up against conservative Black preachers and laymen, employment agency racketeers, White paternalism, a petite Black bourgeoisie class that sought to fleece the masses, fascist exterminators, unscrupulous employers, Uncle Tom Black leadership, and street predators. However, they were not without strength and power against the opposition. Their strength and power came from their spirituality, the spiritual bonds they had forged with other women based on shared assumptions, mutual values, participatory relationships, common suffering, and subordination. They were true "womanists" in the sense that that concept is used by dynamic Black womanhood today. Similar to womanist thinkers and change agents today, these women were able to draw from the past experiences of Black women and reach across class, religious, and racial lines to link oppressed women into a vast intersubjective network that would transform them from victims to agents of change. Inspired by the quest for a better world and a desire for creating community, these women were joined together by a sense of the sacred, a shared consciousness of a nonmaterial, transcendent, and inspired vision that would lift up the spirit of Black women so they could grow in the direction of their own choosing, feed the children of the world, and free the minds of men.

The central question of this work is: What are the implications of Black spirituality for social work today? The purpose of this chapter is to discuss the questions social workers must ask, the assumptions they must make, and the issues they must consider to incorporate Black spirituality into the assessment and intervention process of modern mainstream social work. However, it is first appropriate to reiterate themes throughout this work that are suitable for developing an assessment and intervention framework based on spirituality in the Black helping tradition. It is also appropriate to reiterate themes that tie in historically to the mainstreaming of Black social workers and their turning away from spirituality as a core social work concern.

A REASSESSMENT

The most important theme weaving its way throughout this work is that the Black helping tradition is solidly rooted and grounded in spirituality. We have seen that Black spirituality is so integrated with religiosity that it is difficult to distinguish between the two. Spirituality, communal solidarity, and racial uplift are so intertwined that they are in fact inseparable.

In traditional Africa we saw that the ultimate goal of the traditional African helper was to promote group solidarity; to connect alienated, deviant strands of Black humanity to the group; to maintain a harmonious interplay between the spiritual, the communal, and the destinal selves; and to use this connectedness as the pathway to compassion and caring. We saw that in connecting individuals and groups to a complex spiritual universe and linking them to community, traditional African helping practitioners had to be steeped in their people's history, life, and culture and have a thorough, specialized knowledge of the ways of nature. As Armah (1978) explained, "The healer walks through the same world every person walks through. But he sees signs others don't see. He hears sounds others don't hear" (p. 80). On the slave plantation, we found the healer reappearing in the role of "the conjurer," who gave his oppressed people some feeling of predictability, a belief that their lives were not totally controlled by fate, and an idea that their status was not forever fixed. He brought back to them an African worldview where the forces of nature could be harnessed and the sting could be taken out of the wrath and power of their oppressors. We saw that even after enslaved Africans adopted Christianity, they continued throughout their enslavement to rely on conjure, amulets, charms, dreams, signs, spirit possessions, and other forms of their traditional African spiritual worldview.

We saw on the plantation that when enslaved Africans "turned to Jesus" they found solace in forming a relationship to a God, whom they felt recognized them personally, tended to their day-to-day needs, and moved through human history on their behalf. Enslaved Africans found heroes and heroines in the Holy Bible just as they once had in their own mythical and historical ancestors and gods, and they found in Jesus Christ a wise, loving, and caring ancestor.

We saw that although the slave preacher was put in a position where he often had to wear the mask, he still sought to help his people "make a way out of no way," and inspire his people with visions of "a great gittin up mornin."

Sadly, we also saw that in White religious mythmaking, imagery, and symbolism, Blackness itself had come to represent all that is evil, crude, sinful, and immoral, and that Whiteness had come to represent the contrast conception of Blackness. We saw that even after many enslaved Africans had undergone a life-changing religious conversion, they could not break the religious stranglehold their masters had over their minds. We saw that before they could fully connect their personal interest to the general well-being of their people, they had to adopt the idea that "no religion but that which brings us liberty will we know; no God but He who owns us as his children will we serve" (Delaney, 1861/1970, p. 258).

We saw that in the free Black community, former slaves and slave fugitives inspired Black people born into freedom to devote their lives to "race work." We saw that through race work, free Black people built churches that functioned not only to give them spiritual sustenance but that also served as a social center; a social, therapeutic, and support network; an institution of social control; and an agency of social service. We saw that through their race work, free Black people created quasi-religious African freedom societies that not only took care of orphans, old people, and widows and helped the indigent to bury their dead, but also organized Black people so they could air their grievances, debate their destiny, fight against their enslavement and third-class citizenship, and boycott slave-made products. We saw that the race work of free Black people was guided by a powerful social myth of "Ethiopianism" which cut across all the major race work ideologies of the time to make race men and race women feel that they were copartners with God in the fulfillment of a divine plan.

We saw how W. E. B. Du Bois and his mentor, Alexander Crummell, had given scholarly shape, focus, and coherence to the race work ideology and carried race work ideas of mutuality, teleological optimism, destiny, agency, social debt, and divine gifts over into the budding profession of social work. We saw how early male social workers used Du Bois's and Crummell's mixed bag of race, theology, and sociology to strengthen the service component of the Black church, to build Black moral character, to foster interracial cooperation, and to point out the contradiction between racial, gender, and class oppression in a society professing democratic and Judeo-Christian beliefs. Furthermore, we saw leading Black female social workers that sought to combine spirituality, race work, and class solidarity in their efforts to form fictive kinship with oppressed Black women; break down gender barriers; find Black women their rightful place in the religious, racial, interracial, and international community; and move Black women from the lowly status of victims to the lofty status of agents of social change and the architects of their own destiny.

With this brief reassessment and reiteration of major points highlighted throughout this book, we can now move forward to discuss the mainstreaming of Black social work and the implications of this for spirituality in the Black helping tradition.

THE MAINSTREAMING OF BLACK SOCIAL WORK

The Great Depression of the 1930s took a toll on traditional Black social work practice; by the end of World War II, many Black social workers had moved from blending race work, communal, and spiritual values into their social work practice and had moved into mainstream social work. By "mainstream social work" we mean social work that is sanctioned and legitimized by the status quo. Although there were mainstream Black social workers at the turn of the 20th century, as exemplified by National Urban League social workers, there was a serious strain of Black social work that was largely oppositional social work or social work that operated on the margins. By the end of World War II, this oppositional or marginal strain had almost completely disappeared as Black social workers found considerably more government employment open to them.

Before the Great Depression Black social workers had secured employment in the National Urban League, the Charity Organization Society (which hired its first Black social worker, Jessie Sleet, as a case worker in 1900), the Young Men's Christian Association, the Young Women's Christian Association, Associated Charities, Juvenile and Women's courts, reform schools, orphanages, old age homes, day nurseries, community service agencies, child welfare organizations, Travelers' Aid Societies, playground associations, schools, churches, labor unions, interracial cooperation councils, and Black settlement houses. These workplaces gave them wide latitude in expressing spiritual values, and because Black social workers generally were restricted to working with Black clients only, it also gave them broad opportunity to express race work ideas concerning race unity, race uplift, and collective responsibility. Because the Great Depression almost completely demolished the Black private social welfare sector (the Black settlement houses, the Black orphanages, the Black reform schools, the Black old folks' homes, the Black hospitals, and so forth) many Black social workers had little choice but to work for the government's New Deal administration or leave the profession of social work altogether.

During and after World War II, Black social workers found employment, first as relief workers under New Deal relief programs and later as case workers dishing out the welfare dole to Black recipients of Aid to Dependent Children. These government welfare jobs left little room for Black social workers to express themselves spiritually, racially, or communally. Segregated government jobs in Public Welfare Departments in big cities across America required Black social workers to strictly carry out public welfare policy as written. The bureaucratic roles they played left little room for creativity, imagination, and vision. Absolutely no room was left for radical or militant social activism, race unity, or collective uplift, especially because powerful White politicians were on the prowl with J. Edgar Hoover of the Federal Bureau of Investigation (FBI) to ferret out "red" and "communist agitators" in any collective movement, Black or White, calling for the radical transformation of society. As Black social workers (like social workers in general) became more entrenched in the courts, the police departments, the prison systems, the juvenile detention centers, the state mental institutions, and the public welfare agencies, they also became a more legitimate arm of the repressive machinery of the state (Martin & Martin, 1995). The more they became entrenched, the less they could talk about cultivating the special "gifts" of Black people and moving a hopeful, rising, advancing people toward the fulfillment of a divine mission. The more entrenched they became, the more they began to see their people through the eyes of their White counterparts and bosses. Many of those Black social workers who were brought up in the old race work tradition of Du Bois and who had trouble adjusting to social work as a state sanctioned arm of repression, social containment, punishment, and social control, left social work to become full-time ministers, particularly those who already had theological leanings. Many of those leaning toward sociology gave up social work to become full-time sociologists at Black colleges and universities. Many with radical proclivities left social work to become full-fledged members of communist and socialist organizations. For example, Louise Patterson, who had attended graduate school at the New School for Social Work in New York City, never graduated because she said, "After interning in a charitable organization, I knew I did not want to become a social worker. I was sent to see a psychiatrist because I refused to spy on a client" (Benjamin, 2000, p. 32). After the psychiatrist concluded that Patterson was the sanest person that she had seen in a long time, Patterson gave up social work and joined the Communist Party because it allowed her to express radical desires for militant social activism and social change. Many of those Black social workers who did not leave the profession altogether found themselves working in the "Negro divisions," some as "Negro advisors," of President Roosevelt's Administration. This was about as mainstream as Black social workers could get.

So many Black social workers and other Black professionals had moved in a mainstream direction and away from the radical, militant oppositional stance of the race men and race women of the old days that Du Bois was beginning to seriously question his concept of the "Talented Tenth." He was gravely concerned that Black leadership was in the hands of "a new Negro bourgeoisie" who were aping "the worst of American and Anglo-Saxon chauvinism, luxury, showing-off and 'social climbing'" and who were showing "no arousing care" as to what happened to the masses of Black people (Weinberg, 1970, p. 153). Du Bois was particularly disturbed that his Talented Tenth Black people were beginning to lose faith in "the cultural ability or gifts of Negroes and have no hope nor wish that the mass of Negroes can be raised even as far as the mass of [W]hites" (Weinberg, 1970, p. 190).

Losing faith in the transformative powers of social work, seeing for the first time the limitations of social work in reforming the social structure, and experiencing a keen sense of powerlessness and social impotency, Black social workers began to impose their own bourgeoisie outlook on the impoverished Black masses. They began to give up their roles of advocates and social activists, allowing reactionary politicians to go without a whimper of protest as they used poor people as scapegoats, castigated them as immoral and unambitious, and viciously pursued social welfare policies designed to control, repress, and contain (J. M. Martin & Martin, 1985).

Not all of Black society in the midst of Depression and war gave up the race work tradition. Many Black churches continued to call themselves "race churches" and, led by social workers, stepped up social service activities to meet the massive needs imposed by the Great Depression. Also, many Black civic organizations nationwide operated out of the old race work framework as they fought for social justice and the redistribution of the wealth. Drake and Cayton (1945) said that even when these Black civic groups rarely recorded actual gains, the very activity of fighting in the cause of Black uplift served to bolster the morale and stave off the immobilizing attitudes of alienation, defeatism, and despair (p. 742). However, despite some lingering vestiges of race work and Black life, Black social workers, seeing the massive material suffering of their people, began to lose faith in a spiritual approach. Black social workers, seeing huge numbers of Black people in bread lines and soup lines and foraging city garbage bins for food, began to lose faith in cultivating the divine gifts of the Black masses. They settled for not uplifting Black people on the whole but for rescuing them one Black person at a time; not organizing them in battle for social change but helping them to become better adjusted to their oppression; not freeing them from their poverty and second-class citizenship, but freeing them from their neuroses and psychoses. After Black social workers had reached this level of accommodation, appeasement, and compromise, their mainstreaming was virtually complete.

A FRAMEWORK FOR INCORPORATING
BLACK SPIRITUALITY INTO SOCIAL WORK

The key question before us is: Because Black social work has undergone a vigorous mainstreaming process that has moved away from the old race work spiritual base, how can Black spirituality be incorporated into main-stream social work today? We seek to address this question by creating a theoretical framework drawn from the Black helping tradition. This framework for incorporating Black spirituality and social work focuses on the following crucial areas:

- Scope of the Problem
- Rationale
- Principles
- Ethics
- Assessment
- Intervention
- Desired Outcomes
- Research
- Preparation.

SCOPE OF THE PROBLEM

Black Americans today are among the first African people historically who do not operate from a spiritual frame of reference, one of the few Black generations without a spiritual social myth to guide, inspire, and sustain them, and the first to approach a new century without a spiritual anchor in deeply troubled waters. Black Americans today, to a large extent, are spiritually decentered. By that, we mean that for a large number of Black people, Black youths in particular, spirituality is no longer the dominant motivating force in their lives, the core value upon which their chief moral decisions and critical life choices are based, and the controlling axis around which their lives evolve. Black American life is largely spiritually out of balance, off-center (decentered), and the result has been moral ambivalence and behavioral incongruence. This is, in other words, spiritual fragmentation. Spiritual fragmentation is the incongruence between one's personal, moral, religious, and spiritual beliefs and his or her social acts and communal obligations.

When Black people are spiritually centered, their spiritual lives are in congruence with their culture. If their culture is a caring, empathic culture, then their spiritual lives and behavior will be a reflection of their culture and vice versa. As Figure 3 shows, when Black people are spiritually centered there is a balance between spirituality and culture.

Figure 3: Spiritual Centeredness

Culture

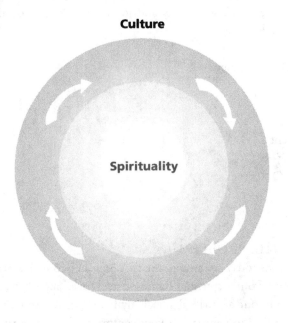

Spirituality

Because spirituality is so grounded in Black culture, spiritual fragmentation also means culture fragmentation. When spirituality is divorced from Black culture, Black people suffer not only spiritual fragmentation but also spiritual alienation. For example, we once attended a rap concert where a popular Black rap artist was singing/rapping his hits. One minute the rap artist would sing about his God's love for all humankind, the next few minutes he would sing about the impact of Malcolm X, and in the next song he started singing about stinking, no-good Black "whores." He had grasped bits and pieces of Black spirituality and Black culture, but he was not spiritually centered, spiritually focused, or spiritually grounded in his culture enough to be spiritually and morally consistent. As Figure 4 shows, spiritual fragmentation takes place when spirituality (represented by the letter "s") and culture (represented by the letter "c") are decentered and out of harmony and form fragments and pieces that are difficult for moral behavior to grasp.

Figure 4: Spiritual Fragmentation

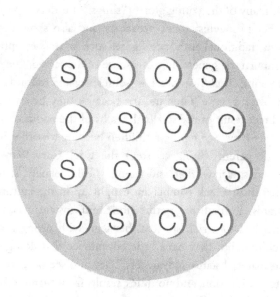

West (1993) believed that Black communities today are plagued by "a pervasive spiritual impoverishment," as indicated by "a collapse of meaning in life," an "eclipse of hope and the absence of love of self and others," "a breakdown of family and neighborhood bonds," and a plethora of "rootless, dangling people with little lines to supportive networks" (p. 5). These are also the results of spiritual fragmentation as spirituality becomes divorced from a caring culture. To speak of a collapse of meaning, an eclipse of hope, an absence of love, the breakdown of neighborhood bonds, and the erosion of supportive networks is to suggest that at some time in history, Black people were driven by a strong sense of purpose, inspired by hope, nurtured by love, and supported by strong communal bonds. It is to suggest that when Black people are spiritually fragmented, they have trouble grasping even bits of spirituality and the pieces of Black culture that they need to sustain meaningful lives.

We stated in the introductory chapter that contemporary Black elders are concerned about the violence among Black youths, the cheapness in which many of them regard human life, their excessive hedonism, their gross materialism, their lack of spiritual concern, and their seduction to decadence. Young Black people with their individualistic "me first" attitudes over the "we first" strategies are deviating from ancient Black ways. The elders are disturbed that many of the young glorify "thugs," "hustlers," "players," "gangsters," and other misogynist street predators, and also show disrespect and disdain towards traditional authority figures such as teachers, preachers, and elders. They mourn the general loss of a sense of the sacred. They mourn the thousands of young Black lives taken so senselessly and callously by so many other young Black people. They mourn because they believe the physical deaths are a direct result of the spiritual deaths of thousands of young Black people on a daily basis. Seeing their children heading toward spiritual death, what are Black parents doing to stem the tide? Gary Ware (2000), an African-centered social worker and mental health expert, stated that the problem is that most Black parents are caught up in the culture that seeks material rewards, immediate gratification, and instant results. They do connect themselves to a rich spiritual heritage with strong roots in Black history and culture, but they have little confidence that doing so will gain their children material status and success. They also see no extrinsic reward, no immediate gratification, and no quick results from turning their children into their spiritual selves. They will not saturate their children with spiritual race work values designed to give them dignity, purpose, identity, and hope because the rewards for doing so are intrinsic and the payoff might be farther down the road. Moreover, the payoff might not be in terms of material status and success but as a commitment to caring and an obligation to repay a social debt.

If the Black community has moved largely away from its spiritual base and if Black parents see no extrinsic, immediate reward in instilling spiritual values, then what must be done by social workers? Given that scholars and the elders are talking about spiritual alienation, spiritual impoverishment, spiritual fragmentation, and spiritual death among Black people, what can social workers today do to address these spiritual concerns? What can social workers do to connect Black people to the ethics of caring that gave Black people in the past a sense of social purpose and a positive sense of racial identity? What are social workers doing in the area of Black spirituality today?

Although social work started out with strong roots in Judeo-Christian principles, it later was guided by an overriding Freudian perspective that convinced social workers that religious or spiritual propensity was a neurotic defense mechanism, an illusory escape from reality, a regression to an infantile state, and a shameless display of primitive, regressive, magical, and archaic thinking. Even those social workers taking a behavioral perspective saw religion as no more than a conditioned response, a biological drive, an environmental stimulus, or a reflex reaction. Today there is a resurgence of spirituality in social work. Social work literature having a spiritual perspective is growing in scope, volume, and magnitude. Social workers have discovered that spirituality is very often the core reality around which people center their lives, that their clients' religio-spiritual orientation could be linked to their presenting a problem or disturbance, and that their clients' spirituality can be used as a resource for coping, healing, and effecting change.

All of this applies to clients in general. However, Black spirituality presents a particular problem to mainstream social work primarily because it is so inextricably connected to racial consciousness and communal solidarity. Black spirituality cannot be studied in a historical vacuum. It must be examined within the historical, experiential context that has given rise to its development. Like Black caregivers and Black social workers of the past, modern day social workers must come to see spirituality as strength in the lives of Black people.

The problem with incorporating Black spirituality into mainstream social work is that many social workers would rather deny the existence of race altogether than deal with this hypersensitive issue (Pinderhughes, 1989). This may explain why the growing body of social work literature on spirituality has largely neglected the growing body of Black literature on spirituality as evidenced in Black liberation theology literature (Cone, 1990; Wilmore, 1998), African-centered literature (Akbar, 1984; Kambon, 1998; Nobles, 1986; Schiele, 2000), and womanist literature (Cannon, 1988; Grant, 1989; Riggs, 1995; Sanders, 1994; Townes, 1994; D. Williams, 1993). Although racism has been deliberate, systematic, and continuous, giving Black people no reprieve, no breathing room, and keeping them constantly in the storm, even leading social work scholars often show great confusion regarding racial matters. For example, one social work scholar who stated he had found racism in 1972 claimed that the civil rights legislation of the 1960s and 1970s had effectively rid the country of racism by 1995. When he "rediscovered" racism in 1997 he posed something as ridiculous as amalgamation as the chief solution (Anda, 1997; Longres, 1973/1995). The key questions, of course, are: What happened to racism between 1972 and the New Millennium? Did White people lose their position of dominance and authority in America? Did their white skin confer upon them less privilege? Did American institutions and authority structures become less racist and more open to Black people and other so-called minority groups? Did White families stop instilling in their children that they were superior to Black people? Did the media stop characterizing Black people in negative ways? Did the passage of a civil rights bill mean that racism was changed in people's hearts, their consciousness, and their value system? Did the situation between Black people and White people so radically change between 1972 and the turn of the 21st century that Black people should rejoice? The answer to each of these questions, of course, is an emphatic "No"!

When social workers pretend "color-blindness," or operate from a belief that race should not even be considered as a critical factor in working with Black clients, they are denying a significant part of their Black clients' reality (McRoy, 1990). This much we can say categorically: Social workers cannot be confused about race and still expect to understand Black spirituality. To be confused about race matters is to be unclear whether Black people's spiritual and religious worldview is a source of support, a source of pain, or sometimes both. To be confused about race matters is not to see the role racism has played in the spiritual fragmentation of Black people. Racism is designed to throw Black people spiritually off-center. Racist religious myths were used to drive Black religious and spiritual content to the limit while racist religious thinking gained center stage in the minds and souls of Black people. Black people, we have indicated, sought to create a counter social myth just to maintain spiritual balance, to keep from teetering off-center.

To deny the racial reality of Black life is also to fail to see that spirituality in the Black helping tradition was never separated from a communalistic perspective or collectivist approach. The chief goals of Black spirituality are to develop community, to connect disorganized aggregates to the corporate body, and to commit the individual to the welfare of the group. For example, poverty and other social tensions have often so overwhelmed and clouded Black spirituality that Black people have sometimes lost sight of the strength of their inner spiritual core. In situations such as these, the Black helping tradition turns to social support to help individuals regain some sense of their own spiritual strength and to give them an emphatic environment where they can incorporate and feed off of the spiritual strength of others. This has been a source of collective therapy that has made the Black church the leading Black caregiving institution, second only to the Black extended family. Social work that has moved markedly in a psychotherapeutic direction at the expense of establishing community-based care (Specht & Courtney, 1994) might have difficulty grasping this fact of Black life.

To show the extent to which social work itself is a part of the problem, we found in an informal survey of the Baltimore, Maryland community that nearly all of the mainstream social work programs for Black youths avoided completely the issue of race, spirituality, and communal or collective strategies. The programs included the Police Athletic League, a Job Corps program, juvenile detention centers, youth residential centers, mentoring programs, and public school social work programs. Practically all of these programs were located outside of the Black community and were administered by White helping professionals with a few Black helping professionals on board. None of these programs focused on immersing these youths in their history, values, and culture. For example, although the federally funded Job Corp programs had 500 Black students and taught these students different trades and offered them courses that led to their obtaining General Equivalency Diplomas, they offered not one course on Black history, Black art, or Black culture. Apparently such emphasis on Blackness made White helping professionals uncomfortable and maybe even threatened. Apparently, too, they believed it was unimportant to help these young people come to grips with what it means to be Black in America.

We also found that none of these mainstream White social work agencies sought to saturate Black youths with Black values. These youths were not being instilled with a sense of social obligation even though many of them had committed antisocial, delinquent, and deviant acts that had alienated them from their communities. Black authority figures such as teachers, religious leaders (such as preachers and imans), social activists, and elderly heads of extended families, who traditionally instilled values and traditions, very seldom had a place in these child welfare agencies and institutions except for maybe being invited for an occasional visit. They were not invited in to instill values geared toward giving the youths a sense of belonging to a community. These youths definitely were not instilled with Black spiritual or religious values despite numerous studies showing that religiosity and spirituality were major determinants in prosocial behavior, productive work, and positive social activities among Black youths (see Hill, 1997, p. 163). They would rather have the Black young people occupying their time playing sports, getting their behavior modified, and having their emotions and actions controlled by drugs than making them aware of their God-given gifts, building off of their spiritual strengths, and giving serious thought to their reason for being God's children.

The helping professionals in those agencies and institutions instilled in Black youths bourgeoisie values that were not much different from the individualistic, materialistic, predatory values that these youths acquired from the mean, big-city streets. They not only sought to impose bourgeoisie values on these poor Black youths, but they were too secularistic to seek to develop in them a spiritual self, too assimilationist and "color-blind" to develop in them a racial self, and too individualistic to develop in them a communal self. Their best hope for these young Black people after leaving their agencies was that they would get a high school education and get a "good job," with a few perhaps going on to college. In the meantime, these youths with no serious connection to their history and ancestry, no sense of a positive race concept, and no sense of communal obligations were expected to behave themselves and to cause as little trouble as possible. All of these agencies working with Black young people seemed to have no understanding that Black youths need to break free from the racist, religious mythmaking today as much as Black people needed to during the days of slavery. Given no sense of divine purpose, calling, or mission and feeling no sense of communal obligation or social debt, it is no wonder that many of these Black young people, particularly those coming out of so-called juvenile and rehabilitation centers, continued to move in a directionless, chaotic, aimless, dead-end direction after they were back on the streets.

What about the Black helping professionals who worked in these child welfare agencies? McRoy (1990) maintained that it is often assumed that Black social workers "are automatically aware of the cultural diversity of Blacks and that they can work with all Black clients" (p. 108). McRoy (1990) acknowledged that it is not unusual for Black social workers to have swallowed wholesale "traditional [W]hite perceptions of the behavior of Blacks" and therefore, "may view Black clients just as stereotypically as some [W]hite therapists" (p. 108). Black social workers in these White-dominated, White-controlled agencies were in a situation that paralleled that of the slave preacher on the slave plantation. Like the slave preacher, they were taught how they were to treat their people by the White people in authority over them. Like the slave preacher they were not to deviate from their White bosses' teachings. Like the slave preacher, they were rewarded or promoted, punished, or demoted according to how consistently they followed White ruling-class policy and ideology. Like the slave preacher, many of these Black helping professionals who worked in White agencies were seeking to maintain peace with their White employers. They were in collusion with their White bosses because they did not want to lose their jobs. Many of these Black social workers did not press for Black youths to become immersed in Black history and culture either. Many of them had also come to feel ill-at-ease with Black history. It conjured up in them images of Black traumas, tragedies, and terrors they wanted to forget. It reminded them of the social debt they still had to pay and the reasons why they were called to social work in the first place. Sadly, many of these Black social workers, like the slave preacher, also had to go through the painful ordeal of wearing the mask. If they did something Black in these agencies they had to do it clandestinely, or in ways that were nonthreatening to the White status quo and definitely in ways that would not incur the wrath of the White people.

RATIONALE

The spiritual impoverishment, spiritual alienation, spiritual fragmentation, and spiritual deaths in the Black community provide a strong rationale for social workers to incorporate Black spirituality into the helping process. Another rationale is that helping professionals must help Black parents understand the long-term benefits and intrinsic rewards of saturating their children with spiritual, culturally based values, and to see that these values are worth pursuing over short-term extrinsic rewards. A major problem, however, as we noted earlier, is that many social workers, Black and White, are still refusing to deal sufficiently with Black spirituality, race, or Black communal obligations and are themselves becoming part of the problem. In the remainder of this chapter, we propose some issues social workers must consider if they are going to become part of the solution and give Black spirituality the treatment it deserves. Of course, the main rationale for incorporating Black spirituality into social work is to better equip social workers for the roles of helping to restore spirituality to its rightful place in the Black community; that is, to make it the potent uplifting force that it was in the lives of Black people in the past.

PRINCIPLES

There are five basic principles social workers must keep in mind as they seek to incorporate Black spirituality into social work practice. Principles are overriding propositions or assumptions that set standards and parameters for thinking about, structuring, and guiding social work practice. Each principle presented here is drawn from the Black helping experience.

- We call the first principle "The Principle of Internal Locus of Control" because it proposes that even when Black people's outer lives are controlled by external oppression, Black people have the space or freedom to control their intrapsychic lives. The Black helping tradition demands that regardless of how circumscribed Black people are politically and economically, they are still responsible for their own moral, intellectual, cultural, and spiritual development.
- The second principle is "The Principle of Personal Responsibility and Collective Reciprocity." This principle states that neither racism nor poverty is an adequate excuse for Black people who do not do all in their power to "look out for one another," particularly to care for the children and to treat caring as a spiritual act.
- The third principle is "The Principle of Social Debt" because it proposes that one way to repay the debt owed to the ancestors for their sacrifices and to repay God for "being good to us" is to help other Black people live and grow in decency, dignity, and self-respect.
- The fourth principle is "The Principle of the Sanctification of Human Life" because it values each human life as sacred and proposes that no problem, no matter how trivial or insignificant, is too small to be given the utmost consideration by the professional helper. In traditional Africa, we pointed out, African helpers believed that even the most trivial problem could be of cosmic significance. African helpers believed that by giving clients so much time and attention, they not only gave their clients an extraordinary value and worth, they also gave themselves a feeling that helping was a sacred enterprise and an ultimate ethical good.
- The fifth principle is "The Principle of a Holistic Approach" because this principle proposes that spirituality is no more the sole domain or exclusive territory of the minister, the rabbi, or the Iman than it is the social worker's and that social workers can no more neglect, ignore, or downplay this significant part of their clients' lives than can the clergy.

ETHICAL CONSIDERATIONS

Social workers can learn much from the Black helping tradition about the ethical considerations they must take into account. First, they can learn that they must be extremely cautious that they are sensitive to their clients' religio-spiritual worldview even when it differs from their own. For example, although Reverdy C. Ransom and R. R. Wright, Jr., were both ministers in the African Methodist Episcopal Church and early pioneering Black social workers, they never turned down Black clients seeking help when they belonged to religious denominations different from their own. In fact, they believed that denominationalism was the chief obstacle to the Black church providing social services to the community on the whole. One cannot imagine Harriet Tubman refusing to lead an enslaved African to freedom just because his or her religious beliefs differed from her own.

Second, social workers can learn that they must make a conscious effort to avoid imposing their own spiritual values or religious beliefs on their clients. For example, S. Willie Layten was a Baptist social worker, but in seeking to form fictive kinship ties with Black women she never sought to persuade, indoctrinate, or coerce Black women to adopt her own Baptist beliefs. Eva Bowles, also an early Black social worker, sought to empower Black women in the Young Women's Christian Association regardless of their religious beliefs and affiliations.

Third, social workers can learn from the Black experience that they must always show respect to their clients' spiritual leaders and never seek to demean them, undermine their credibility, or usurp their authority (Richards & Bergin, 1997, p. 150). Social workers must be aware that in the Black experience, Black people will often turn to their spiritual leaders before they will turn to social workers. Also, it is often necessary for social workers to form collaborative relationships with spiritual and religious leaders in a team effort to solve their clients' problems.

Fourth, the Black helping experience can teach social workers that an ecumenical approach is the most ethical approach to take in dealing with clients from a variety of religious and spiritual backgrounds and lifestyles. A denominational approach may be appropriate if both the social worker and the client share the same denominational background and religious affiliation. However, an ecumenical approach is "one that is appropriate for clients of diverse religious and spiritual beliefs and affiliations" (Richards & Bergin, 1997, p. 191). For example, 19th-century race workers of different ideological stripes often sought to organize Black people to their cause on a nonsectarian basis. For example, Delaney (1861/1970) encouraged his band of fictive Black insurrectionists to say: "Our ceremonies ... are borrowed from no denomination, creed or church; no existing organization, secret, secular, nor religious; but originated by ourselves, adopted to our own condition, circumstances and wants" (p. 258).

Fifth, the Black helping tradition can teach social workers that although Black helpers in the past were careful not to violate their clients' value autonomy and were open to making their own values and beliefs explicit to their clients when appropriate, they did not operate from a value-free or value-neutral stance. It was clear that their value preference was in the direction of promoting altruistic, communally oriented, caregiving values and lifestyles. Early Black caregivers and professional Black helpers had a distinct value bias toward caring and believed that whether one was Buddhist, Muslim, Christian, Jewish, or a practitioner of traditional African religions, the common denominator was the emphasis each placed on human compassion and caring. They clearly believed that some spiritual values and religious beliefs were in the interest of Black people and were not on a personal or a collective level. The early black caregivers and professional black helpers reserved the right to confront their clients on the basis of what they believed to be faulty or pseudo-religious/spiritual values and beliefs or when they thought that their clients' religious beliefs were clearly driven by mental illness. For example, based on the Black experience, social workers should have no more tolerance for clients telling them that they abuse their children or batter their wives because God told them to than early Black caregivers had for Black people who believed that God had made them hewers of wood and drawers of water forever. If early Black caregivers and pioneering social workers sought to impose any values and beliefs on their clients, it was the value of race uplift, race unity, and race identity. Nineteenth-century Black people were saturated with the race uplift value. It was preached in their churches, schools, benevolent societies, and so forth. Through character building, it was to become an integral part of their personality. They clearly believed that social workers should have no more tolerance or respect for some values and beliefs than Harriet Tubman and Frederick Douglass had for Black people who believed that slavery was ordained by God or that God had imposed slavery on Black people as punishment for past sins. To tolerate or to let such faulty religious/spiritual beliefs go unchallenged would be in itself unethical.

ASSESSMENT

When assessing their clients' social functioning, many social workers examine every crucial aspect of their clients' background but their religiosity and spirituality. They look at their personal and family history, their economic and educational status, their physical and cognitive functioning, their social stressors and social supports, and their behavior and conduct, but seldom seek to understand the extent to which religion and spirituality are significant in their clients' lives or even the extent to which religiosity and spirituality may impinge on the problems their clients bring to them. If social workers in the postmodern age are to follow the lead of early Black caregivers and pioneering Black social workers, they will have to consider spirituality as a significant, vital, and crucial part of Black life.

The Black helping tradition suggests that social workers must not only fully see the importance of spirituality in Black life and explore it as a possible resource for meeting needs but must also include religious and spiritual matters in the assessment process. In traditional Africa, native helping specialists assessed all social problems in terms of spiritual causes and spiritual solutions. For example, if a family was experiencing abject poverty and other misfortunes while families around it were thriving, that family was not likely to have its situation assessed in terms of environmental circumstance, fate, personal defects, a culture of poverty, or other familial shortcomings but in terms of disharmonious relationships to an infinitely superior, invisible, spiritual force. Many early Black American caregivers did not conduct a religious history of their Black clients because they generally took their religiosity and spirituality for granted. Social workers today should neither assess all problems in spiritual terms nor take Black religiosity and spirituality for granted.

Social workers today cannot assume that all Black people are religious in the sense of believing in a deity or belonging to a religious institution such as a church, synagogue, or mosque. They cannot even assume that those Black people who are religious are all Christians, even though the great majority of religious-oriented Black people in America adhere to the Christian religions. However, they belong to so many different Christian denominations, sects, and cults that these differences must be also taken into consideration. Black Americans belong to practically every religious faith and belief found on American soil. To name a few, there are Black Buddhists, Shintoists, Confucionists, Yoruba practitioners, and Muslims. The point we are making is that whether or not Black people are religious and whether they are affiliated with one religion or another, social workers should at least approach the topic. Assessing their clients' religious history, background, and worldview will give them a fuller understanding of both their clients and their clients' problems. This means that whether a client is a Black Muslim or Christian, a Rastafarian or a follower of Vodoun, a Yoruba or a Christian fundamentalist, social workers should have a thorough working knowledge of their client's religious affiliation. Mendes (1982) wrote that if helping professionals fail to gain an understanding of their Black clients' religious and spiritual beliefs, values, and lifestyles, they should enlist the help of religious consultants. For example, if a client believes that someone has put an evil spell or "hex" on him or her, the social workers may have to call on the expertise of someone knowledgeable about such matters and the rituals for combating the evil influence.

While social workers cannot assume that all Black people are religious, they are on safer ground if they assume that in the African sense it is difficult for even the most nonreligious Black person to be totally devoid of spirituality. While spirituality may not be in the blood or the genetic make-up of Black people, it has long and deep roots in the culture and history of Black people, and it is defined so broadly in the traditional African experience and in the African American helping tradition that it embraces most, if not all, Black people.

In the Black helping tradition, spirituality refers to more than just those transcendent experiences of oneness with God, nature, or the universe, more than just the existential probing of the meaning of life, death, good, and evil. Spirituality in the Black experience involves having a communally oriented, caregiving sense of destiny, purpose, and mission; having a hopeful, positive, optimistic outlook on life even in the midst of oppression and despair; feeling a warm, emphatic sense of group belonging; experiencing an inner sense of responsibility for self and others; feeling a core sense of peace within oneself; experiencing an unshakable feeling of self-confidence, human dignity, and self-worth; having a cool head and a warm heart; having a powerful sense of inner self-control; experiencing a keen sense of the sacredness of life; feeling that families are sacred, elders are sacred, children are sacred, parents are sacred, and that Black life in general is sacred. Spirituality in the Black experience also involves reaching one's God-given potential, and realizing one's God-given talents and "gifts"; feeling a strong kinship relationship with the ancestors; feeling a sense of oneness with one's history and culture; believing that anger toward one's people, particularly hidden anger, is an evil that must be expulgated; and believing that hatred toward one's people is hatred toward oneself.

As we said earlier, because Black spirituality is inseparable from racial and communal connections, Black people historically and traditionally could hardly perceive that a person may not have a spiritual self. One's spirituality may be weak, hidden deep in the inner recesses of his or her being, overwhelmed by all manner of strains and stresses, trials and tribulations, thrown off by society's excessive materialism, hedonism and individualism, and even distorted, twisted, and turned adversely upon the self or others by emotional distress or mental illness. However, one was seldom viewed altogether as a spiritless, soulless being. Black helping practitioners in the past spent considerable time trying to lift the spirit, feed the spirit, feel the spirit, and be one with the spirit of their people. To not have a spiritual self, they believed, was not to have life itself.

In their assessment of Black people's spirituality and religiosity, social workers should rely on a number of techniques drawn from the Black experience:

• They will find it helpful to do a content analysis of Black language because the language of Black clients is often peppered with religious metaphors, symbolism, and themes. Black clients often say such things as, "I was born in the church" or "I am a child of God" or "God will make a way" or "I'm blessed" or "I have to pray on it" or "God is able" or "God is willing" or "If God is willing" or "God will provide." They often end sentences with the exclamatory phrase "Thank you, Jesus," "Thank the Lord," or "Have mercy, Jesus." Such statements provide social workers with an opening and an opportunity to probe further into their client's religious background and to assess the extent of their religiosity.
• Social workers will find it helpful to analyze their clients' dreams. Many Black people believe strongly that their dreams represent or symbolize messages that come from the spirit world. Many Black people have had dream experiences where they have been visited by people they know are dead. In most cases, they believe that these deceased persons, particularly if they are beloved relatives, are trying to warn them of and advise them on how to avoid some impending disaster. Just as traditional African helpers believed dream content revealed critical information about their

clients' problems, social workers today must also pay careful attention to the dream content of Black people.

• Social workers will find it helpful to examine how their Black clients perceive or visualize God. Black people's image of God or representations of God might have significant influence on their personality and on their relationship with other people. We saw in Chapter 4 the pathological consequences of enslaved Africans' perception of God as an all-powerful White man just like their slave masters or perceptions of their master as a god or the elect of God. We saw that early Black caregivers and early Black social workers were generally highly critical of any religious beliefs that caused Black people to believe that they were cursed, damned, unworthy, and inferior, or made Black people content with oppression. Black caregivers and early Black social workers were also generally highly critical of any religious beliefs that induced Black people to wait on a great emancipator, fate, or divine intervention to save them rather than make the effort and take the risk of liberating themselves, or that made them concerned only about their own personal salvation and caused them to lose confidence in their own ability to rise. In this regard, the Black church was often the target of their most vituperative critique. Nineteenth-century Black people believed that they needed to be culturally saturated with the belief that God was on their side as well as immersed in Black history to combat the constant barrage of racist propaganda that portrayed them as worthless, shiftless people. What is the significance of a Black person viewing God as harsh, vindictive, and impersonal? What is the impact of a Black person seeing God as the representation of a mean, abusive parent? What is the impact of seeing God as kind, loving, nurturing, forgiving, and understanding? For example, one friend of ours told us that she always views God as being like her grandmother, willing to accept her as she is and willing to do anything for her when the entire world seems against her, someone she always felt she could turn to for love, nurturing, advice, and assistance when she could turn to no one else. It is crucial for social workers seeking to incorporate Black spirituality into their practice to be keenly aware of the God image, God idea, and God representation of Black people. Such information will give them a clearer understanding not only of their clients' problems, but also their personality and their interpersonal relations.

• Social workers will find it helpful to become knowledgeable of the role Black spirituality plays in major life events such as weddings, baptisms, holiday celebrations, funerals, family reunions, and memorials. These Black life events are often teeming with Black religion and spiritual overtones that have deep meaning to Black people. For example, family reunions, which are growing in popularity in the Black community, provide a veritable storehouse of Black spirituality across the generations. As Black families assess their own place and space in the world, social workers are given a great opportunity to assess spiritual links between the old and the young, the living and the dead, and between family history and Black history.

• Social workers will find it helpful to assess both religiosity and spirituality as a potential source of strength and support, and as an intervention resource. As we stated earlier, race work scholars such as W. E. B. Du Bois and Alexander Crummell created the Black strength perspective, and they created it around spirituality. Also, although they are seldom given credit for it, Black scholars such as Andrew Billingsley (1968), Robert Hill (1971), and Joyce Ladner (1971) created the strength perspective in social work long before such a perspective became popular in social work literature during the 1990s. Each of these sociologists/social workers viewed spirituality as a strength or primary source of Black social support. By finding out whether their clients pray, attend church, meditate, and read scriptures, social workers can find out the effectiveness of these religious and spiritual techniques in solving their clients' problems. They can even find out which technique is most effective with different types of problems and clients.

While social workers are examining spirituality as a source of strength; taking a religious history; listening for religious imagery, metaphors, symbolism, and themes in the language of Black clients; analyzing dreams; drawing portraits of their clients' God image; ascertaining the role religion and spirituality plays in major life events; and having a working knowledge of the religious affiliation of their clients, spirituality in the Black experience also indicates that they should be starkly aware of the depth of their own spirituality and religiosity. Early Black caregivers and Black social work pioneers knew where they stood religiously and spiritually in their own lives, and they had no problem letting their clients know where they stood. Today, even when Black social workers themselves are highly religious and spiritual people, they have been conditioned by their social work education and training to feel uncomfortable in addressing the religiosity and spirituality in their clients and letting clients know where they stand in this regard. Mendes (1982) cited a case of a Black female social worker who did group work with several Black women at a Black church. Apparently everything was going well until two of the women asked the social worker if she was "saved." The social worker, obviously feeling that she should keep her own spiritual views separate from her helping practice, believed that the question was not relevant to what she was doing and refused to answer, viewing her own religious beliefs as a private matter. The women concluded from her failure to give a clear answer to the question as proof that she was not a "born again" follower of Jesus Christ and they were highly reluctant to be influenced by a nonbeliever. They dropped out of the therapy session, taking the other Black Christian women with them, which severely demoralized the therapy group. While early Black social workers did not always tell the clients what their spiritual beliefs and values were, they had no problem telling them when they were asked and they had no problem making use of their own spiritual and religious lives in the service of their clients.

Many Black social workers in contemporary society are as spiritual and religious as their Black ancestors, but they have been so heavily indoctrinated with the notion that spiritual and religious ways of viewing the world are not scientific, empirical, objective, rational, and logical, that they are reluctant to use their spirituality and religiosity in the service of their clients. Black social workers have reported being totally uneasy when clients have asked to pray with them or to be prayed for, even when they themselves personally and privately believe in the power of prayer. Early Black caregivers and early Black social workers usually were so in tune with the spiritual and religious lives of their people that they generally had no such misgivings and welcomed the opportunity to commune with their people on a spiritual basis.

INTERVENTION

If social workers today are to follow the lead of early Black caregivers and pioneering Black social workers in the area of spiritual intervention, they must follow the dictum we expressed earlier. That is they can no longer act as if spiritual concerns are the sole province of the clergy. We saw already that at the turn of the 20th century, some of the leading, pioneering Black ministers were also trained, professional social workers.

The first lesson from the Black experience to social workers is that Black ministers today are calling for social workers and other professional caregivers to help them solve the myriad social problems brought to their doorsteps because they know they cannot solve them alone. Problems of illegal drugs, alcohol addiction, crime, delinquency, AIDS, family deterioration, and a number of social ills are just as overwhelming to Christian, Muslim, and other Black religious leaders as the problems the Southern Black migrants presented to Black ministers nearly 100 years ago. Many Black religious leaders themselves are taking social work courses. The point here is that just as Black religious leaders recognize that they must be trained in social work to be more effective, up-to-date ministers equipped to deal with problems concerning their members, social workers have to understand that they must deal with spiritual matters if they are going to have a full understanding of their clients' needs.

The second lesson for social workers is that not to explore the appropriateness of using spiritual intervention is to deprive themselves of a potential helping and healing resource. Smith (1997), a prominent psychologist and pastoral counselor, gives some indication of the importance of tapping into the spirituality of Black clients and using it as a resource for generating emotional and even physical strength. He cites a case of how a Black nurse assistant found a way to help a Black cancer patient deal with her depression when psychotherapists, social workers, and ministers were at a loss as to what to do. He said that in going about her assigned duties the nurse assistant began to stop and visit the sick woman and offer her encouragement, care, and time. Learning quickly that she and the sick woman were both members of a Black church and both knew scriptures and the spirituals, the nurse assistant easily established "rapport" with the despairing woman on spiritual grounds. Soon they were singing spirituals and praying together and expressing their faith in God and a firm belief in God's love. Smith (1997) stated, "The nurse assistant was faithful in that she was consistent. She moved physically close, i.e., would sit at Martha's bedside, talk to her, and softly hum a spiritual" (p. 93). Even after completing a full evening's work, the nurse assistant would visit and reach out to the sick woman and tap into the common spiritual resource. Soon the sick woman overcame her depression, regained a sense of intrinsic worth, and started to feel better emotionally and spiritually. Her health condition also improved markedly. Her cancer was rediagnosed and found to be treatable, and the woman left the hospital with a new determination and a stronger "commitment to spiritual renewal and social uplift" (Smith, 1997, p. 85).

The third lesson social workers must understand is that even in situations where spirituality is low, repressed, or seems nonexistent among Black individuals and groups, social workers must not assume that it is not there for them to draw from. In a personal interview with us, a Black social worker recounts the dilemma he faced as to what to do in a case involving collective grief. He was called in to help a predominantly Black high school deal with grief after a popular Black male student had been murdered, leaving students in a state of disbelief and shock. He found that the grief among the victim's classmates and close personal friends was especially acute, and he was at a loss as to how to handle the situation. As he was pondering how to apply the training he had had in group therapy, crisis intervention, and dealing with traumas, one of the young men asked the students to join him in singing church hymns. They did. Soon they were all singing religious hymns and spirituals interspersed with prayers and testimony. The social worker said that he was surprised at how well these students knew the words of the religious songs. Some he discovered had learned them in church, and others had learned them from just hearing them sung in their own homes. He said that neither he nor the teachers had realized the depth of their spirituality. They, too, had bought into the media image that these youths were bitter, hostile, violent, uncaring, materialistic, and ungodly members of the "lost generation." Through these students, this Black social work professional started the process of getting back in tune with his own spiritual heritage and feeling comfortable with tapping into this rich therapeutic resource.

A fourth lesson from the Black helping tradition to social workers is that spirituality brings to social work a wide variety of change options. It gives social workers intervention techniques with which Black clients are familiar, such as prayer, forgiveness, scripture reading, religious bibliotherapy, religious storytelling, mediation, collaboration with spiritual leaders, and the use of the clients' religious community as a source of therapy and social support. None of the spiritual intervention techniques supersedes the psychodynamic, behavioral, cognitive, humanistic, and ecological-systemic perspectives of social work. They complement, rather than oppose, the various social work methods of intervention.

The fifth lesson for contemporary social work is that the Black helping tradition suggests what intervention roles social work should play to incorporate Black spirituality in the helping process. Just as 19th-century race work had its various intervention roles such as those of sacrificer, moral developer, mental developer, protestor, builder, and vindicator, early Black caregivers and professional social workers also played various roles as they sought to use spirituality in their helping practice. Among these are the following five spiritual intervention roles:

1. the clarificationist role
2. the connective–supportive role
3. the confrontational role
4. the collaborationist role
5. the cooperationist role.

Social workers must also perform the non-Black traditional clinical role to deal with cases where spirituality and religiosity are associated with mental disorders.

DESIRED OUTCOMES
Each of these Black traditional intervention roles corresponds to the desired outcome early Black caregivers and social workers sought as they used spirituality in the helping process.

• The clarificationist intervention role is designed to help Black people clarify and affirm their spiritual, religious, and moral values and beliefs. For Black people to believe in "nothing and nobody" is antithetical to Black history and culture. The clarificationist role seeks to help Black people become more spiritually focused and spiritually centered, and to create greater congruence between their moral, spiritual, and religious values and beliefs and their actions, aims, behavior, and conduct. It also seeks to help Black people gain greater clarity of their spiritual mission or life purpose.

• The connective–supportive intervention role is designed to link deviant, alienated, lost, and confused strands of Black humanity to community by providing them with communal identity and support. The connective intervention role seeks to bring Black individuals in harmony with their families, the ancestors, and their communal life, and to get them to view these life forces as sacred. We wrote that the chief goal of Black spirituality is to provide a caregiving, emphatic milieu in which Black people can build a community. We said that Black leaders in the past made considerable use of positive, sustaining sociospiritual myths to help Black people overcome feelings of alienation, bitterness, defeatism, and despair, and to feel a sense of belonging to a community. For instance, the Garvey movement was able to take Ethiopianism to unprecedented heights and organize more than 4 million Black people worldwide. The Garvey movement gave Black people a positive sense of Black identity and Black self-esteem, and a powerful vision of being involved in a great social movement of apocalyptic proportions. In other words, Garveyism provided a sense of mission and social purpose. It gave followers a great sense of belonging to a nurturing, supportive community as they organized under the motto: "one God, one aim, one destiny." Today, few Black groups are better able to organize deviant Black elements, instill in them a vigorous sense of purpose, and give them a sense of belonging to community than the Nation of Islam. The Nation of Islam also operates around a powerful religious–racial mythology that calls for Black people to recognize their true enemies and regain their rightful place in the world through the communal process of "doing for self." Social workers have much that they can learn from the Nation of Islam in reforming and rehabilitating drug addicts, drug dealers, thieves, thugs, prostitutes, convicts, and other so-called dregs of society.

• The confrontational intervention role is to challenge irrational, harmful religious thinking and beliefs. For example, by the turn of the 20th century, the old magical thinking of the conjurer had fallen in disrepute, although numerous pockets of Black people tended to believe in this kind of thinking. By this time, the conjure man, the voodoo man, or the hoodoo were beginning to be seen at best as sources of amusement and curiosity, as fortune-tellers, palm readers, and readers of bones and tea leaves and at worst as fakes and frauds seeking to play on the ignorance of superstitious Black people. Black caregivers and professional helpers were beginning to confront Black people who laid claims that their social misfortunes were due to hexes and fixes or who believed that their fortune and fate in life relied on charms, lucky numbers, or gris-gris bags. Magical thinking was seen largely as faulty thinking that kept Black people from taking responsibility for their own lives. Social workers must be able to determine when magical thinking is just harmful, irrational, defeatist thinking and when it is a legitimate part of their Black clients' religious beliefs.

• In the collaborationist intervention role, the social worker seeks to form a partnership with religious leaders and spiritual advisors to help clients solve problems and build on their spiritual strengths and support systems.

• The cooperationist intervention role emphasizes using spirituality to promote interracial cooperation. In earlier periods, Black caregivers believed it was basically impossible for White people not to be racist given the power of racist propaganda. They believed that the psychological esteem White people experienced because of their belief that they were the elect of God and appointed by providential design to rule over the Earth was generally too much for them to let go. They were aware that even White people who were fair-minded and believed in justice, truth, and equality found it difficult not to think of Black people as inferior, given how deeply racist mythmaking had permeated White society. Nevertheless, the general thrust of early Black caregivers and Black social workers was toward interracial cooperation. Black helpers were practitioners of cultural diversity decades before social workers recognized the need to be prepared in this area. Du Bois wrote as early as 1897 that "we believe that ... it is entirely feasible and practicable for two races ... to develop side by side in peace and mutual happiness, the peculiar contributions which each has to make to the culture of their common country" (Du Bois, 1897/1970, p. 261).

Early Black social workers placed great emphasis on interracial cooperation even though they were skeptical at times. Overall, the racial consciousness of early Black social workers was based neither on subjugation of other races nor on revenge for wrongs done to them. They believed that if Black people and White people could not get along on the basis of race they should at least be able to cross the racial divide on the basis of common spiritual strivings. Black pioneering social workers such as Edmund Haynes staked their entire professional lives on this premise. Eva Bowles ended her social work career in frustration over this matter because White YWCA officials had no vested interest in interracial cooperation. Black social workers who had incorporated the race work social philosophy into their social work practice believed that because Black people had been endowed with rich gifts of spirituality, part of their mission was to seek the spiritual uplift of White America. Ransom (1935) wrote that "out of the depths of this highly spiritual and emotional nature, we shall prophecy to the dry bones of our civilization until they are united, clothed with flesh that knows no distinction of race, pulsate with the warm blood of our common human brotherhood and be made alive by the spirit of God dwelling in their hearts" (p. 7).

The misguided notion that racism is no longer a significant factor in holding Black people down leads to such suppositions as it must be something within Black people themselves that is doing so—perhaps their "culture of poverty," perhaps their "deteriorating families," perhaps "their laziness or lack of ambition," or perhaps the problem lies within their "genes."

Overall, the desired spiritual outcomes early Black caregivers and social workers sought are relevant to social work today. Taking a lead from the Black helping tradition, social workers should play a vital role in creating spiritually sensitive, spiritually focused, spiritually centered, spiritually whole Black people who have a spiritual purpose or mission; who are one with their ancestors, history, culture, families, and communities; who are willing to collaborate and cooperate with other Black people and people of other races in an effort to strengthen themselves internally, empower others, and change society; and who, if they believe, are copartners with God or a higher power to create a better world.

RESEARCH

Because incorporating Black spirituality into the social work practice is a relatively new area, considerable research is needed.

- Social workers must do a thorough review of the literature on Black religiosity and spirituality in order to gain insight into the significance of a religio-spiritual worldview in the lives of Black people.
- Social workers should use qualitative research methods to learn firsthand from Black people about the importance of spirituality and religiosity in their lives. This includes ethnographic studies, biographical reports or narratives, case studies, client self-reports, interviews, and so forth. For example, R. R. Martin (1995) wrote that "oral histories are of value in expanding social workers' comprehension of the uniqueness of

individual, cultural, and value orientation" (p. 28). Oral histories are particularly effective in gaining insight into Black spirituality across the generations. With such data, social workers can compare spirituality among the Black elderly with that of other Black age grades, particularly Black youths. Black people can also gain insight on the extent or continuity of spiritual values and religious beliefs in their own family histories. There is a definite need for qualitative studies that provide information comparing spirituality among Black people in the past with Black people today with the purpose of examining the extent to which Black people have maintained spirituality and religiosity. Longitudinal studies that examine spirituality throughout the life cycle with respect to gender and socioeconomic status will also be helpful to social workers.

• Quantitative research methods are needed to test empirically a number of relationships between Black religiosity, Black spirituality, and a number of variables. For example, it would be insightful to have more studies that test the relationship between religiosity and Black caregiving, to see whether there is a negative, positive, or zero relationship between religion and social problems such as those for alcohol abuse, drug abuse, premarital sex, teen pregnancy, and crime and delinquency with mental health, and to determine the extent to which spirituality and communal support go hand-in-hand. There are already numerous general studies in this area, but more studies are needed on Black populations in this regard. For example, Marx's study on Black religion and Black protest speaks of the concerns that early Black social workers had about Black religiosity. He found that Black religiosity as a compensatory spiritual force that emphasizes personal salvation and freedom from sin could serve as an inhibitory factor to Black protest. Marx (1967) concluded that "when one's religious involvement includes temporal concerns and acceptance of the belief that men as well as God have a role in the structuring of human affairs, then, rather than serving to inhibit protest, religion can serve to inspire and sustain it" (p. 105).

• Phenomenological and existential research methods are needed to explore the spirituality role and religiosity in terms of what meaning, purpose, and value Black people give to their lives, what they get out of life, what they give to life, what stands or attitudes they take toward life, and what place they envision for themselves in the world. These methods are needed to find out how Black people deal with life and death, good and evil, and other matters pertaining to their existence on earth.

- Evaluation research methods are needed to test the effectiveness of spiritual intervention strategies, paradigms, and techniques in helping Black people solve social problems. Whenever any spiritual technique is used in the intervention process, it needs to be evaluated in terms of how well it achieves the desired output and outcome. Although it may be difficult to test the effectiveness of prayers and other spiritual techniques, because their benefits might not be immediate or apparent, one can evaluate such spiritual techniques for the affective and psychological impact they have on the clients in terms of peace of mind, serenity, self-esteem, feeling of emotional security, catharsis, a positive outlook on life, and hope. Evaluation research can also determine what spiritual intervention techniques tend to work best for different problems. This will provide feedback to social workers on which spiritual techniques they need to reconsider or discard altogether for particular problems and which ones they need to modify and refine for greater use in the change process.

PREPARATION

Research will help social workers tremendously in preparing to incorporate Black spirituality into their social work practice. Social workers seeking to achieve the desired outcomes of Black spiritual intervention roles must again take a lead from the Black helping tradition and immerse themselves in Black history and culture; saturate themselves with Black caregiving and communal values; participate in Black ritual, social, and institutional experiences such as attending Black churches, funerals, and family reunions; and develop personal relationships, contact, and communication with real Black people instead of relying solely on theories and perspectives of Black people in textbooks.

SUMMARY

Figure 5 provides a summary of the Martin and Martin framework for incorporating Black spirituality into social work practice.

In an area as broad as spirituality, we are certain that our framework for incorporating Black spirituality into mainstream social work leaves many critical areas unexplored. However, we feel confident that this framework, despite its limitations, covers broadly the crucial areas the Black helping tradition demands.

Figure 5: Martin and Martin Framework for Incorporating Black Spirituality into Social Work Practice

Problem	Rationale	Principles	Ethics	Assessment	Intervention	Desired Outcome	Research	Preparation
(a) spiritual decenteredness; (b) spiritual fragmentation; (c) spiritual alienation and spiritual death; (d) disillusion-ment of elders for younger generation; (e) White social worker, neglect of spirituality and denial of the existence of racism when working with Black clients; (f) collusion of Black social workers; (g) Black parental neglect of spirituality; and (h) mourning the loss of spirituality in materialistic, hedonistic, and individualistic American culture	(a) to overcome spiritual alien-ation, spiritual fragmentation, and spiritual death; (b) to help Black parents understand long-term benefits and intrinsic rewards of instilling spiri-tual values; (c) to help social work-ers see the impor-tance of spirituali-ty and to give it the treatment it deserves in the helping process; and (d) to restore spirituality in the Black community	(a) the principle of internal locus of control; (b) the principle of personal and collective responsi-bility; (c) the principle of spiritual debt; (d) the principle of the sanctification of human life; and (e) the principle of a holistic approach	(a) cautious not to be insensitive in the assessment process; (b) make a conscious effort to not impose spiritual values or religious beliefs on clients; (c) show respect for spiritual leaders of clients; (d) take a basically ecumenical approach; (e) develop value preference in the interest of promoting spirituality and communal uplift; (e) make appropriate use of communal, altruistic, communal, and caregiving values and lifestyles; (f) avoid confrontation of pseudo religious/spiritual values and beliefs	(a) include spiritual matters in the assessment; (b) avoid assumption that all Black people are religious and Christians; (c) assume all Black people who have a spiritual based on Black tradition-al concepts of spirituality; (d) see Black spirituality as being inseparable from racial identi-ty and communal work; (e) make appropriate use of (1) content analysis; (2) interpretation of dreams; (3) examine Black people's image of God; (4) acknowledge Black life rituals and celebrations; (5) assess spirituality as a source of strength	(a) to not see spiritual interven-tion as the sole province of the clergy; (b) to not overlook spiritu-ality as an inter-vention resource; (c) to not assume spirituality is not there in Black clients; (d) to explore spiritual interven-tion for the vari-ety of options it brings to social work; (e) to view spiritual interven-tion techniques as complementary to social work methods; (f) to play intervention roles drawn from the Black experi-ence such as the clarificationist, connective-supportive, confrontational, collaborationist, and coopera-tionist roles; (g) to also explore the clinical roles	(a) to develop spiritually centered, spiritu-ally focused, spiri-tually whole Black persons; (b) to develop Black persons who have a spiritual mission or purpose; (c) to develop Black people; (d) to develop Black persons who are one with their ancestors, history, culture, family, spirituality, and other vari-ables; (e) to develop Black people who are willing to collaborate and cooperate with others for social change; (f) to develop Black people who, if they are believ-ers, see them-selves as copart-ners with God or a higher power	(a) to do thorough review of Black literature on culture; (b) to use qualitative research methods to learn firsthand from the inti-mate, personal, and institutional experiences; (c) to use quantitative methods to test relationships between religiosi-ty, spirituality, and other vari-ables; (d) to use phenomenologi-cal and existential methods to explore the meaning and purpose spiritual-ity gives to Black life; (e) to use evaluation methods to test the effectiveness of spiritual intervention strategies, paradigms, and techniques	(a) immersion in Black history and culture; (b) satura-tion in Black caregiving and communal values; (c) participation in Black ritual, social, and institutional experiences; (d) personal communication and contact with Black people

B ecause spirituality in the Black helping tradition is oriented toward developing a positive racial self-concept and communal caregiving, it is oppositional to mainstream social work's use of secular tools solely on the basis of empirical explanations that exclude spirituality, advance a mythical color-blind perspective, and take an individualistic approach. Mainstream social work feels uncomfortable in incorporating spirituality into the helping process, inadequate in addressing the highly sensitive issue of race, and reluctant in calling for collective approaches to build viable families and communities. Two social work approaches that support the call of Black spirituality for racial and communal connectedness and wholeness are the African-centered approach (also known as the Afrocentric paradigm) and the Black experience–based social work approach. Both of these social work approaches see spiritual, racial, and communal self-development as crucial to collective Black survival and general well-being and see social work as a major tool for advancing these aims. This chapter will examine the main principles of each perspective and analyze how each uses spirituality in problem solving on the micro, mezzo, and macro levels.

EARLY BLACK SOCIAL WORKERS AND AFRICA

Early Black social workers took a great interest in Africa. They were influenced by Du Bois and Garvey in this regard. Du Bois, a leading Pan-African scholar, had written definitive histories of Africa (1915, 1930, 1939) and had encouraged social workers and other helping professionals to emulate the communalism of traditional African village life. Du Bois (1940) wrote:

In the African communal group, ties of family and blood, of mother and child, of group relationship, made the group leadership strong, even if not always toward the highest culture. In the case of the ... American Negroes, there are sources of strength in common memories of suffering in the past; in present threats of degradation and extinction and the determination to prove ability and desert. Here in subtle but real ways the communalism of the African clan can be transferred to the Negro American group. (p. 219)

Du Bois also saw African communalism as a way African Americans could make a significant contribution to America and the world. He said, "I can conceive no more magnificent nor promising crusade in modern times. We have a chance here to teach industrial and cultural democracy to a world that bitterly needs it" (p. 219).

Drake and Cayton (1945) said, "Garvey didn't get many Negroes back to Africa, but he helped to destroy their inferiority complex, and made them conscious of their power" (p. 752). Maymie De Mena, a Garvey follower who perfected the technique of community organization, naturally had Africa foremost on her mind. However, other Black social workers also had Africa on their minds. Thyra J. Edwards, a pioneer in international social work, was interested in the plight of Africa's women and children, and Eva Bowles was interested in developing YWCAs in Africa. Reverdy C. Ransom, R. R. Wright, Jr., and Monroe N. Work were interested in Africa from a spiritual point of view.

Ransom (1935) believed that African Americans had inherited rich spiritual gifts from their African heritage but when they submerged themselves "into the rigid forms of the [W]hite man's spiritual expression" their spirit died (p. 24). Ransom (1935) believed that in order for Black America and White America to be saved, Christianity had to become "Africanized" (p. 72).

As a missionary in South Africa, R. R. Wright, Jr. (1965) was particularly intrigued by the Africans' sense of hospitality and communalism. He wrote: "My wife and I found that all through Africa, particularly through the rural sections, our belongings were always safe. We neither locked doors nor suitcases. We found genuine courtesy, and sympathy and those other human virtues without which none can be great." Wright (1965) said he learned more than he taught in Africa:

When I came home and told so many good things about the Bantu to some of our church leaders, they said facetiously, "We sent Bishop Wright to convert the heathens and it looks like the heathens have converted him." The latter was to a large extent true. (p. 252)

Wright not only propagated African culture among African Americans but he believed that America's White supremacy mythology was the primary reason why Christian missions failed in Africa, Asia, and the South Sea Islands. According to Wright, hundreds of students from Asia and Africa had gone back to their native lands with great disappointment because of their experience with America's virulent racism against people of color. Overall, the Black American churches on African soil were often more popular among Africans than those run by Europeans because Black missionaries were far less patronizing than White missionaries, allowed Africans to occupy positions of responsibility when White churches usually did not, and had no problem socializing with members of their African congregations as equals (Wamba, 1999, p. 140). Wamba (1999) believed that certain African nationalistic ideas that would later find expression in anti-colonial movements could be attributed to concepts popularized by Black American missions in Africa (p. 312).

Monroe N. Work was also fascinated with Africa. He presented copious facts about the African past and present circumstances; gathered an extensive bibliography on practically every facet of African history, life, and culture; wrote numerous articles on the African family; and took a special interest in African religion, proverbs, and folktales. Work concluded that African Americans should draw inspiration from their African past and feel proud of their physical features. Work (1916) said that "the genuine African of the interior bears no resemblance to the accepted Negro type" of the caricature of Black people with jet black skin, thick red lips, shiny white teeth, and big bulging white eyeballs (p. 321). Work, the generally objective and detached social scientist, even sounded a note of Ethiopianism when he maintained that if Black people develop along "their own special line and in their own peculiar ways," their "achievements can be such that once more Blacks will be dignified and the fame of Ethiopia again spread throughout the world" (Work, 1916, p. 326).

George Edmund Haynes, the chief promoter of professional social work training among Black Americans, in 1947 visited 15 African territories for the World's Committee of the Young Men's Christian Association. He wrote a 500-page study that examined African educational, cultural, economic, religious, and political life, including the brutal colonial exploitation of African people. Haynes was concerned that colonialism had broken down the "rigid visions and inner controls of the old tribal life" (Haynes, 1950,

p. 449). Haynes (1950) proposed that a Christian and democratic strategy must bring hope and guidance to Africans by helping them to "conserve the values of their old culture" and "to replace the weaknesses of their old life with values from the Christian and democratic way" (p. 451). Haynes (1950) believed that the extent to which Africans are able to "build upon the best in past traditions" will determine whether they will be "regarded as men, who are ends in themselves or as 'boys,' as tools for the use of their superiors" (p. 452). Haynes saw Africa as the continent of the future.

Early social workers studied not only the rich spirituality of African people and the prevalence of the ethos of mutuality but also the poverty, the internecine tribal conflicts, the crisis of African leadership, and other complexities still plaguing the African continent today. While early Black social workers took an interest in Africa, they did not develop the Afrocentric or African-centered approach. By the time the Afrocentric approach was created in the 1970s, Black social workers were just beginning to break somewhat out of their bourgeoisie mold and become more radicalized and Africanized because of the civil rights and the Black consciousness movements of the 1960s.

THE AFRICAN-CENTERED APPROACH

The African-centered approach was developed by Molefi Asante, an African studies professor and Pan-African scholar. Asante (1990) stated that Afrocentricity "seeks to uncover and use codes, paradigms, symbols, motifs, myths, and circles of discussion that reinforce the centrality of African ideals and values as a valid frame of reference for acquiring and examining data" (p. 6). Asante (1990) stated that "the uses of African origins of civilization and the Kemetic high culture of a classical starting point are the practical manifestations of the ways the scholar secures centrism when studying Africa" (p. 14). Therefore, the Afrocentric perspective gives primacy to the study of African civilizations such as Kemet (Egypt), Nubia, Axum, and Meroe. Afrocentric scholars, following the lead of the Senegalese Egyptologist, Cheik Anta Diop (1974), lay claim to the African origin of ancient Egyptian civilization. Therefore, ancient Egypt has been the subject of considerable Afrocentric scholarship (Karenga & Carruthers, 1986). A major feature of Afrocentrism is its critique of the "Eurocentric" approach that has dominated Western epistemological, axiological, and aesthetic thought. For centuries, Eurocentric thought has viewed African people as backward, barbaric, and inferior and has shown little interest in African thought. Afrocentric scholars charge that Eurocentrism has aggressively promoted an individualistic, racist, materialistic, and secularistic worldview that is radically at odds with the communalistic, humanistic, and spiritualistic worldview of Afrocentricity. Eurocentrism represents a form of cultural and intellectual imperialism that seeks to relegate Afrocentric thought to metaphysics, mysticism, and myth. Asante (1990) wrote:

> The religion of science, with its rituals, priesthood, orthodoxy, apostates, liturgy and converts, is the dominant outlook of the Western world .... In a real sense, this religion sees everything as profane and natural, nothing is sacred and supernatural. With this view of the world European man assumed himself to be a God. The scholar becomes the priest, the assistant professor the altar boy, and Newton, Darwin and Freud are made saints to be worshipped. (pp. 91–92)

Afrocentrism takes basically a historical, cultural, and spiritual approach. While Mbiti (1970) wrote, "Christianity in Africa is so old that it can be rightly described as an indigenous traditional and African religion" (p. 300), advocates of Afrocentrism show more favoritism toward traditional African religions than they do toward either Christianity or Islam. Afrocentrism seeks the development of African consciousness on the basis of an authentic African way of life. It calls for Black people to immerse themselves in ancient African history, particularly Kemet (Egypt). It not only calls on the Black community to saturate itself with African communalistic and spiritual values but also to adopt Afrocentric lifestyles. Afrocentrism has had wide appeal not only to Black historians and intellectuals but also to Black helping professionals.

Afrocentrism is also heavily connected ideologically and politically to Pan-Africanism. Drake (1970) wrote that with the gradual secularization of Black leadership in the United States, the Caribbean, and Africa, Pan-Africanism gradually replaced "Ethiopianism" as the new energizing social myth and symbol around which powerless Black people gathered for social action. Kambon, a leading Afrocentric Black psychologist, stated categorically in 1998 that "the overarching ideology value of Pan-African Nationalism philosophy must govern African-to-African relations internally/locally or domestically, as well as around the world" (p. 416).

Essentially, the chief goal or objective of Afrocentrism is reclamation or cultural recovery. Afrocentric scholars seek to reclaim African ideas, beliefs, worldviews, mythologies, and histories that were lost in the ordeal of slavery or that repressed, distorted, or covered up racism and Eurocentric hegemony. They also seek to claim that which they believe was stolen by Eurocentric scholarship and mythmaking, particularly the myriad contributions ancient Egypt made to Western Civilization. As one Afrocentric-oriented thinker said on her return from Egypt, "I have reclaimed my history, my archetypes—my kings and queens and gods and goddesses, my priests and principles and legends. I am reconnected with my origins. That which had been stolen and then denied is reclaimed" (Jones, 1973, p. 213).

AFRICAN-CENTERED PSYCHOLOGISTS
Black psychologists such as Nobles (1986), Akbar (1994), Azibo (1996), Myers (1989), and Kambon (1998) not only seek to reclaim Africa's cultural heritage but use it in solving emotional and psychological problems confronting Black people. They have taken the lead in covering a wide range of psychological issues from the African-centered perspective. In their efforts to create African-centered psychological intervention paradigms, Afrocentric psychologists have recognized spirituality as a central component of African mental health, psychological functioning, and the development of an authentic African personality. In addressing spirituality, African-centered psychologists have focused particular attention on the Kemetic concept "Ma'at." Asante (1990) wrote that "Ma'at is the cumulative appearances of the divine properties that function as the celebration of harmony and balance in the life of African people"(pp. 88–89). Kambon (1998) wrote, "The concept of Ma'at refers to cosmic order and balance as the cardinal principles governing the dynamic functioning of all aspects at all levels of the universe," including "personal human behavior and functioning" (p. 44). Afrocentric psychologists maintain that the emphasis Ma'at placed on order, justice, righteousness, and balance suggests how people should relate to one another, to nature, and to the universe. Their approach to promoting psychic health and wholeness is designed to help individuals reach the Kemetic quality of Ma'at of establishing harmony and balance in their interpersonal lives.

African-centered psychologists also believe it is crucial for Black people to achieve an authentic sense of African identity. They often speak of the racial self in terms of the "African personality," "African self-consciousness," or "African self-concept." From the Afrocentric psychological perspective, an authentic African identity is crucial for African people if they are to work toward their communal interest of nation building and Pan-African development. Also, they must develop an authentic African identity to be capable of maintaining collective resistance to forces threatening Black survival and general well-being. African-centered psychologists view African consciousness as communal consciousness, as the individual's awareness of his or her collective responsibility to the welfare of the group. This idea is expressed in African-centered psychological literature in terms of "the extended self" (Nobles, 1980), "the community of self" (Akbar, 1985), the "African self extension orientation" (Kambon, 1998), "the collective Black mind" (R. L. Williams, 1981) and "WEUSI, meaning 'we, us, and I'" (R. L. Williams, 1981). Within their Afrocentric framework, the spiritual, racial, and communal selves are blended together to form a healthy African personality.

AFROCENTRIC SOCIAL WORK

Jerome H. Schiele, a Black social work educator and scholar, is the leading exponent of the African-centered perspective in social work. Taking the lead from African-centered psychologists, Schiele's (2000) *Human Services and the Afrocentric Paradigm* provides a ground-breaking application of Afrocentric principles to social work education and practice. According to Schiele (2000), the Afrocentric paradigm of human service is particularistic in that it addresses the distinctive liberation needs of African people and universalistic in that it fosters "the spiritual and moral development of the world" (p. 11). Although Schiele's Afrocentric paradigm is centered around culture—the celebration of cultural differences, the promotion of cultural pluralism, and the struggle against cultural oppression—culture is never separated from a focus on spirituality. Schiele's definition of spirituality is consistent with the traditional African spiritual worldview that endows people, nature, inanimate objects, worldly and other-worldly forces with spiritual essence, connecting them to an ultimate supernatural source. He believes that the positivistic, materialistic, secular Eurocentric worldview has "bastardized" spirituality and has created a cultural climate that has made helping professionals apprehensive in using it as a tool of intervention. This climate has also made them "conceive of the soul as something to avoid when planning social and mental health services" (Schiele, 2000, p. 35).

Schiele also believes that the Eurocentric worldview has "objectified" God, thus making it difficult for people to feel a subjective close relationship with a personal God who is interested in their daily lives. The objectification of God not only separates the material from the spiritual but also separates morality from spirituality, leading to "the injudicious use of power and the intellectualization of morality" (Schiele, 2000, p. 69). Schiele maintains that after human service professionals recognize the soul as an unseen, transdimensional, natural element connecting human beings to a transcendental source, they will be able to design services "to help tap into an often unexplored source of power and self-affirmation" (Schiele, 2000, p. 35).

Spirituality is a central theme that runs throughout Schiele's Afrocentric paradigm of human services and social work. He also sees the integral connection of spirituality to African identity and community. The spiritual self, the racial self, and the communal self discussed throughout this study are talked about in Schiele's Afrocentric paradigm in terms of "African self-consciousness" or the state of awareness that gears Black people toward fostering the collective survival, advancement, and prosperity of African people on the continent of Africa and throughout the African Diaspora (Schiele, 2000, p. 19).

AFROCENTRISM AND MICRO, MEZZO, AND MACRO SPIRITUAL INTERVENTION

African-centered psychologists and social workers have no problem working spirituality into their intervention paradigms on the micro, mezzo, and macro levels. We examine briefly Linda Myers's micro-level Afrocentric paradigm; Paul Hill, Jr.'s mezzo-level Afrocentric paradigm; and Schiele's macro-level Afrocentric paradigm—all three of which view spirituality as a central component to their helping practices.

Case 1: A Micro-Level Afrocentric Program

Myers, a clinical psychologist, proposes an Afrocentric "optimal psychology" that is designed to help Black individuals gain greater self-knowledge and become more conscious of the choices that they make. She believes that, "the problems of humankind are derived from a worldview through which we see ourselves as separate from God," the supplier of health, power, life, peace, and love, the source of all good (Myers, 1989, p. 25). The Afrocentric paradigm assumes that reality is at once spiritual and material; that material life without a spiritual core is illusory, temporal, and chaotic; that Black people are inextricably connected to ancestors, nature, the community, and the yet unborn; and that it is through the process of human and spiritual networks that individuals achieve their goals. Myers (1989) believes that these Afrocentric assumptions rebel against the segmented, "suboptimal" thinking that prevents a unification of the physical and transphysical (spiritual) selves and that keeps individuals from being conscious of themselves and their world "as manifestations of infinite spirit" (p. 24).

Myers's (1989) "optimal psychology" provides a holistic worldview that operates against materialism, competition, and individualism, which are "the primary values of the segmented worldview" (p. 44). This suboptimal, fragmented worldview, she said, defines reality by what people see, touch, taste, smell, and hear, in other words, by material existence, which Myers believes deprives them of a sense of oneness and wholeness. Only when individuals gain an optimal perspective that sees the universe as a unified, interdependent, and integrated whole can they become conscious of being one with themselves and one with their history and community.

Because optimal psychology posits human consciousness as the indisputable determinant of a universe known to us by direct and immediate self-knowledge, its chief goal is the cognitive restructuring of consciousness. It seeks to help clients to gain self-knowledge and to understand the consequences of their chosen belief systems and worldviews. To help clients structure maximally positive worldviews through the conscious, purposeful search for their true inner selves, Myers uses what she calls Belief Systems Analysis (BSA). BSA is a tool that helps facilitate openness and honesty in helping clients examine and articulate their beliefs, discover how their worldviews affect them, and explore their capabilities for self-healing and sustained development toward their fullest potential as human beings (Myers, 1989, p. 78). BSA raises questions related to identity, purpose of being, the role of consciousness, human nature, responsibility, and more specific questions about conceptual change. Myers also believes that hypnosis, dream analysis, relaxation exercises, astrology, and other activities are useful in increasing self-awareness, self-knowledge, and human understanding. Moreover, Myers views readings in ancient history, African religion, metaphysics, human potential, and other areas of transpersonal literature as helpful in this regard.

After clients supplant a faulty, fragmented, mechanistic, suboptimal world-view with a holistic optimal worldview, Myers believes that they will gain greater self-worth and identity; become more in tune with the whole; develop an extended conception of self and communalism; become more relaxed, enthusiastic, and loving; cease to allow their feelings to be defined as reactions to circumstances; become critical thinkers questioning and challenging faulty assumptions; become more equipped to synthesize ancient wisdom and contemporary thinking; and become better able to rely on faith and draw from God all that they need to lead normal, healthy, happy, productive lives.

Case 2: A Mezzo-Level Afrocentric Program

Hill, a Black social worker, uses an African-centered approach in his African American male Rites-of-Passage program. Conscious of the high murder, unemployment, and incarceration rates among young African American males, Hill uses his Rites-of-Passage program as an ongoing socialization process to prepare young Black males for adulthood. Hill proposes to help Black males rethink their ways of doing and thinking and to replace their confused self-concept with an African self-concept; cultural incompetence with cultural competence; ambivalent behavior with positive behavior; depreciated character with transcendental character; adaptive behavior with self-awareness; confused group loyalty with group loyalty; medium/low self-esteem with high self-esteem; and reactionary behavior with liberated behavior (Hill, 1992, p. 59). In this process of maturation, the Rites-of-Passage program focuses on creating and maintaining three "senses" among young Black males:

1. The Sense of History
2. The Sense of Community
3. The Sense of Supreme Being.

Hill (1992) wrote:

The Sense of Supreme Being helps us understand that there is power and a will that is greater than all else. The Sense of the Supreme Being helps us realize that just as the natural path of living plants is to grow toward the sun, our natural path is to grow in understanding toward the Supreme Being. (p. 75)

In seeking to develop a spiritual sense in young Black males, Hill's Rites-of-Passage program takes the initiates through an intensive education process where they are required to discuss spirituality; to distinguish between "religion" and "spirituality"; to discuss the role spirituality has played in the lives of Africans of the Diaspora; to discuss creation stories; to identify the Pharaoh Akenaten (the father of monotheism); to discuss traditional African religion; to discuss the significance of traditional African rituals and libation; to discuss how Africans were denied the worship of their traditional religion by White missionaries and colonizers; to discuss the Egyptian 42 Negative Confessions and the relationship to the Ten Commandments; and to discuss the contribution of African people to religion (Hill, 1992, p. 111).

Hill's Rites-of-Passage ceremonies also draw heavily from traditional African spirituality. For example, ceremonies include pouring libation to honor the ancestors; using music (particularly drums), dance, and poetry; drawing from the wisdom and experiences of the elders (participants have to develop a family tree and interview elders); using various rituals to symbolize the death of boyhood and the rebirth of manhood; and using various myths, stories, and proverbs to convey to young people some ancient truth, meaning, and wisdom. Hill states that the Rites-of-Passage program does not focus on Africa as a reference point to recreate Africa in America but to "internalize the concept of Africa as part of our perspective and to point out the contribution of Africa and Africans to our development" (Hill, 1992, p. 82). Hill also believes that a focus on Africa gives the initiates a "spiritual kinship" that links them to African people not only on the continent of Africa and in America but also to Africans throughout the Diaspora.

Hill's Rites-of-Passage program makes extensive use of Maulana Karenga's Nguzo Saba or Seven Principles (unity, self-determination, collective work and responsibility, cooperative economics, purpose, creativity, and faith) as guiding values. It involves initiates in an intensive study of Black history, a rigorous physical fitness regimen and study of health and hygiene, and an intensive study of the cooperative economics. The program also seeks to sharpen the leadership, decision-making, and personal planning skills of the initiates.

After initiates go through the five to seven months of the Rites-of-Passage program, the desired outcome is that they have achieved a sense of their true identity and a feeling of belonging and commitment to the Black community and Diaspora; a level of social maturity and awareness that will enable them to function in a racist society without engaging in self-defeating behavior; masculine roles that are satisfying, responsible, and consistent with acceptable cultural norms and values; a philosophy of life that allows them to function in a responsible and mature manner; and an ability to relate positively to their parents, peers, extended families, teachers, and elders (Hill, 1992, pp. 90–91).

Case 3: A Macro-Level Afrocentric Program

Schiele (2000) also developed an Afrocentric program that deals with Black youths (pp. 73–96), but it is his macro-level program on substance abuse that this chapter discusses. Schiele (2000) believes that the excessive and abusive use of drugs in society can be explained in terms of "the tripartite framework" of political economic oppression, spiritual alienation, and cultural misorientation (p. 97). Oppressed and exploited people of all racial and ethnic backgrounds, Schiele writes, use drugs as a temporary, illusory escape from economic pressures. He says that excessive drug use among the poor serves the status quo by keeping poor people from organizing politically to critique, challenge, and change the system that oppresses them.

People who define themselves as lone individuals who are primarily material and physical beings without the "vibrant entity called the soul" are also highly prone to turn to drugs. These people, according to Schiele, suffer from spiritual alienation and use drugs in a futile attempt to fill their spiritual emptiness. Spiritual alienation is defined as "the disconnection of non-material and morally affirming values from concepts of human self-worth and from the character of social relationships" (Schiele, 2000, p. 81). Spiritually alienated people rely solely on sensory perception to define reality and feel no sense of divine mission or purpose. They turn to drugs out of a sense of spiritual meaninglessness, purposelessness, and worthlessness.

Schiele believes that to be fully successful in working with substance abusers, programs using spiritual paradigms, such as Alcoholics Anonymous (AA) and Narcotics Anonymous (NA), must "subjectify, rather than objectify God." That is, they must see the totality of their clients as a spiritual, divinely inspired part of the cosmic whole with the potential to tap into the creator's power, sagacity, and creative genius. Schiele (2000) maintains that the Afrocentric view of spirituality differs from the 12-step programs of AA and NA in that it offers a "sociospiritual critique of American culture" (p. 117).

Besides seeking to escape the pressures of political and economic oppression and suffering from spiritual alienation, African American drug abusers also generally suffer from "cultural misorientation" (Schiele, 2000, p. 123). This means that they have internalized the oppressive materialistic, individualistic, hedonistic values of the dominant culture that socialize them to shun the communalistic, caregiving culture of their ancestors. This adoption of callous cut-throat ideology that shows little respect for human compassion causes Black people to define themselves largely as material beings and to develop insular, detached identities devoid of any sense of group commitment or communal obligations. These disconnected souls suffer a profound lack of racial identity and cultural self-esteem, which makes them highly vulnerable to abusing drugs.

Schiele's recommendation for substance abuse prevention and treatment includes social policies that address social inequities and power disparities in the American society, strengthen the spiritual bond between individuals and their wider and intimate social milieus, and help abusers achieve greater spiritual wellness and development. He recommends that drug treatment programs based on the Afrocentric or the African model should help African Americans become aligned with their cultural heritage. Cultural alignment will help them gain a more positive ethnic/racial identity, develop in them an African self-consciousness (that is, a level of group commitment to the people of Africa), and help them to develop and maintain "a standard of conduct of resolute and uncompromising resistance to all things anti-African." Schiele proposes that social workers and other helping professionals who work in such programs express empathy for their clients; avoid judging, criticizing, or blaming them; point out to their clients the discrepancies between their present behavior and broader goals; encourage clients to assume responsibility for decisions about their recovery process; point out their clients' strengths and competencies as they gently guide them toward full recovery; and make them aware that their recovery is related not just to their own wellness but to the healing and advancement of the African American community on the whole.

Table 3 illustrates schematically the micro, mezzo, and macro Afrocentric approaches of Myers, Hill, and Schiele, respectively.

Table 3: Micro, Mezzo, and Macro Afrocentric Spiritual Approaches

	Human Nature	Target Group	Problem	Objectives and Goals	Intervention Process / Methods / Techniques	Desired Outcome
Myers's Micro Approach	Spiritual/natural with spirituality gaining ascendancy	African individuals in general	Suboptimal fragmented or segmented thinking and worldviews that separate spirituality from material existence	To develop optimal cognition and worldviews that see the spiritual and the material as a unified whole	Cognitive restructuring techniques; belief systems analysis; dream analysis; hypnosis; relaxation exercises; readings in ancient African history, religion, and metaphysics	Create in client a holistic, optimal worldview that will lead to greater self-worth and identity, a sense of oneness of self and community; ability to synthesize ancient wisdom and contemporary thinking; and greater reliance on God
Hill's Mezzo Approach	Spiritual/natural with spirituality gaining ascendancy	Young African Men	Inadequate socialization in hostile environments, that leads to immature, self-defeating behaviors and lifestyles	To help Black men achieve mature masculine identities so they can feel a sense of belonging to family and community and function responsibly in society	Use of Nguzo Saba; lessons in spirituality, physical fitness, hygiene, cooperative economics, leadership, etc.; use of African rituals, symbols, myths, etc.; use of elders as mentors and spiritual guides	Create initiates who will feel a sense of commitment to community; operate maturely and responsibly in society; relate positively to parents, peers, extended families, teachers, and elders; and feel spiritual kinship with African people wherever they may be in the world
Schiele's Macro Approach	Spiritual/natural with spirituality gaining ascendancy	Individuals with drug abuse problems/ mainly African Americans	Political oppression, spiritual alienation, and cultural misorientation, that leads to excessive drug use	To address social inequities and power disparities; to promote spiritual wellness and development and a subjective view of God, and realign Black people with their communalistic caregiving cultural heritage	Advocacy for social policies that address societal inequities, development of empathic, nonjudgmental relationship with clients; building on clients' strengths and competencies; strengthening clients' spirituality; and creating awareness of clients' responsibility to community	Create spiritually strong, culturally aligned, and conscious Africans with a sense of obligation to community and a strong commitment to the struggle for social change

Afrocentrism has inspired a great deal of activity directed toward strengthening the Black community. It is in harmony with other trends and movements in the Black community that seek to claim African heritage for the use it may have toward Black uplift today. Many Black social workers operating in the contemporary Black church are integrating Afrocentric paradigms into their social work practice. These social workers believe that the God who spoke to Black people in their African past is speaking to Black people in the contemporary Black community and that God's message is liberation. Many Black churches are beginning to "Africanize" Christianity in the sense that Ransom suggested years ago. Following the lead of Reverend Albert Cleage and his Black Madonna Church in Detroit and the Imani Temple in Washington, DC, Black churches are gradually portraying Black biblical figures and are also blending Christianity with traditional African practices. For example, Dr. Johnny Ray Youngblood, a Baptist minister with an Afrocentric outlook, incorporates African rituals into his services, particularly making liberal use of the Akan "Sankofa" symbol that expresses the importance of using the past as the guide to the future. Every year he leads his congregation in commemorating the Middle Passage by pouring libation to the ancestors who died in that horrific sea voyage. His congregation also reenacts scenes from the "Maafa" (a Kiswahili word for the Middle Passage). Wamba (1999) wrote that "Youngblood was one of many contemporary Black ministers who retained a tradition of applying an African sensibility to spiritual leadership in various African American communities in the 1990s" (p. 319).

Besides Africanizing Christianity, there has been a trend since the 1970s of Black Americans seeking spiritual alternatives to Christianity. Many of them have given up mainstream Black churches altogether to become practitioners of traditional African religions. For example, Yoruba, which has thrived in South America and the Caribbean, is now gaining a solid footing in the African American religious experience as Black people in major cities across America are beginning to practice their own version of this highly resilient, traditional West African religion. This means that more and more African Americans are mourning with their ancestral heritage through their service to numerous African Gods, divination, spirit-possession, and other spiritual mediums.

Also, many Black social workers are making wide use of Maulana Karenga's secular celebration of African culture. Karenga is the creator of Kwanzaa, which has become a national holiday celebrated by millions of Black Americans and a growing number of African people worldwide.

Kwanzaa is based on seven principles called the "Nguzo Saba." These principles and their Kiswahili names are: unity (Umoja), self-determination (Kujichagulia), collective work and responsibility (Ujima), cooperative economics (Ujamaa), purpose (Nia), creativity (Kuumba), and faith (Imani). Black social workers often use the Nguzo Saba in mentoring and African rites-of-passage programs that deal with Black youths. A number of rites-of-passage programs and mentoring programs around the country are based on the Nguzo Saba as Black youths are coming under the care and authority of Black social workers who are growing more comfortable with exposing them to their cultural and spiritual heritage.

Whether Black Americans are in mainstream Black Christian churches or practitioners of traditional African religions or secular versions of African spirituality, more and more of them are paying homage to the ancestors through pouring libations, building shrines to the ancestors, and other rituals. Just the emphasis Black people are placing on Black history suggests a desire to make an ancestral connection. To cite Bambara (1984/1999), an increasing number of Black people are beginning to realize that it cannot be natural, sane, healthy, wholesome, or in their interest "to violate the contract/covenant we have with our ancestors, each other, our children, ourselves, and God" (p. 204).

BLACK EXPERIENCE-BASED SOCIAL WORK

Black experience-based social work, developed by Martin and Martin (1995), rests on the belief that Black people in today's society are lacking a dominant, unifying worldview that is powerful enough to counter the vicious, racist propaganda that saps them of self-esteem and causes them to identify with their oppressors. It mourns the fact that the myth of Ethiopianism that gave inspiration, hope, and divine assurance to countless generations of 19th-century and early 20th-century Blacks has been effectively destroyed by contemporary versions of the Holy Bible. If we recall, the Ethiopian myth was based on Psalms 68:31 of the King James Version of the Holy Bible, which simply reads: "Princes shall come out of Egypt, Ethiopia shall soon stretch out her hands unto God." Modern versions of that statement give the biblical passage all kinds of interpretations. For example, in one contemporary English version of the Holy Bible (1995) Psalms 68:31 reads: "Force the Egyptians to bring gifts of bronze; make the Ethiopians hurry to offer presents" (*The Holy Bible: Contemporary English version*, p. 594). In another version of the Bible (1985), Psalms 68:31 is interpreted: "Envoys will come out of Egypt; Cush will submit herself to God" (*The NIV/KJV Parallel Bible*, p. 725). Yet another version of Psalms 68:31 reads: "Egypt will send gifts of precious metal; Ethiopia will stretch out her hand to God in adoration" (*Life Application: The Living Bible*, 1968, p. 68). The White slave masters would have been more comfortable and would have gained more inspiration from these contemporary biblical interpretations than enslaved and oppressed African Americans.

Black experience–based social work raises the issue or question of what happens to a people when they have no unifying social myth or electrifying worldview to energize them and spur them to action. Like Afrocentrism, Black experience–based social work seeks a sustaining sociospiritual worldview that will sustain Black people in their continuing storm and that will serve as a guide to social work practice. Like Afrocentrism, Black experience–based social work places heavy emphasis on spirituality. Martin and Martin (1995) wrote:

> Although contemporary social work practice tends to be primarily a sec-
> ular profession, this can be said categorically: there can be no social work
> based on the Black experience that does not consider both the secular
> and the sacred world of Black people. Thus, Black experience–based
> social work is primarily a secular practice with a deep spiritual emphasis.
> It does not operate from a theological framework, but it recognizes that
> Black people historically are a spiritual people not only in the religious
> sense but also in terms of the role of historical empathy, ancestral con-
> nectedness, and faith and hope. Black experience–based social work
> advances the idea that it is imperative for any social workers working with
> Black people to recognize the primary role and important function of the
> sacred as well as the profane in Black life. (p. 201)

Black experience–based social work has its roots in the "Black perspective" of social work developed by such social work scholars and educators as
Leon Chestang, Lawrence Gary, Robert O. Washington, Audrye Johnson, Will
Scott, Robert B. Hill, Andrew Billingsley, Maggie Jackson, Millie Charles, and
others. It also has roots in the sociology of E. Franklin Frazier, Charles S.
Johnson, Hylan Lewis, Allison Davis, and Oliver C. Cox. While it has gained
much from the Afrocentric approach, it is narrower in focus and does not
have as its starting point the mystery systems of ancient Egypt. Black experience–based social work is derived from a most unlikely source, the enslaved

Africans of North America. It draws its values, method of intervention, and inspiration from the musical form developed by enslaved Africans in America known as the spirituals and from the Black musical form called the blues. The blues provided the reality check or reality principle to the spirituals and kept them from moving too far in a Utopian, sentimental, illusory direction that distorts the way things really are as opposed to the way Black people want them to be. In Black experience–based social work, the spirituals and the blues go hand-in-hand to form a rich Black helping philosophy, but the central emphasis of Black experience–based social work is on the spirituals.

Spirituals can be traced to the musical, storytelling, spiritual heritage of traditional Africa and to the artistic genius of enslaved Africans that responded creatively to their plight on the American soil. Spirituals helped enslaved Africans to move from a religion of "servant-obey-your-master" to one of jubilee. Liberty-minded enslaved Africans gained inspiration from Leviticus 25:9,10 of the King James Version of the Holy Bible, which reads:

> Then shalt thou cause the trumpet of the jubilee to sound ... and ye shall hallow the fiftieth year, and proclaim liberty throughout all the land unto all the inhabitants thereof; it shall be a jubilee unto you; and ye shall return every man unto his possession, and ye shall return every man unto his family.

The spirituals were called jubilee songs before they were called spirituals because they were songs proclaiming liberty, hope, renewal, redemption, transformation, and rebirth. Spirituals were born in slavery but they have shown amazing resilience in transcending time. They have helped Black people to endure the horrible experience of slavery and have inspired many of Black history's greatest artists—singers such as Paul Robeson, Roland Hayes, Marian Anderson, Leotyne Price, and Mahalia Jackson; composers and arrangers such as R. Nathaniel Dett, William Grant Still, William Levi Dawson, Hall Johnson, and Harry T. Burleigh; and writers such as James Weldon Johnson and James Baldwin.

The spirituals survived slavery to inspire generations of oppressed Black people. For example, during the modern civil rights era they were revised and updated for use in delivering Black people from the evil bondage of segregation. The spirituals have given people all over the globe inspiration, fortitude, hope, and courage in the face of brutality, terror, and death. Lovell (1972) wrote, "There is no continent on [E]arth (and few countries) where the African American spiritual has not been sung .... No matter how far from the original the singing gets, the spiritual has brought millions of people over the world their own special brand of freedom feeling, joy, compassion, religious faith, human identification, and sweet sorrow" (1972, pp. 552–553). Denard (1995) gave a moving testimony of how the spirituals and other sacred Black music helped her grandmother defy Alzheimer's disease. She said that her grandmother had deteriorated to the point that she could only moan. She said that one day when she and her sister were visiting their grandmother, they started singing old living hymns they used to sing in church. As they started one song, they had forgotten the words and kept repeating "a charge to keep have I ... a charge to keep I have." Denard then leaned over to her grandmother, and this woman who had been frozen in a sitting position for years and unable to talk answered, as clear as a bell, "A God to glorify. A charge to keep I have, a God to glorify." Denard called it a miracle and after that was able to sit with her in all her confusion and lack of memory and sing "Jesus Keep Me Near the Cross," "What a Fellowship," "Blessed Assurance," and other songs her grandmother had sung in church and "to fit her troubles as she took refuge in her kitchen" (Denard, 1995, p. 135). Denard (1995) wrote that although the songs did not prevent the continued deterioration of her grandmother's body and her eventual death:

> They gave her a way to articulate and bring forth her deepest inner spirit ... and maybe when she spoke out so clearly in the backyard that day, the spirit was just breaking through to affirm the words that were describing the nature of her present spiritual journey and the bedrock promise she had made to herself and to God a long time ago. When called upon to testify, she broke through the moans, the confusion and the tangled and unconnected sentences and spoke out clearly her spiritual mission. She had a charge to keep, she had a God to glorify. It was a promise that not even Alzheimer's, the demon of memory, could make her forget. (pp. 135–136)

Alice Walker (1983) raised a chilling question in her brilliant, moving essay, "In Search of Our Mother's Gardens":

How was the creativity of the Black woman kept alive, year after year and century after century, when for most of the years Black people have been in America, it was a punishable crime for a Black person to read or write?

And the freedom to paint, to sculpt, to expand the mind with action did not exist. Consider, if you can bear to imagine it, what might have been the result if singing, too, had been forbidden by law. (p. 234)

We maintain that if the spirituals have managed to be a source of inspiration, strength, and healing to people across the generations throughout every continent, and if they have become embedded in the psychic structure of our ancestors as the only articulation of their souls the law would allow, then why could they still not be of use to Black people in their current state of social, economic, and political distress? Why couldn't social work use this great resource not only to help Black people but others who suffer from spiritual alienation and communal disconnectedness? The Black experience–based social work paradigm particularly draws from three main themes or metaphors of the spirituals: moaning, mourning, and morning. Moaning represents the cry of Black people for deliverance and redemption. It symbolizes the Black primal scream heard throughout the sojourn of Black people in North America. Spirituals were often called "moaning songs" by enslaved Africans. Du Bois called them sorrow songs (1903/1961, pp. 181–191). Mourning represents the collective efforts of enslaved Africans to heal the emotional wounds caused by the trauma of separation and loss. Black people had to undergo the work of mourning on the personal, family, community, and historical levels before they could have a clear, expanded vision of the future. Therefore, morning represents a vision of a better day. Enslaved Africans sang, "One of these mornings bright and fair I'm going to lay down my heavy load." As Martin Luther King, Jr. (1963) wrote, enslaved Africans believed that their present circumstance was more tolerable when they could envision that the midnight reality of rawhide whips, auction blocks, and families torn asunder would eventually turn to the dawning of a new day (p. 66). King stated:

I'm so glad trouble don't last always. Oh my Lord, O my Lord, what shall I do. Their positive belief in the dawn was the growing edge of hope that kept the slaves faithful amid the most barren and tragic circumstances. Faith in the dawn arises from the faith that God is good and just. When one believes this, he knows that the contradictions of life are neither final nor ultimate .... Even the most starless midnight may herald the dawn of some great fulfillment. (p. 66)

Lovell (1972) saw the unity of moaning, mourning, and morning. He also saw that although Black people believed in incremental change, taking one step at a time, moving inexorably "lak a poor inch worm" day-by-day toward their goal, they were also open to cataclysmic, revolutionary, apocalyptic change:

"My Lord, what a morning" is sometimes delivered, "my Lord, what a mournin." In either case, it is the beginning of a great day of justice, accompanied by falling stars, moaning sinners, thundering trumpets, nations awakening underground, and, of course, shouting Christians gliding toward heav'n. (p. 368)

Mourning allowed enslaved Africans to identify with one another; to purge themselves of their shame, guilt, and hatred of self; to heal wounds caused by their victimization; to draw closer together in a spirit of caring, compassion, and trust; and to become one with one another in the present and one with their ancestors of the past.

If the essential goal of Afrocentrism is reclamation of the rich Black cultural heritage, then the essential goal of Black experience–based social work is to achieve cultural–historical connectedness. It seeks to connect Black people to their ancestors in the past and to connect them to one another in the present. By turning backward in time to revitalize the spirituals, Black experience–based social work is connecting Black people to a rich Black healing and helping resource of their past. Also, it realizes that just as traditional Africans could not feel normal, healthy, whole, or sane without drawing from their historical–mythological past, enslaved Africans could not feel normal, healthy, whole, and sane until they drew from the Holy Bible's Hebrew experience a helping/healing paradigm to sustain them in slavery. Black people in the 21st century cannot be normal, healthy, whole, or sane without retrieving their history and culture that represents their lost, unfulfilled selves.

The major objective of Black experience–based social work is to help Black people rediscover their lost historical selves by developing the sense of timelessness conveyed in the spiritual, "Were you there when they crucified my Lord?" Thurman (1975), the renowned Black theologian, called this timelessness "the sense of tomorrow" while Cone (1972), another renowned Black theologian, called it the experience of the "transcendent present" (p. 83). Cone said that to enslaved Africans it "meant that God's future had broken in the slave's historical present" giving them "a foretaste of the freedom which is to be fully revealed in the future."

Black experience–based social work uses numerous strategies to help Black people achieve a sense of timelessness that harmonizes their past, present, and future. Through cultural memory, storytelling, reconstructing the lives of revered ancestors and historical personalities, immersion in Black history, pouring libation to the ancestors, music, dance, life scripts, fiction, art, folklore, and mythology, Black experience–based social work seeks to tap into the energy and spirit of the past so that Black people can move forward in the present toward a viable, revitalized vision of an open-ended, alternative future. This process begins in an empathic communal setting with individuals that begin to put together the shattered pieces of their own broken spiritual and psychic selves and realign themselves personally to their own damaged racial and communal selves.

By bringing the past and the future into the present, Black experience–based social work seeks to inspire, motivate, and encourage Black people to realize their unique gifts, strengths, potential, and promise to create the sense of community that is necessary for them to work through the difficulties of their current circumstance. As Figure 6 shows, the aim of the moaning–mourning–morning process is to help Black people bring their past suffering (moaning) and their open-ended future prospects (morning) to bear on their present plight (mourning). In the effort of Black experience–based social work to connect deviant, broken, alienated Black people to their history and to their communities in the present, we examine micro-level, mezzo-level and macro-level interventions based on the Black experience–based paradigm.

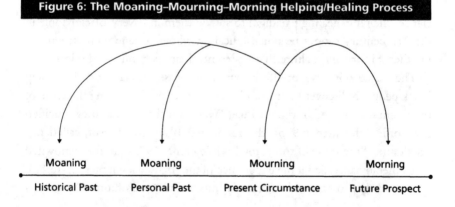

Figure 6: The Moaning–Mourning–Morning Helping/Healing Process

| Moaning | Moaning | Mourning | Morning |
| Historical Past | Personal Past | Present Circumstance | Future Prospect |

Case 1: Micro-Level Black Experience–Based Social Work Program
One of the chief goals of Black experience–based social work is to get young Black people to start thinking seriously about their future, to stop making excuses for why they are not moving forward in their lives, and to stop expressing self-defeating behaviors and attitudes. Black experience–based social work has created what we call Spirituals/Blues Analysis, which is a therapeutic, counseling technique based on the philosophy expressed in the spirituals and the blues. The spirituals are a method of giving solace, meaning, and collective support to a people during a terribly trying time. They can be best understood if they are viewed as the words, chants, prayers, poetic utterances, advice, confessions, cries, sermons, shouts, and sacred testimonies of enslaved African people in individual or group therapy sessions. If one sees spirituals not as songs but as people talking to other people, the messages of spirituals exhorting enslaved Africans to "let nobody turn you around" or "hold out to the end" or "keep your hand on the plow, hold on" can immediately be seen as a counseling session where oppressed people are giving encouragement, hope, and support to one another. When enslaved Africans sang "Mary, don't you weep, don't you moan/Pharaoh army done drown in the Red Sea," they were giving comfort to enslaved African women who were in grief over the loss of loved ones who had been sold, driven away, or murdered by slave masters. This song was therapeutic counsel to grieving souls. It reminded Black women that they still had communal support, and that God was still on their side. It assured them that God would punish their enemies just as providence had meted out divine justice to Pharaoh's army, that nothing is fixed forever, and that a change will always come in the morning.

Spirituals, we said earlier, embrace revolutionary change but basically are about incremental change, small steps, and counseling the individual to get through one day at a time. By identifying with the suffering, oppression, and redemption of the Hebrew people, enslaved Africans saw their struggle as a protracted struggle. They did not look for quick solutions. Like Moses and the Hebrew people wandering in the wilderness for 40 years, enslaved Africans believed that they had to develop the mental toughness, spiritual strength, and moral resilience to keep moving forward. Being a forward-looking people, enslaved Africans gave praises to God for even the smallest steps toward positive change. Even incremental steps toward freedom were something for which they could thank God. As they took their plight on a day-by-day basis, they believed that God was on their side so long as day-by-day their lives in some way were getting better. Enslaved Africans sang:

We are climbing Jacob's ladder;
We are climbing Jacob's ladder;
Every round goes higher, higher.

Spirituals then are basically about incremental movements, a moral or spiritual step higher up the heavenly ladder, a mountain to climb or move out of the way, a river to cross, a train to catch in the great gittin' up mornin'. Spirituals posit that everybody no matter how oppressed, down-trodden, and distressed, has the "freedom of movement," as Thurman (1975, p. 50) called it to move forward in a positive direction.

Like the spirituals, the blues present a philosophy of mental, moral, and spiritual toughness. The blues acknowledge the rawness and brutality of life, but like the spirituals, blues songs are not songs of complaint, self-pity, blame, or despair. They are songs that affirm that life is not always fair, that setbacks, troubles, defeats in life are inevitable, and that one had better be prepared morally, mentally, and spiritually to deal with the raging storms when they come so he or she can move in life. The blues also indicate that no one moves forward in this life without "paying dues" and that there is a price each person must pay just for the benefit of being alive.

With Spirituals/Blues Analysis, Black experience–based social work seeks to instill the spiritual and blues philosophy or outlook on life in young Black people, particularly the troubled ones brought into the therapeutic/counseling environment. It gets them to tell their life story through writing narratives or the oral tradition (through talking, poems, songs, etc.) and mourns with them through their trials and traumas. It gets them to prepare a life script that details step-by-step plans to realize their life goals, what barriers they are likely to be faced with, and how they will overcome these barriers with realistic, achievable, manageable plans of actions. It confronts any defeatist, immobilizing, alienated thinking or any thinking that does not hold the client as an agent responsible with the support of others (right now, in this case, the social worker) for his or her own destiny. It asks them about the specific actions they are willing to take and the dues they are willing to pay to achieve intrinsic rewards with no immediate, extrinsic benefit. It even gets them to memorize spirituals and blues songs they like and enjoy chants, prayers, songs of meditation, and relaxation and affirms to help them to bear life and to move forward one step at a time.

An indispensable tool of Spirituals/Blues Analysis is inspiration, a traditional Black helping art form that has been lost to Black helping professionals today. Inspiration as a helping tool has been largely turned over to ministers, motivational speakers, and writers of devotional literature, not social workers. Black experience–based social work retrieves this great traditional helping technique and uses it to inspire young people—to dig deep within themselves to find their spiritual center, to take themselves seriously as human beings, to recognize their God-given talents and gifts, in short, to lift their spirit. After all, that was the main purpose of the spirituals—to set the souls of Black people on fire, to reenergize them for struggle, to inspire them to higher levels of achievement, and to awaken in them a greater conception of themselves. Another major purpose of the spirituals was to inculcate hope, and this is what Spirituals/Blues Analysis also seeks to do. Inspiration and hope in the Black experience go hand-in-hand. If faith is the substance of things hoped for and the evidence of things not seen, then hope is the fervent belief that nothing under God's sun is fixed forever, that it is never too late to change, and that with God as a copartner one can be the architect of change for the better. Spirituals/Blues Analysis seeks to have young Black people understand that hope is what gave Black sacrificers their reason for being. Enslaved parents, elders, and other Black sacrificers who knew that they would never taste freedom themselves held out hope that their children or their grandchildren or great grandchildren would experience that which they could only envision in their imaginations. Hope was the only wealth they had to bequeath to the future Black generation.

This is why Spirituals/Blues Analysis also relies heavily on Black history as a source of both inspiration and hope. Many Black people, particularly young Black people, are afraid to study Black history, to connect themselves to the past because they believe that they will be confronted with nothing but an endless drama that depicts suffering and pain. However, Black experience-based social work takes them through a moaning–mourning–morning process where they discover that it is not until they have gone through the terror (moaning) that they will find the beauty, genius, strength, and support (mourning) and ultimately the achievements (morning). We find that after Black young people find their way, past the trauma to triumph, through victimization to victory, they are usually exhilarated. They see Black courage, not so much as the courage of war generals but as the courage of ordinary Black people, sacrificers, builders, and barrier breakers. They see the courage Black people had to have just to survive on a daily basis in America, just to hold on until another generation could gain ground. They also see the courage they must develop so that they can withstand the daily storms of being Black in White-dominated America and the courage they must develop to take a stand that will not lead to defeat or to a social dead end.

Spirituals/Blues Analysis as a one-on-one therapeutic and counseling method works particularly well with young Black people who have not given any thought to the meaning and purpose of their lives or have any thoughts about their future. It works well for young Black people who are wandering aimlessly in life toward economic, social, and spiritual dead ends as if they are cultural amnesiacs with no history, culture, or support systems to draw from to show them the way inside themselves.

Case 2: Mezzo-Level Black Experience–Based Social Work Program

As we mentioned earlier, a key concept of Black experience–based social work is the concept "mourning." Mourning in the Black experience goes beyond grieving over loss. It also involves collective empathy, emotional catharsis, the inculcation of faith and hope, and a keen focus on objective conditions for any opportunity to relieve the suffering of others. The problem is that many Black people in the modern urban materialistic, individualistic, dog-eat-dog culture have lost an ability to mourn. Martin and Martin (1995) wrote that there are many Black youths in the cool world of big-city streets who suffer from the psychology of terminal illness. Many of these youths have no hopes that they will live to see tomorrow. They have grown bitter and callous and have adopted the attitude that they do not "give a damn" about anybody, often including themselves. These youths clearly show an inability to mourn the plight of Black people.

Black experience–based social work proposes a program (it is not yet in operation at the publishing of this book) to get Black youths suffering from a psychology of cultural terminal illness to work with elderly Black people who are terminally ill (or even young people who are terminally ill). By working with either the terminally ill elderly or youth, the objective is to get these young Black people to develop a sense of the preciousness and sacredness of life and to teach them the ability to mourn. These young people can be referred to the program from the juvenile court system, or the public schools can refer young people who frequently make life miserable for other people.

To prepare these youths for working with the terminally ill, Black experience–based social work will have them undergo extensive Spirituals/Blues Analysis with its chief tools of inspiration and hope. It will immerse them in their Black history so that they can see slave ships and lynchings and traumas that Black people have suffered and endured. It seeks to inculcate the concept of "social debt" in these young people. Since many of these youths come from "broken," fatherless homes, they will be provided adult mentors, particularly comprised of Black elders for intergenerational continuity and involvement. A great deal of time will be devoted to helping these young Black people manage anger. This is keeping within the framework of the Black helping tradition. We recall in Chapter 3 that the Taita people of Kenya saw anger, especially hidden anger, as the root of all evil and went to great lengths to cast it out. Seeking to manage anger was a widespread practice all over traditional Africa. The Zulus of South Africa, for example, had their warriors undergo various rituals of resocialization after each battle that were designed to keep them from bringing the hostility they had directed toward the enemy back into Zulu society. Some African societies held annual festivals and ceremonies that involved entire communities in rituals where they were allowed to express their anger to the ones they were angry with, including elders, chiefs, kings, and queens. The purpose was to free themselves of the anger before it disrupted communal life, or worse, opened the door for sorcery and witchcraft.

The spirituals operate within the scope of this African tradition. Although a few do exist, it is extremely difficult to find a spiritual that expresses anger. The great majority of spirituals are remarkable in that they are totally free of hatred, anger, or any rancor whatsoever. Black experience–based social work draws from this and helps Black young people develop cognitive perspectives of the impact of Black anger on the Black family and community and of how variant anger is with traditional Black values and norms. If Black youths are to be angry, Black experience–based social workers want them to be angry with social injustice, poverty, hunger, and other social ills and only then in a politically sophisticated and mature way.

In working with Black youths with an inability to mourn, Black experience-based social work also makes use of "ancestral assignments" where each youth must relate to an ancestor (a historical or mythological hero or heroine), know the story, carry a picture of the ancestor (if available) around in their wallets or pocketbooks, feel the ancestor's spirit, and imagine the messages the ancestors would convey and the advice they would give to these young people. Again, we are taking a cue from the spirituals. The spirituals allowed enslaved Africans to find heroes and heroines in the Holy Bible to guide their own actions and behaviors, to frame their responses to their condition, and to define their relationship with their people and with God. Roberts (1989) wrote, "Throughout the spiritual song tradition, they portrayed biblical heroes who confronted enslavers and persecutors and who were forced by circumstances to protect the identity and values as well as their physical well-being in situations not unlike those known to the African slave community" (p. 148). Enslaved Africans believed that if God intervened in human history on behalf of the Hebrew people, there was no reason, given their faithfulness to God during the storm, that he would not also intervene on behalf of the enslaved Africans of North America. Through their spirituals they could prophesize a new day coming and could sing with great jubilation that "soon I'll be done with the troubles of the world."

While enslaved Africans used spirituals to portray biblical heroes and heroines as models of inspiration and hope and exemplars of behavior and conduct, Black experience-based social workers use modern hermeneutics to interpret spirituals that feature nonbiblical Black heroes and heroines. Black experience-based social work views national heroes such as Harriet Tubman, Malcolm X, and ancestors on the family or community level in terms of the principles and messages expressed in the spirituals. The ancestors drawn from nonbiblical Black history within the contexts of the spirituals and the blues serve as ancestral role models and mentors to these youths and even serve as "transitional objects" for missing parents and support systems as young people form a kindred spirit with them.

Case 3: Macro-Level Black Experience–Based Social Work Program
In the Black experience, spiritual intervention is generally connected to the practical day-to-day needs of the people. Early Black social workers/ sociologists/ministers believed that material impoverishment led to

impoverishment of the human spirit and vice versa and that it was a sin and an obscenity for the Black church to seek to save people's souls while leaving them in abject poverty.

Not only do spirituals suggest that helping professionals should see small steps towards healing and wholeness as a sign of making progress but also that they should not divorce Black people's spiritual needs from their material needs. Black people in America have always been among the wretched of the earth; but they have always aspired toward high self-fulfillment and material comfort. Lovell (1972, pp. 348–350) explained that even as enslaved Africans sang of heaven, they expressed their yearnings for relief from physical and material suffering in this world. They sang of wearing well-fitting long white robes in heaven to replace the worn out rags they wore in slavery, fine golden slippers to replace worn-out shoes and bare feet; mansions with plenty of room instead of the broken-down, overcrowded shacks with leaky roofs and mud floors; crystal fountains instead of muddy streams and old wells; milk and honey, corn and wine—gospel feasts—instead of the standard Black diet of fatback, cornmeal, and molasses; golden chariots instead of walking around everywhere; pearly gates instead of being held in by barbed wire fences guarded by patrollers; and wings with which to rise above poverty, hardship, and suffering.

A macro-level Black experience–based social work program that is up and running successfully concerns an attempt at Black community development through Black youth development. We have created a youth program that places low-income Black youths in a Black history museum (The Great Blacks in Wax Museum, which is founded and owned by the Martins). The museum itself does not function to impart knowledge for knowledge's sake. It serves as a social weapon to combat ignorance, self-hatred, feelings of inferiority, and low self-esteem. The museum trains youths ranging in age from eight to 17 in every phase of museum operations and pays them a weekly salary to act as curators, sales clerks (in the gift shop), reservationists and so forth. They learn cooperative economics and both the business and the cultural end of running the nation's first Black history wax museum. These young people are required to immerse themselves in the history and culture offered by the museum, to know the life story of all the figures in the museum, and to make ancestral connections. They have to assess the role of spirituality in the lives of each of these "great Blacks." Since the museum has an auditorium, which is used frequently by singers, dancers, poets, lecturers, and so forth, these young people get exposed to a rich variety of Black cultural influences. Also, by being around professional people, these youths gain insight into professional standards and decorum.

The aim is to connect these youths to community, to instill uplifted values in them, and to prepare them for future leadership in the museum and for future leadership in the community. By connecting them to community and providing them with a nurturing, supportive, self-environment in which they can develop and grow, the goal is to keep these young people from being among those who believe that nobody cares about them, nobody knows they exist, and nobody cares whether they live or die. The goal is to help them, like race workers of old, to gain a sense of divine mission and sacred purpose and to feel a sense of obligation to repay the social debt owed to their ancestors and to God through service. Table 4 illustrates the micro-, mezzo-, and macro-level Black experience–based social work interventions presented in this chapter.

Table 4: Micro, Mezzo, and Macro Black Experience–Based Spiritual Approaches

	Human Nature	Target Group	Problem	Objectives and Goals	Intervention Process/Methods/Techniques	Desired Outcome
Micro–Level Approach	Spiritual/natural	Black youths in general	Lack of serious thought about future; self-defeating behaviors and attitudes; aimless wandering toward a dead end	To instill spiritual and blues philosophy of life; to prepare a life plan	Life narrative; Spiritual/Blues Analysis (SBA); inspiration and hope; life plan; confrontation of defeatist thinking; memorization of spiritual and blues songs to be used as prayers, chants, affirmations, etc.	To produce serious, mature, goal-directed, focused young people; to energize young Black people; to inspire young Black people in the here-and-now with thoughts, plans, ideas, and visions of a future, a transcendent present, and a sense of tomorrow
Mezzo–Level Approach	Spiritual/natural	Alienated Black youths; Black youths suffering psychology of cultural terminal illness; Black youths with an inability to mourn	Inability to mourn psychology of cultural terminal illness	To help young alienated Black youths gain the ability to mourn by getting them to identify with terminally-ill Black people and to instill concept of social obligation and social debt	Spiritual/Blues Analysis; immersion in Black history; ancestral assignments; elders as mentors; inspiration and hope; anger management techniques and rituals	To produce Black youths who feel a sense of oneness and belonging to community, and connection to a past and who have an optimistic outlook toward the future and the ability to withstand social pressures and take a stand
Macro–Level Approach	Spiritual/natural	Black youths in low-income neighborhoods	Impoverished, underdeveloped neighborhood leaving young Black people with few career and employment options and little feeling of hope	To bring young people into a supportive, nurturing, educative environment in which they can prepare for leadership roles; engaging young people in community work; instilling inspiration and hope; instill ideas of social obligation and social debt, and develop the community by developing young Black people	Black history immersion; culture saturation, use of professionals as role models and mentors; hands-on business training; engaging young people in community work; instilling inspiration and hope; developing leadership skills	To produce young Black people who feel loved and cared for and who feel a sense of social debt, an obligation to community uplift, and a desire to become future community leaders

CONVERGENCE OF BLACK EXPERIENCE-BASED AND AFRICAN-CENTERED SOCIAL WORK APPROACHES

Overall, experience–based social work is in convergence with the Afrocentric approach. Both approaches seek to promote and develop a sense of awareness among Black people that will bring them in harmony with one another and with their ancestors. Both would thrive better in community-based programs where they could enjoy creativity, flexibility, and autonomy in developing programs that will serve Black people (and maybe the nation on the whole) as social balm in Gilead. Both use historical immersion and awareness of Black people's current plight, critique of the Eurocentric perspective, and promotion of social activism and African consciousness, and both seek greater unity among Black people. Both center on the belief that spirituality is the essence of African life and has to be a major focus of any profession that seeks to help African people. Afrocentric scholars follow the spiritual principle of Ma'at, whereas Black experience–based social work follows the spirituals that are probably a derivative of Ma'at. Both paradigms make extensive use of songs, dance, drama, history, proverbs, metaphor, autobiography, and imagery in the helping process. From Black autobiography, both draw from the lives of Black people, past and present, who have gone through the spiritual journey of moaning, mourning, and morning.

Black experience–based social work is more narrow in focus in that it seeks to saturate Black people, particularly Black youths, with the caring, communalistic, liberation values that are expressed in the spirituals and the blues. Spirituals, above all else, seek a sense of place where Black people can be themselves instead of imitating and identifying with their oppressors. They also seek a space of freedom that will allow even poor, oppressed people the movement to build strong Black families and communities and develop character through right living, finding meaning and purpose in their lives, and feeling communally committed and socially responsible for the well-being of other Black people. In the quest for place and space, the spirituals also emphasize that any steps, great or small, that are taken by Black people to move away from oppressive circumstances are steps toward healing, health, and wholeness. Therefore, Black experience–based social work, drawing from its rich African and African American spiritual heritage, extols the determination of Black people to struggle for justice, to resist oppression, to find meaning and purpose through service, to live in harmony and peace with others, and to hold fast to dreams. Like the Afrocentric helping paradigm, Black experience–based social work maintains that it is imperative for Black people to dig deep into their own spiritual, historical, and cultural well to create that great "gittin' up morning" where the darker children of God can be healthy, whole, safe, secure, happy, and free and can let their little lights shine everywhere they go.

Abimbola, W. (1997). *IFA: an exposition of Ifa literary corpus*. New York: Athelia Henrietta Press.

Ades, B. (1953). Eulogy of Thyra Edwards Gitlin. *Thyra J. Edwards Papers*. Chicago: Chicago Historical Society.

Adler, K. S. (1996). "Always leading our men in service and sacrifice": Amy Jacques Garvey, feminist Black nationalist. In E. N. Chow, D. Wilkinson, and M. B. Zinn (Eds.), *Race, class and gender: Common bonds, different values*. Thousand Oaks, CA: Sage Publications.

Akbar, N. (1984). *Chains and images of psychological slavery*. Jersey City, NJ: New Mind Productions.

Akbar, N. (1985). *The community of self*. Jersey City, NJ: New Mind Productions.

Akbar, N. (1994). *Light from ancient Africa*. Tallahassee, FL: Mind Productions and Associates.

Anda, D. D. (Ed.). 1997. *Controversial issues in multiculturalism*. Boston: Allyn and Bacon.

Aptheker, H. (1952). *American Negro slave revolts: Nat Turner, Denmark Vesey, Gabriel and others*. New York: International Publishers.

Armah, A. K. (1978). *The healers*. Portsmouth, NH: Heinemann.

Asante, M. K. (1990). *Kemet, Afrocentricity and knowledge*. Trenton, NJ: African World Press.

Azibo, D. A. (1996). *African psychology in historical perspective and related commentary*. Trenton, NJ: African World Press.

Baltazar, E. R. (1973). *The dark center:* A process theology of Blackness. New York: Paulist Press.

Bambara, T. C. (1999). Salvation is the issue. In H. A. Ervin (Eds.), *African American literary criticism: 1773 to 2000.* New York: Twayne Publishers. (Original work published 1984)

Barbour, S. B. and Strong, J. E. (1981, December 5). Mme. De Mena works hard to get all factions together. *The Negro World,* p. 1.

Bardolf, R. (1959). *The Negro vanguard.* New York: Rinehart.

Benjamin, L. (2000). *Three Black generations at the crossroads: Community, culture and consciousness.* Chicago: Burnham.

Bernard, J. (1967). *Journey toward freedom: The story of Sojourner Truth.* New York: The Feminist Press, City University of New York.

Billingsley, A. (1968). *Black families in White America.* Englewood Cliffs, NJ: Prentice-Hall.

Blassingame, J. W. (1972). *The slave community.* New York: Oxford University Press.

Bracey, J. H., Meier, A. and Rudwick, E. (Eds.). (1970). *Black nationalism in America.* New York: Bobbs-Merrill.

Bradford, S. H. (1971). *Scenes in the life of Harriet Tubman.* New York: Books for Libraries Press. (Original work published 1869)

Broughton, V. (1907). Twenty year's experience of a missionary. In *Spiritual narratives.* New York: Oxford University Press.

Burkett, R. K. (1978). *Garveyism as a religious movement: The institutionalization of a Black civil religion.* Metuchen, NJ: Scarecrow Press.

Burroughs, N. H. (1927). Glorify Blackness. In G. Lerner (Ed.). *Black women in White America: A documentary history.* New York: Pantheon Books.

Campbell, J. T. (1998). *Songs of Zion: The African Methodist Episcopal Church* in the United States and South Africa. Chapel Hill: The University of North Carolina Press.

Canda, E. R. (1997). Spirituality. In R. L. Edwards (Ed.-in-Chief), Encyclopedia of Social Work (Supplement 19th ed., pp. 299-308). Washington, DC: National Association of Social Workers.

Cannon, K. (1988). Black womanist ethics. Atlanta: Scholars Press.

Carlton-LaNey, I. (1996). George and Birdye Haynes' legacy to community practice. In I. Carlton-LaNey and N.Y. Burwell (Eds.), African American community practice models: Historical and contemporary responses. New York: Haworth Press.

Clarke, J. H. (1991). African world revolution: Africans at the crossroads. Trenton, NJ: Third World Press, Inc.

Cone, J. H. (1972). The spirituals and the blues: An interpretation. Maryknoll, NY: Orbis Books.

Cone, J. H. (1990). A Black theology of liberation, twentieth anniversary edition Maryknoll, NY: Orbis Books.

Conrad, E. (1942). Harriet Tubman: Negro soldier and abolitionist. New York: International Publishers.

Cook, M.V. (1998). Woman's place in the work of the denomination. In P. S. Foner and R. J. Branham (Eds.), Lift every voice: African American oratory 1787-1900 (pp. 663-676). Tuscaloosa, AL: The University of Alabama Press. (Original work published 1887)

Cox, O. C. (1948). Caste, class and race. New York: Monthly Review Press.

Crummell, A. ([1891] 1969). Africa and America: Addresses and discourses by Alex Crummell. Miami, FL: Mnemosyne Publishing, Inc. (Original work published 1891)

Crummell, A. (1985). The need of new ideas and new aims for a new era. In J. R. Oldfield (Ed.), Civilization and Black progress: Selected writings of Alexander Crummell on the South (pp. 120-133). Charlottesville, VA: University Press of Virginia. (Original work published 1885)

Crummell, A. (1992). The destined superiority of the Negro. In W. J. Moses (Ed.), *Destiny and race: Selected writings 1840-1898 Alexander Crummell*. Amherst, MA: University of Massachusetts Press. (Original work published 1877)

Crummell, A. (1992). The social principle among a people, and its bearing on their progress and development. In W. J. Moses (Ed.), *Destiny and race: Selected writings 1840-1898 Alexander Crummell* (pp. 254-268). Amherst, MA: University of Massachusetts Press. (Original work published 1875)

Crummell, A. (1992). The work of the Black priest. In W. J. Moses (Ed., 1992), *Destiny and race: Selected writings 1840-1898 Alexander Crummell*. Amherst: University of Massachusetts Press.

Crummell, A. (1995). At Hampton Institute. In J. R. Oldfield (Ed.), *Civilization and Black progress: Selected writings of Alexander Crummell on the South* (pp. 185-194). Charlottesville, VA: University Press of Virginia. (Original work published 1896)

Crummell, A. (1995). Civilization the primal need of the race. In J. R. Oldfield (Ed.), *Civilization and Black progress: Selected writings of Alexander Crummell on the South* (pp. 195-199). Charlottesville, VA: University Press of Virginia. (Original work published 1897)

Crummell, A. (1995). Incidents of hope for the Negro race in America. In J. R. Oldfield (Ed., 1995), *Civilizations and Black progress: Selected writings of Alexander Crummell on the South* (pp. 174-184). Charlottesville, VA: University Press of Virginia. (Original work published 1895)

Crummell, A. (1995). Tracts for the Negro Race. In J. R. Oldfield (Ed.), *Civilization and Black progress: Selected writings of Alexander Crummell on the South* (pp. 215-226). Charlottesville, VA: University Press of Virginia. (Original work published 1879)

Delaney, M. R. (1970). *Blake or the huts of America*. Boston: Beacon Press. (Original work published 1861)

Denard, C. C. (1995). Defying Alzheimer's: Saving her spirit in song. In Gloria Wade-Gayles (Ed.), *My soul is a witness* (pp. 131-136). Reston, VA: Beacon Press.

Deren, M. (1953). *The divine horseman: The living gods of Haiti*. Kingston, NY: McPherson.

Diop, B. (1975). Spirits. In E. C. Kennedy (Ed.), *The Negritude poets: An anthology of translations from the French* (pp. 152-154). New York:Viking Press.

Diop, C.A. (1974). *The African origin of civilization*.Westport, CT: Lawrence Hill.

Douglass, F. (1963). *Life and times of Frederick Douglass*. Secaucas, NJ: Citadel Press. (Original work published 1881)

Douglass, H. F. (1998). I do not believe in the antislavery of Abraham Lincoln. In P. S. Foner and R. J. Branham (Eds.), *Lift every voice: African American oratory 1787-1900*. Tuscaloosa, AL: The University of Alabama Press.

Drake, S. C. (1970). *The redemption of Africa and Black religion*. Chicago: Third World Press.

Drake, S. C. (1990). *Black folk here and there* (Vol. 2.). Los Angeles: Center for Afro-American Studies, University of California.

Drake, S. C. and Cayton, H. R. (1945). *Black metropolis: A study of Negro life in a northern city* (Vol. 2.). New York: Harcourt, Brace and World.

Du Bois, W. E. B. (1907). *Economic Co-operation among Negro Americans*. (Atlanta Study No. 12). Atlanta: Atlanta University Press.

Du Bois, W. E. B. (1908). *The Negro American family*.(Atlanta Study No. 13). Atlanta: Atlanta University Press.

Du Bois, W. E. B. (1909). *Efforts for social betterment among Negro Americans*. (Atlanta Study No. 14). Atlanta: Atlanta University Press.

Du Bois, W. E. B. (1915). *The Negro*. New York: Henry Holt.

Du Bois, W. E. B. (1920). On being Black. In Weinberg, M. (Ed.), *W. E. B. Du Bois: A reader*. New York: Harper and Row. (Original work published 1920)

Du Bois, W. E. B. (1922). *The gifts of Black folk.* Boston: Stratford.

Du Bois, W. E. B. (1930). *Africa: Its geography, people and products.* Giraud, KA: Haldeman-Julius.

Du Bois, W. E. B. (1939). *Black folk: Then and now: An essay in the history and sociology of the Negro race.* New York: Henry Holt.

Du Bois, W. E. B. (1940). *Dusk of dawn: An essay toward an autobiography of a race concept.* New York: Harcourt and Brace.

Du Bois, W. E. B. (1960). Whither now and why. In H. Aptheker (Ed.), *The education of Black people: Ten critiques, 1906-1960, by W. E. B. Du Bois.* (pp.144-153). New York: Monthly Review Press. (Original work published 1960)

Du Bois, W. E. B. (1903a, Reprinted 1961). *The Souls of Black folk.* Greenwich, CT: Fawcett Books. (Original work published 1903)

Du Bois, W. E. B. (1899, Reprinted 1967). *The Philadelphia Negro.* New York: Schocken Books. (Original work published 1899)

Du Bois, W. E. B. (1968). *The autobiography of W. E. B. Du Bois.* International Publishers.

Du Bois, W. E. B. (1970). Africa and the Negro intelligentsia. In Weinberg, M. (Ed., 1970), *W. E. B. Du Bois: A reader.* New York: Harper and Row. (Original work published 1954)

Du Bois, W. E. B. (1970). Character. In D. L. Lewis (Ed.), *W. E. B. Du Bois: A reader* (pp. 440-441). New York: Harper and Row. (Original work published 1947)

Du Bois, W. E. B. (1970). The conservation of races. In J. H. Bracey, A. Meier, & E. Rudwick (Eds.), *Black nationalism in America* (pp. 250-263). New York: Bobbs-Merrill. (Original work published 1897)

Du Bois, W. E. B. (1971). The talented tenth. In J. Lester (Ed.), *The seventh son: The thought and writings of W. E. B. Du Bois* (Vol. 1, pp. 33-75). New York: Harper and Row..

Edwards, T. J. (1935). Let us have more like Mr. Sopkins. *Crisis, 42,* 72, 82.

Edwards, T. J. (1936, July). Attitudes of Negro families on relief. *Opportunity,* 14, 213-215.

Fauset, A. H. (1938). *Sojourner Truth: God's faithful pilgrim.* New York: Russell & Russell.

Foner, P. S. (1983). *Black socialist preacher.* San Francisco: Synthesis Publication.

Ford, C. W. (1999). *The hero with an African face.* New York: Bantam Books.

Ford-Smith, H. (1991). Women in the Garvey movement in Jamaica. In R. Lewis and P. Bryan, (Eds.), *Garvey: His work and impact.* Trenton, NJ: African World Press.

Frazier, E. (1926, August 18). Garvey: A mass leader. *Nation, 123,* 147-148.

French, A. M. (1862). *Slavery in South Carolina and the ex-slaves: Or the Port Royal Mission.* New York.

Freud, S. (1856-1939). *The psychopathology of everyday life.* New York: Norton.

Fry, G. (1991). *Night riders in Black folk history.* Athens, GA: The University of Georgia Press.

Fullwinder, S. P. (1969). *The mind and mood of Black America.* Homewood, IL: Dorsey Press.

George, C. V. R. (1973). *Segregated sabbaths: Richard Allen and the emergence of independent Black churches 1700-1740.* New York: Oxford University Press.

Gerber, D. A. (1988). Peter Humphries Clark: The dialogue of hope and despair. In L. Litwack and A. Meier (Eds.), *Black leaders of the nineteenth century.* Chicago: University of Illinois Press.

Gilkes, C. T. (1994). If it wasn't for the women ... : African American women, community work, and social change. *In M. B. Zinn and B. T. Dill* (Eds.), *Women of color in U. S. Society* (pp. 329-346). Philadelphia: Temple University Press.

Grant, J. (1989). *White woman's Christ, Black woman's Jesus.* Atlanta: Scholars Press.

Harper, F. E. W. (1998). The great problem to be solved. In P. S. Foner and R. J. Branham (Eds., 1998), *Lift every voice: African American oratory, 1787-1900* (pp. 564-576). Tuscaloosa, AL: The University of Alabama Press. (Original work published 1875)

Harris, G. G. (1978). *Casting at anger.* Great Britain: Cambridge University Press.

Haynes, G. E. (1922). *The trend of the races.* New York: New York Council of Women for Home Missions and Missionary Education Movement of the United States and Canada.

Haynes, G. E. (1950). *Africa, continent of the future: Its people, problems and prospects.* New York: The Association Press.

Henson, J. (1962). *Father Henson's story of his own life.* New York: Corinth Books. (Original work published 1849)

Herkovits (1941). *The myth of the Negro past.* Gloucester, MA: Peter Smith.

Higginbotham, E. V. (1993). *Righteous discontent: The women's movement in the Black Baptist church, 1880-1920.* Cambridge: Harvard University Press.

Hill, Paul L. Jr. (1992). *Coming of age: African American male rites of passage.* Chicago: African American Images.

Hill, R. B. (1971). *The strengths of Black families.* New York: Emerson Hall Publishers, Inc.

Hill, R. B. (1997). *The strengths of African American families: Twenty-five years later.* Washington, DC: R and B Publishers.

Jagers, R. J. and Mock, L. O. (1993). Culture and social outcomes among inner-city African American children: An Afrographic explanation. *Journal of Black Psychology, 22,* 429-442.

James, W. (1890). *Principles of Psychology.* New York: Henry Holt and Co.

Johnson, J. W. (1968). *Along the way*. New York: Viking Press.

Jones, R. S. (1973). Proving Blacks inferior: The sociology of knowledge. In Ladner, J. A. (Ed.), *The death of white sociology*. New York: Vintage Books.

Kamalu, C. (1998). *Person, divinity and nature: A modern view of the person and the cosmos in African thought*. London: Karnak House.

Kambon, K. K. (1998). *African/Black psychology in the American context: An African-centered approach*. Tallahassee, FL: Nubian National Publications.

Karenga, M. and Carruthers, J. H. (Eds.). (1986). *Kemet and the African worldview: Research, rescue and restoration*. Los Angeles: Sankore Press.

Kenyatta, J. (1965). *Facing mount Kenya*. New York: Vintage Books.

King, M. L. K. (1963). *The strength to love*. New York: Harper and Row.

Ladner, J. (1971). *Tomorrow's tomorrow*. New York: Anchor Books.

Lerner, G. (1972). *Black women in White America: A documentary history*. New York: Pantheon Books.

Levine, L. C. (1977). *Black culture and Black conscience*. New York: Oxford University Press.

Life application: The living Bible (1986). Wheaton, IL: Tynsdale House Publishing.

Locke, A. (1925). *The new Negro*. In A. Locke (Ed., 1925), *The new Negro: An interpretation*. Salem, NH: Ayer.

Loewenberg, B. J. and Bogin, R. (1976). *Black women in nineteenth century American life*. University Park, PA: The Pennsylvania State University Press.

Longres, J. (1973). The impact of racism on social work education. In J. A. Goodman (Ed.), *Dynamics of racism in social work practice*. Washington, DC: National Association of Social Workers.

Longres, J. (1995). *Human behavior in the social environment.* Itasca, IL: F. E. Peacock Publishers.

Lovell, J. (1972). *Black song: The forge and the flame.* New York: Paragon House Publishers.

Luker, R. E. (1991). *The social gospel in Black and White: American racial reform, 1885-1912.* Chapel Hill, NC: The University of North Carolina Press.

Martin, C. L. (1993). Biblical theodicy and black women's spiritual auto-biography. In E. M. Townes (Ed.), *A troubling in my soul* (pp. 13-36). Maryknoll, NY: Orbis Books.

Martin, E. P. and Martin, J. M. (1995). *Social work and the Black experience.* Washington, DC: National Association of Social Workers Press.

Martin, J. M. and Martin, E. P. (1985). *The helping tradition in the Black family and community.* Washington, DC: National Association of Social Workers.

Marx, G. T. (1967). *Protest and prejudice: A study of Black belief in the community.* New York: Harper and Row.

Mattis, J. S. (1997). The spiritual well-being of African Americans: A preliminary analysis. In R. J. Watts and R. J. Jagers (Eds.), *Manhood development in urban African American communities* (pp. 103-120). New York: The Haworth Press, Inc.

Mbiti, J. S. (1969). *African religion and philosophy.* New York: Anchor Books.

McMurry, L. O. (1985). *Recorder of the Black experience: A biography of Monroe Nathan Work.* Baton Rouge, LA: Louisiana State University Press.

McRoy, R. (1990). *Cultural and racial identity in Black families. In* S. Logan (Ed.), *Social work practice with Black families* (pp. 97-111). New York: Longman.

Mead, G. H. (1934). *Mind, self and society.* Chicago: The University of Chicago Press.

Meier, A. (1996). *Negro thought in America 1880-1915.* Ann Arbor, MI: University of Michigan.

Mendes, H. A. (1982). The role of religion in psychotherapy with Afro Americans. In B. A. Bass, G. E. Wyatt, and G. J. Powell (Eds.), *The Afro American family: Assessment, treatment, and research issues* (pp. 203-210). New York: Grune and Stratton.

Morris, C. S. (1990). *Reverdy C. Ransom: Black advocate of the social gospel.* New York: University Press of America.

Moses, J. M. (1978). *The golden age of Black nationalism, 1850-1925.* New York: Oxford University Press.

Moses, J. M. (1982). *Black messiahs and uncle toms: Social and literary manipulations of a religious myth.* University Park, PA: The Pennsylvania State University Press.

Moses, J. M. (1989). *Alexander Crummell: A study of civilization and discontent.* Amherst: University of Massachusetts Press.

Moses, J. M. (1998). *Afrotopia: The roots of African American popular history.* Cambridge: Cambridge University Press.

Muse, E. T. (1931, February 21). New Orleans division enjoys exciting days with Mme. De Mena. *The Negro World*, p. 3.

Myers, L. J. (1989). *Understanding an Afrocentric worldview: Introduction to an optimal psychology.* DuBuque, IA: Kendall-Hunt Publishers.

Nobles, W. W. (1980). Extended self: Rethinking the Negro self-concept. In R. L. Jones (Ed.), *Black psychology* (2nd Ed.). New York: Harper and Row.

Nobles, W. W. (1986). *African psychology: Toward its reclamation, reascension and revitalization.* Oakland, CA: Black Family Institute Publication.

Ogbonnaya, A. O. (1994). Persons as community: An African understanding of the person as an intrapsychic community. *Journal of Black Psychology, 2,* No. 1, 75-87.

Owens, L. H. (1976). *This species of property.* New York: Oxford University Press.

Painter, M. I. (1996). *Sojourner Truth: A life, a symbol.* New York: Norton.

Parris, G. and Brocks, L. (1971). *Blacks in the city: The history of the national urban league.* Boston: Little, Brown and Company.

Patterson, O. (1998). *Rituals of blood: Consequences of slavery in two American centuries.* Washington, DC: Civitas/Canterpoint.

Pinderhughes, E. (1989). *Understanding race, ethnicity and power: The key to efficacy in clinical practice.* New York: The Free Press.

Potts, R. (1991). Spirits in the bottle: spirituality and alcoholism treatment in African American communities. *Journal of Training and Practice in Professional Psychology, 5,* 53-64.

Raboteau, A. W. (1978). *Slave Religion.* New York: Oxford University Press.

Ransom, R. C. (1935). *The Negro: The hope and despair of Christianity.* Boston: Ruth Hill Publisher.

Ransom, R. C. (1949). *Pilgrimage of Harriet Ransom's son.* Nashville, TN: Sunday School Union.

Ransom, R. C. (1983). The Negro and Socialism. In P. S. Foner (Ed.), *Black socialist preacher: The teachings of Reverend George Washington and his disciple, Reverend G. W. Slater, Jr.* San Francisco: Synthesis Publications. (Original work published 1897)

Richards, P. S. and Bergin, A. E. (1997). *A spiritual strategy for counseling and psychotherapy.* Washington, DC: American Psychological Association.

Richmond, M. (1917). *Social diagnosis.* New York: Sage Foundation.

Riggs, M. (1995). *Awake, arise, and act: A womanist call for Black liberation.* Cleveland: Pilgrim Press.

Roberts, J. W. (1989). *From trickster to badman: The Black folk hero in slavery and freedom.* Philadelphia: University of Pennsylvania Press.

Romero, P. W. (Ed.) (1978). *I too am America: Documents from 1619 to the present.* Cornwells Heights, PA: Association for the Study of Afro American Life and History.

Rose, J. A. (1989). *Lugenia Burns Hope: Black southern reformer.* Athens, GA: The University of Georgia Press.

Sanders, C. (Ed.). (1994). *Living the intersection: Womanism and Afrocentrism in theology.* Minneapolis: Fortress Press.

Schiele, J. H. (2000) *Human services and the Afrocentric paradigm.* New York: The Haworth Press.

Smith, A. (1997). *Navigating the deep river: Spirituality in African American families.* Cleveland, OH: United Church Press.

Smith-Irvin, J. (1989). *Marcus Garvey's foot soldiers of the universal Negro improvement association.* Trenton, NJ: African World Press.

Somé, M. P. (1998). *The healing wounds of Africa.* New York: Jeremy P. Tarcher/Putnam.

Specht, H. and Courtney, M. E. (1994). *Unfaithful angels: How social work has abandoned its mission.* New York: Free Press.

Starling, M. W. (1981). *The slave narrative: Its place in American history.* (2nd ed.). Washington, DC: Howard University Press.

Steiner, R. (1990). Braziel Robinson possessed of two spirits. In A. Dundes (Ed.), *Mother Brit from the laughing barrel* (377-379). Jackson, MS: University Press of Mississippi.

The Holy Bible: Contemporary English version (1995). New York: American Bible Society.

The NIV/KJV Parallel Bible (1985). Grand Rapids, MI: Zondervan Publishing House.

Thurman, H. (1975). *Deep river and the Negro spiritual speaks of life and death.* Richmond, IN: Friends United Press.

Townes, E. (1994). *Womanist justice, womanist hope.* Atlanta: Scholars Press.

Walker, A. (1983). *In search of our mothers' gardens: Womanist prose.* New York: Harcourt Brace and Company.

Walker, D. A. (1993). *David Walker's appeal to the coloured citizens of the world.* Baltimore: Black Classic Press. (Original work published 1839)

Wamba, P. (1999). *Kinship: A family's journey in Africa and America.* New York: Penguin Putnam.

Webber, T. L. (1978). *Deep like the rivers: Education in the slave quarters community 1831-1865.* New York: W. W. Norton.

Weinberg, M. (Ed.) (1970). *W. E. B. Du Bois: A reader.* New York: Harper and Row.

Weiss, N. J. (1974). *The National Urban League 1910–1940.* New York: Oxford University Press.

West, C. (1982). *Prophesy deliverance: An Afro-American revolutionary Christianity.* Philadelphia: The Westminster Press.

West, C. (1993). *Race matters.* Boston: Beacon Press.

West, C. (1999). *The Cornell West leader.* New York: Basic Civitas Books.

White, D. E. (1999). *Too heavy a load: Black women in defense of themselves 1894-1994.* New York: W. W. Norton.

Williams, D. (1993). *Sisters in the wilderness.* Maryknoll, NY: Orbis Books.

Williams, R. L. (1981). *The collective Black mind: An Afrocentric theory of Black personality.* St. Louis: Williams and Associates.

Wilmore, G. (1998). *Black religion and Black radicalism: An interpretation of the religious history of African Americans.* Maryknoll, NY: Orbis Books.

Work, M. N. (1923, April). *The contribution of Black people to the Kingdom of God.* The Student World Special Number 61, April 1923. New York: World's Student Christian Federation.

Work, M. N. (1928). *Bibliography of the Negro in Africa and America.* New York: H. W. Wilson.

Work, M. N. (1970). The passing tradition and the African civilization. In J. H. Bracey, A. Meier, and E. Rudwick (Eds.). *Black nationalism in America.* New York: Bobbs-Merrill. (Original work published 1916)

Wright, R. R. (1916, April 13). African methodism and the second century. *The Christian Recorder, 64.*

Wright, R. R. (1922). Social service. Philadelphia: *The Christian Recorder.*

Wright, R. R. (1925a, May 28). Editorial. *The Christian Recorder, 73* (12).

Wright, R. R. (1925b, September 10). Editorial. *The Christian Recorder, 73,* 26.

Wright, R. R. (1925c, November 26). *Editorial. The Christian Recorder, 73,* 37.

Wright, R. R. (January 21, 1926). Editorial. *The Christian Recorder, 74* (45).

Wright, R. R. (1965). *Eighty-seven years behind the Black curtain: An autobiography.* Philadelphia: Rare Book Company.

INDEX

A

Abolitionism, 108–109, 147–148

Accommodationism, 108, 110

Addams, Jane, 143, 144

Africa, early Black social workers and, 227–230

African-centered approach, 230–232

    convergence of Black experience-based social work and, 258–259

African-centered psychologists, 232–233

"African Corner," 52

African identity, 232–233. *See also* Racial self

African Methodist Episcopal (A. M. E.) Church, 140, 142, 151.

    See also Ransom in New York, 98

    in Philadelphia, 97

Afrocentric programs, 234, 240

    macro-level, 238–242

    mezzo-level, 236–238, 240

    micro-level, 234–236, 240

Afrocentric social work, 233–234

Afrocentrism, 231

    essential goal/objective, 232, 247

    and micro, mezzo, and macro spiritual intervention, 234–242

Agency, human, 124–125, 134, 139, 160

Alcoholics Anonymous (AA), 238–239

Allen, Richard, 97, 100–102, 104

Ancestors, 20–22, 242

"Ancestral assignment," 254

Ancestral/reincarnated self, 30, 66

    making peace with, 16

Anger management, 253

Armah, A. K., 9, 31, 193

Freedom fighters, 63, 93. *See also specific individuals*
French, A. M., 57–59
Freud, Sigmund, 74
Future, looking to the, 130–131

G
Garnet, Henry Highland, 102
Garrison, William Lloyd, 100
Garvey, Amy Jacques, 178–180
Garvey, Marcus, 177–186
Garveyism and Garvey movement, 177–185, 220
George, David, 97, 103
"Gifts"
    divine, 121–124, 134, 140
    race work, 158–160
Gifts of Black Folk, The (DuBois), 123–124
Gikuyu, 24–25
Gilkes, C. T., 95
God, 3, 6. *See also* Worship
    assessing clients' image/perception of, 214
    belief in, 3, 59, 76
    Christian, 45–46
    and destiny, 118
    high, 18–19
    objectification of, 234
    relationship with, 6, 83–84, 88, 234
God-determination, 10
Gods, African, 19–20, 35, 40, 66
    sacred covenant with, 18
Government, repression by, 196–197
Great Awakening, The, 44, 45
Great Blacks in Wax Museum, 255
Great Depression, 10, 182–183, 185, 187, 195–196

H
Hamitic myth, 65
Harper, Francis Ellen, 109, 122

"Preventive social work," 172

Priests, 47, 48

Prosser, Gabriel, 99

Prosser, Martin, 99

Protest, 129–130

Protestant evangelicalism, 44–45

Protestors, 112

Providential intervention, 134

Psychologists, African-centered, 232–233

Psychotherapy, conflict between Black religion and, 10

Puritans, 65

R

Raboteau, A. W., 45, 47, 53–55, 57

Race
    divine "gifts" inherent in each. See "Gifts"
    spiritualizing the concept of, 116

Race destiny, 96

Race relations, 134. See also specific topics

Race work, 95. See also Church(es), Black; specific topics
    defined, 11
    and destiny, 95–96
    transition to social work, 131–134

Race work "gifts." See also "Gifts"
    and Black social work "strengths," 158–160

Race work ideologies, Ethiopianism and, 108–109

Race work paradigm, 134

Race work social philosophy of Du Bois, 116, 195, 197

Race work values and roles, 109–110

Race workers, types of, 110–112

Racial consciousness, 203

Racial cooperation, 182

Racial self, 90. See also African identity
    development of, 6, 66, 119, 206

Racism, 64, 94, 222. See also specific topics

Racist mythmaking paradigm, 134

Racist religious mythomania, 63–66, 74, 75, 89–90, 107, 204, 206